CHILD CARE
A to Z

the first five years

Dr. Richard C. Woolfson

Meadowbrook Press
Distributed by Simon & Schuster
New York

Library of Congress Cataloging-in-Publication Data

Woolfson, Richard C.
    [A to Z of child development]
    Child care A to Z : the first five years / Richard C. Woolfson.
        p. cm.
    Originally published: A to Z of child development. Toronto, Canada :
Stoddard, 1995.
    Includes index.
    ISBN 0-88166-274-7 (Meadowbrook).
    ISBN 0-671-57497-3 (Simon & Schuster)
    1. Child psychology--Dictionaries. 2. Infant psychology--Dictionaries.
3. Child development--Dictionaries. 4. Infants--Development--Dictionaries.
I. Title.
BF721.W59 1997
649' . 123'03--dc21   96-39512
                                                                   CIP

Editor: Liya Lev Oertel
Production Manager: Amy Unger
Desktop Publishing: Danielle White
Text and Cover Design: Amy Unger

Published by Meadowbrook Press, 5451 Smetana Drive, Minnetonka, MN
55343.

BOOK TRADE DISTRIBUTION by Simon & Schuster, a division of Simon and
Schuster, Inc., 1230 Avenue of the Americas, New York, NY 10020.

The contents of this book have been reviewed and checked for accuracy and
appropriateness by professionals in the field of child development. However,
the authors, editors, reviewers, and publisher disclaim all responsibility arising from any adverse effects or results that occur or might occur as a result
of the inappropriate application of any of the information contained in this
book. If you have a question or concern about any of the information in
this book, consult your health care professional.

00 99 98 97   4 3 2 1

Printed in the United States of America.

To Esta and Maurice

Acknowledgements

Thanks to Lisa, Tessa, and Eve for their love and support.

Contents

V

W

X

Y

Z

Preface

I will never forget that moment when we left the hospital with our first child, Tessa. As we stood on the threshold, with the caring support of the nursing staff behind us and the vast outside world in front of us, I was momentarily terrified. Suddenly, I was aware of the awesome responsibility of parenthood, of wanting to do the best for our new baby and yet not knowing how. Suddenly, the prospect of parenthood no longer seemed the straightforward assignment I had previously imagined.

The memory of that moment will always be a permanent reminder that parents are expected to do so much, with so little experience—and they are expected to get it right! It's rather ironic that people have to undergo extensive training to be allowed to drive a car along a road for a few seconds, and yet parents don't have to undergo any training at all to look after a child twenty-four hours a day, for many years.

Of course, there isn't a particular "right" way to raise a child (although there are plenty of wrong ways). So many decisions regarding your child depend on your own values as parents, and so what may be appropriate for one family may not be appropriate for you and yours.

Child Care A to Z, therefore, isn't a rule book for parents. It doesn't provide a set of incontrovertible solutions for every problem you are likely to experience with your child. What it does do is highlight many of the issues that you will face with your child during the next few years, issues upon which you will have to act. It gives ideas for action, as well as information to further your understanding of your child's development. You can read this book either section by section, literally from A to Z, or you can read any entry on its own (most are cross-referenced to other related topics). An index will direct you to specific points within each entry.

Dr. Richard C. Woolfson

Additives An American medical practitioner Ben Feingold was the first to suggest a link between additives in children's food and hyperactivity. He claimed that if an overactive, disruptive child eats only natural foods, without any added chemicals and without salicylate (which occurs naturally in tomatoes), then the child's behavior will improve. In Feingold's view, hyperactivity can be cured by putting the child on an additive-free diet.

Some parents have found this strategy effective. They discover that when their child eats foods containing artificial coloring, preservatives, excessive amounts of sugar, or monosodium glutamate (MSG), he becomes miserable and unpredictable, with sudden mood swings; he changes from being cheerful and happy to being a child out of control. But when the child follows an additive-free diet, his behavior settles within a few days.

Such arguments do not convince all the experts, however. For every apparent success involving an improvement in behavior following a change of diet, there are dozens of cases where a change of diet has no effect at all. A number of controlled studies have been carried out, but most of them conclude that diet is a relatively unimportant factor in causing hyperactivity.

A British study has found that food allergies can have a significant adverse effect on children's behavior. When a group of children (categorized as hyperactive) was placed on an additive-free diet, the following results were observed:

- A quarter of the children improved so much that their parents described their behavior as "normal."
- Over half of the children showed a significant decrease in their level of hyperactivity.
- Most of the children experienced an alleviation of related difficulties, such as headaches and pains.

The most pronounced changes in behavior resulted from eliminating foods containing tartrazine and other food colorings and preservatives, followed by cow's milk and chocolate. Many parents and teachers have also noticed a link between the amount of sugar consumed and the activity levels and attention spans of small children.

You will have to make up your own mind on this issue. Bear in mind, though, that despite the lack of scientific evidence, a junk-free, balanced diet will not do your child any harm. Additives to be avoided include artificial colors, antioxidants, preservatives, MSG, and sulfites. Ask your pediatrician or family doctor to provide you with a comprehensive and detailed diet for your child. This diet will probably exclude candy, corn chips and potato chips, pretzels, soft drinks, cakes, and cookies. Keep your child on the diet for at least three weeks before you make an assessment of its effectiveness.

See also Fussy Eaters; Healthy Eating; Hyperactivity; Snacks.

Age Gap Most parents worry about jealousy between their children, and some parents think they can minimize jealousy by having either a very small age gap between siblings or a very large one. This view is supported by psychological research, which has found that an age gap between children

- of seventeen months or less tends to produce less jealousy;
- between two and four years tends to produce a higher level of jealousy;
- of five years or more tends to produce a lower level of jealousy.

You shouldn't assume, however, that things will automatically work out that way. A large age gap can still result in jealousy because the older child may become too accustomed to being the center of her parents' attention—and she'll not easily share her parents with anyone else. A very small age gap can also result in jealousy, because the children are likely to have similar interests and are more likely to compete with each other.

Jealousy between your children, whatever the age gap, can be reduced by the following strategies:

- *Encourage siblings to play together, and to share their toys.* The more they enjoy each other, the less likely they are to be jealous of each other.
- *Give each child a turn to have new items of clothing or toys.* Make sure it's not always your oldest who gets the new item. Let it be the younger one sometimes.
- *Don't tell a child how different she is from her brother or sister.* Jealousy will only be increased if one child feels she is constantly being compared with someone else in the family.
- *Spend a few minutes every day with each child, just the two of you together.* Jealousy will be reduced when you give all of your children some individual attention each day.

A small age gap can be cost-effective. Your biggest financial outlay is with the first child, mainly because of all the equipment necessary for adequate care of a new baby. A second child who closely follows the first-born will be able to use most of these items since they'll not have been given away to friends—something that often happens when there is a large age gap between the children. And if your second child is the same sex as your first, most of your older child's baby clothes will still be suitable.

Some couples deliberately plan a large age gap between their children, purely because of economic considerations. These parents believe that raising two children closely together would mean one parent being away from work for perhaps five or six years, which would result in a loss of income over a long period, and possibly even a loss of career. With a large age gap, they reason, one parent would be able to return to work soon after the first child is born, allowing the couple to accumulate savings before they have their second child.

A large age gap has the advantage that each child can enjoy undiluted attention and stimulation from her parents, which is helpful for intellectual development in the preschool years. Practical constraints dictate that in large families with three children under the age of five, the mother and father have only a limited amount of time to play with, talk to, and stimulate each child. However, parents can overcome this problem by making a special effort to ensure that whenever time is available, each child gets individual attention.

When the age gap between the youngest child and the next child in the family is more than five years, the youngest child might have a tendency to be selfish, and to have difficulty mixing with other children. This potential disadvantage of a large age gap can be avoided by ensuring that the youngest child plays with other children of her own age as often as she can, preferably at a playgroup or nursery school. At home the child should be encouraged to share her toys with her friends when they come over to play. This will help offset any detrimental effect of being the "baby of the family."

"Family spacing" should also take your own feelings into account. Some couples find raising their first child to be so demanding, so time-consuming, that they feel they couldn't cope with two young children at the same time. It may be far better for a couple to be honest about it—to wait a few years before having their second and subsequent children—than to have more children before they are emotionally ready.

Deciding on the age gap between your children means weighing all these different factors. Remember, age gaps don't always turn out the way parents plan! In addition, with our modern "recombined" families, added factors of birth order in both families muddy the waters even more.

See also Birth Order, First-Born Jealousy; Jealousy; Sibling Rivalry.

Aggression
Every child is aggressive at one time or another. Sometimes aggression is desirable (for example, when he has to protect himself), acceptable (for example, when he is trying to win a game), and sometimes it is unacceptable (for example, when he hits another child in order to grab a toy). Children must be taught how to judge when aggression is acceptable, and they also must be taught how to control their aggression.

Sigmund Freud believed that every baby is born with aggressive instincts, and that parenthood involves teaching a child to repress these hostile impulses. Freud also maintained that no matter how well parents do their job, such impulses are always there in the child, just lying under the surface waiting to be triggered. Yet we all know at least one child who is very docile, who would never fight back even to save himself from injury. Children like this seem to lack all aggressive urges, even when they themselves are at risk. If human aggression was solely a matter of instinct, then such children wouldn't exist.

You may be worried that some television programs encourage your child to be aggressive. Current studies indicate that you have cause for concern. Consider these basic psychological facts:

- Young children model the behavior they see.
- Young children are unable to distinguish fantasy from reality.
- Young children do not understand the meaning of death.

Educators report that violence portrayed in the media contributes to violence perpetrated by children and against other children. Most vulnerable are underprivileged children whose caregivers often do not have the time or resources to supervise television viewing, interpret the messages given, or provide recreational alternatives. Often the TV set is the household baby sitter. Statistics indicate that the average North American preschooler watches twenty-five hours a week of television. This statistical average includes children who watch no television and children who live in homes where the television is never turned off.

Through mainstream television programs, children are exposed to attractive individuals, cartoon characters, and even toys that are violent and engage in acts of physical harm, sexual violence, brutality, and verbal abuse. Peaceful or intellectual people are usually portrayed as boring nerds. Think about some of the messages children may receive:

- Violence is fun.
- Guns are toys.
- Problems can be resolved by violence.
- You are only attractive when you are violent.
- You are only attractive when you have a muscular body.

- You are only attractive when you are thin.
- Violence is entertainment.
- Violence is attractive.
- The more violent you are, the greater your prestige.
- Being a caring or intelligent person or a negotiator means you are a loser.
- Men only look and act in certain ways.
- Women only look and act in certain ways.

Educators report children are confused when they receive conflicting messages once they get out into the real world:

- In nursery school: "It's not nice to hit Johnny."
- In kindergarten: "Kung fu and karate kicks are not allowed."
- In grade school: "It is NOT okay to swarm a child on the playground because he appears different from the others."
- In high school: "If you bring a gun to school you are expelled. Permanently."

Whenever you allow young children to see violent television, discuss the violence and values presented.

Parents also influence the development and expression of their children's aggression. Extreme forms of discipline at home—whether overly strict or overly permissive—are more likely to cause your child to be aggressive than are more-balanced forms of discipline. Children who are spanked when they misbehave have a higher level of aggression. One study shows that hitting a child as a form of discipline gives the child a "hitting license"—the child learns behavior that is not tolerated at work, play, or outside the home. Physical punishment becomes an increasingly violent cycle that results in such long-term effects as physical damage, higher death rates, and stunted mental and emotional growth. Children who are hit are more likely to abuse their own children. In North America, spanking is becoming less and less acceptable as a form of discipline, and can lead to charges of physical assault against an abusing parent, with sentences of six months to three years.

Most children have aggressive emotions from time to time. This is normal. There is nothing wrong with your child feeling angry and hostile toward someone, especially when that person has deliberately hurt him. What is wrong, however, is for your child to act on these feelings. Your child must learn how to express aggressive urges in an indirect way, without assaulting other people. So never be outraged when you see your child angry. Instead, help him dissipate that fury without hurting anyone.

The most socially acceptable way for young children to release aggression is any form of physical exercise, such as running, playing soccer, swimming, playing on playground equipment, playing catch, jumping, skating, and skipping. Other socially acceptable—and psychologically healthy—ways of releasing pent-up emotions include active playground games, such as tag, and all creative activities: painting, singing, dancing, playing in a sand box, playing with water, clay-modeling and working with Play-Doh. Every day in playgroups, nurseries, schools, and homes you will find children slapping clay around most vigorously, or perhaps enthusiastically splashing paint.

See also Bullying; Discipline; Fighting; Spanking; Sociable Play; Television.

Allowance Most children older than five receive an allowance each week from their parents. Giving your child an allowance will enable her to learn how to spend money, save for a large purchase, or donate to a worthwhile cause to help others. A child under five doesn't have an understanding of money, so there is little point in giving her a regular amount. Having an allowance gives your child some responsibility for minor purchases, a sense of independence, and an idea of the value of money.

There is no fixed amount that your child should receive at any specific age, although some parents find that a dollar a week for every grade of school will work for a while. (Kindergarten is worth fifty cents a week.) You will soon learn a universal law regarding an allowance—no matter how much you give your child, her friend always gets more! Conduct a brief survey of other parents to determine the average amount for someone of your child's age, but expect to find a broad range. Some parents give a larger amount and expect their child to buy candy, comics, and their entertainment with it, while others give a smaller amount but give the child extra money for these treats. It doesn't matter which system you use, as long as you make the rules clear to your child. Tell her what things you expect her allowance to cover.

Parents often use an allowance to introduce their child to the concept of saving. Ensure that the saving element doesn't eliminate the child's spending money! Probably the best strategy is to encourage your child to save a portion of her pocket money each week (for example, a third) and to spend the rest in a planned way. A child aged five or six needs her parents' help to budget money, because her natural inclination will probably be to spend it all as soon as she gets it. Explain to your child why she should save (for example, so she can buy a bigger toy, later) and discuss with her how and when the remaining sum might be spent. You can offer to "match" whatever she deposits in her savings account as an additional incentive to save for the two-wheeler she desires.

Never threaten to withdraw your child's allowance as a method of discipline.

See also Independence.

Attention Deficit Disorder (ADD) It is esti-
mated that up to 3 percent of the general population is affected by Attention Deficit Disorder (ADD). ADD is defined as developmentally inappropriate inattention, impulsiveness, and hyperactivity, and is identified far more frequently in boys than in girls. ADD can appear without hyperactivity—in fact, the child may be quite lethargic—and hence, ADD can be misdiagnosed. ADD usually appears before the age of seven, with about half of all cases appearing before the age of four. Usually ADD is recognized in the classroom when the child starts school. The exact cause has not been identified, but there appear to be both genetic and environmental components.

The course of the disorder is influenced by home and school

environments and experiences, life events, stress, and intervention and treatment. Many cases are helped by adolescence, due to the increased self-awareness and self-control that come at that age. Sometimes attention deficits continue throughout life, possibly surfacing during periods of stress and excitement.

A child with ADD may

- seem rude, lazy, irresponsible;
- appear inattentive, careless, noisy, messy;
- display behavior problems;
- be aggressive toward other children;
- be very creative;
- fight authority;
- try to control others;
- be manipulative and demanding;
- have problems accepting boundaries and limits;
- be an academic underachiever;
- have problems completing and organizing his work.

Some findings on ADD include the following:

- Symptoms of ADD may appear only in some environments; at other times the child may show no symptoms.
- The child may appear normal in one-on-one situations with an adult.
- The child may appear normal when sufficiently challenged.
- The child may appear normal in new or novel situations.
- ADD may not show up in a clinical testing situation.

Some of the strategies for treating ADD include special education for the child, including small-group instruction. Educators often have to present such a child with new learning strategies, as well as several learning styles. Family counselling is often recommended, and parents are advised to provide a stable environment, including a calm household and consistent discipline. Parents are encouraged to focus their child's intellect and emotions on the discovery and pursuit of his own goals and objectives. Parents should encourage their child's sustained attention on tasks and details of organization.

Often, doctors prescribe the drug Ritalin for a child with ADD. Ritalin is a stimulant that increases concentration span and curbs impulsiveness. As mastery and control come to the child, the medication can be regulated, so the child only takes it as needed. Some of the side effects of Ritalin include insomnia, decreased appetite, irritability, nervousness, increased heart rate, and abnormal movements.

Some experiments in using neural feedback to treat ADD have also shown success; children with ADD were able to control their own brain-wave patterns.

See also Learning Difficulties; Hyperactivity.

Attention-Seeking Behavior Young children seek
attention. Attention ensures the survival of very young children. However, children can also push their parents to the absolute limit with their demands to be the star attraction. Some children are able to turn any situation to their own advantage—as though they have an intuitive knowledge of their parents' weak spots. In these circumstances, you may feel you are at the end of your tether, especially when such behavior appears in public.

You can change the way your attention-seeking child behaves, without becoming too extreme. The first step to take when trying to counter your child's demands—whether she's a three-month-old infant or a three-year-old child—is to have a closer look at what is happening. Because an element of learning is involved in your child's behavior, to evaluate her behavior properly you have to understand three basic principles of learning theory:

- *If something that your child regards as positive immediately follows one of her actions, then there is a high probability she will repeat the action.* When the link between your child's behavior and the result is favorable, she will repeat the behavior.

- *If something that your child regards as negative immediately follows one of her actions, then there is a lower probability she will repeat the action.* When the link between your child's behavior and the result is unfavorable, she probably won't repeat the behavior.

- *Your child may like some aspect of what's happening, even though you don't.* Many babies and young children would rather have any form of parental attention than be ignored. Although you may think that screaming at your child, as you jump up and down having your own tantrum, will discourage your child's inappropriate behavior, the reprimand may be attractive from her point of view. Any attention is better than no attention at all, and besides, you're giving her a good show.

From these principles arise the following practical suggestions for managing an attention-seeking child. First, give your child what she wants—that is, attention—but give it at varying times for different actions. If you pay attention to your child only when she is disobedient, then she will quickly learn to act up every time she wants your attention. She should be given attention spontaneously, when she is not expecting it. That's why it is crucial for you to play with your child when she is settled and contented, and to praise her when she is behaving well. That takes away your child's desire to misbehave to get your attention.

Second, ignore negative attention-seeking behavior, when possible. On many occasions, punishment has no effect whatsoever, except, perhaps, to encourage your child to continue misbehaving. Ignoring the undesirable behavior can be very effective—though, admittedly, this is a very difficult strategy, requiring strong resolve and assessment of the immediate situation. One North American expert recommends intervening when the behavior is "life threatening, morally threatening, or harmful to others." Remember, a solid refusal to respond to your child's negative attention-seeking behavior can discourage such behavior.

No method of management is guaranteed to work every

time with every child, and the above suggestions will not necessarily bring about an instant improvement in your child's behavior. They are simply strategies to provide a starting point for more effective ways of coping with your child's difficult behavior. In time, if such strategies are applied consistently, they will have a positive effect. Otherwise, try a new approach. Usually, a three-week trial period will show the impact of a new strategy.

See also *Breath-Holding; Crying Baby; Discipline; Ignoring; Praise; Punishment; Spanking; Tantrums; Victim; Whining.*

Attractiveness Our culture is obsessed with physical appearance. We are constantly bombarded by advertisements, television programs, and films that create a link in our minds between beauty and success, between slimness and attractiveness, between sports prowess and fame, between youth and intelligence. The media's nonstop message is that physical appearance is everything, and that personality characteristics, intelligence, and wisdom are inconsequential.

Maybe this obsession is an inevitable side of commercialism, but it has the undeniable effect of making impressionable young viewers think that they have to be young, beautiful, successful, attractive, and good in sports—plus have a perfect body—before they can feel good about themselves. Of course, the other message being delivered is that if you have a large body type (or wear glasses, or are confined to a wheelchair, or vary in any way from an unreachable physical ideal), you are unacceptable.

This sort of media pressure can make children think there is something wrong with them, when there isn't. Unfortunately this kind of thought pattern may contribute to the ever-increasing occurrence of anorexia and bulimia among young women. It may also contribute to overeating and obesity among both sexes. ("I will never be perfect, so why not eat this tub of ice cream or bag of candy?") Use of steroids is ever-increasing among young men, who hope to get the desirable "muscular" superhero, athletic body. This type of thinking has dire effects on the future physical development of our children.

This point was brought forcefully home by the results of a wide-ranging survey that explored the views that nine-to-four-teen-year-old girls hold about their ideal body image. Boys were not included in the study, unfortunately. The results are worrying:

- Girls as young as nine diet because they are unhappy with the shape of their body, even when they are not overweight.

- Children who diet usually think that dieting is the only way to have a slimmer body, and that people who don't diet will have an unattractive body shape.

- Although some of the girls who admitted they were dieting really were overweight, at least half of them had normal body weight.

- While the younger girls were too young to be concerned about the size of their chest, they expressed concern about the size of their hips, the width of their legs, arms, thighs, and shoulders, and the shape of their noses.

- Many of those who dieted had mothers who also dieted, and had probably learned the strategy from them.

- In a few instances, dieting was so extreme that it impaired growth, may have led to anorexia, and delayed puberty.

Other studies have shown that boys, too, are vulnerable to this sort of pressure, though for males, the emphasis tends to be on physical skills and strength rather than good looks. Boys' role models are usually muscle-bound sportsmen, or macho, super-strong adventure heroes. Any body shape remotely approaching fatness is definitely out.

If you want to discourage your child from linking physical attractiveness to feelings of personal worth, then do the following:

- *Encourage your child to consider a wide range of personal features, not just good looks, when judging whether someone is nice.* Tell your child to think about the person's kindness, thoughtfulness, friendliness, knowledge, and so on.

- *Encourage your child to be physically active.* If your child can have fun with sports, and have an active body, he will feel good about his body.

- *Try to select children's stories that don't emphasize a relationship between beauty and success, or between ugliness and failure.* Read your child stories about ordinary children who have interesting adventures.

See also Self-Confidence.

Autism Autistic children have difficulties forming relationships with other people. They seem to be cut off, living in a world of their own. Although the condition was first identified in the eighteenth century, it was not until 1943 that American psychiatrist Leo Kanner called it "early infantile autism" (from the Greek word *autos* meaning "self"). Kanner used this term because of the autistic child's withdrawn behavior and disinterest in others.

Statistics confirm that approximately four or five children per 10,000 have classic autism, and approximately fifteen to twenty per 10,000 have autistic-like features. Autism—the cause of which is unknown—affects four times as many boys as it does girls.

Experts on autism emphasize that the condition affects the child's whole system of communication. A typical autistic baby doesn't show awareness of her mother's presence, screams constantly unless rocked rhythmically all the time, and doesn't look at the world around her; at the toddler stage, the autistic child appears not to understand the meaning of speech, and is late learning to talk. Secondary problems usually develop, such as resistance to change (routine becomes very important), absence of imaginative play, socially difficult behavior (destructive, aggressive actions), and learning disabilities. Many parents of autistic children think their child is potentially intelligent, if only she could communicate with them.

Some autistic children make no progress at all and remain withdrawn all their lives. The majority show some improvement, however, especially between the ages of six and twelve years, but only 15 percent are able to lead an independent life in adulthood.

In recent years, new treatments aimed at helping autistic

children have been developed (for example: holding therapy, in which an adult hugs the child tightly during a distressed outburst; aural training, which uses the Tomatis method of ear and voice instruction and practice; neuro-feedback training, which uses monitoring of brain-wave patterns; or daily life therapy, pioneered in Tokyo, which relies heavily on group dynamics, modeling, and physical activity). While it is generally agreed that early intervention is best, the effectiveness of these programs has still to be evaluated properly and may vary according to the needs, personal and community resources, and, unfortunately, finances of each autistic individual and her family.

See also Language Difficulties.

B

Baby Sitters and Nannies Early on in your child's life, you will probably start to use baby sitters, either to allow you to resume your own social life once again or simply to give you a well-earned break from the routine of parenting. Some parents employ full-time help, such as a day nanny or a live-in nanny. No matter how much time this caregiver spends in your home, your child has to feel comfortable with him or her. You may find that at first your child resists the idea of you leaving him with another person, but he will gradually get used to the idea.

Here are some strategies to help your baby, toddler, or young child adjust to being left in the temporary care of another adult:

- *Make sure the caregiver is capable and sensitive.* You should be fully satisfied that the person you employ is the sort of person you want to look after your child. Don't rush the selection process, or take second best.

- *Let your child meet the baby sitter or nanny before you hire.* Your child will have a more positive attitude if he thinks that he was involved in the selection process (even though you made the final choice).

- *Tell your child beforehand that you will be going out for a while.* Your child would probably prefer to know in advance that someone else will be looking after him, rather than being informed at the last moment.

- *Use a positive tone of voice when telling your child about the baby sitter or nanny.* Your child is more likely to have a positive attitude toward his new baby sitter or nanny when he thinks that you are positive about this person, too—your child's feelings reflect yours.

- *Reassure your child that he'll be fine.* He may be anxious at the last moment, just as you are about to leave. If so, calm your child down, and remind him of all the fun activities that he and the caregiver will do together while you are away.

- *Tell your child you will be back soon.* Your child's sense of time may be different from yours, so tell him you will be back soon. This is essential, as he may not realize you intend to return home.

- *If your child becomes upset at the separation, calm him and then go.* Don't be surprised if your child becomes slightly upset just as you are about to leave. Give him a quick cuddle, remind him you will see him soon, and walk out with a smile on your face. He'll be fine.

- *Praise your child when you return home.* Whether he was settled in your absence or not, give your child lots of praise when you come back. Make it clear how pleased you are with him, and ask him what he did while you were out.

See also *Playgroup/Nursery School.*

Bath Time Bath time can be such fun for you and your baby; a time for loving physical contact, a time when your baby can relax in the comforting warmth of the water. But it can also be a time for tears, especially when your baby feels insecure and frightened.

Look at it from her point of view—it is hardly surprising that bath time might cause your baby to feel terror rather than pleasure. The removal of clothes may increase her sense of vulnerability, the slippery surface of the bath may make her feel unsettled and afraid, the splashing of the water on her body may surprise her, and the soap in her eyes during hair washing may be distinctly unpleasant, even painful. So, try to remove as many barriers to an enjoyable bath time as possible.

First, try to make bath time a relaxed event, one in which you don't rush. Smile and appear relaxed to create a happy atmosphere for your baby. Second, undress your baby slowly, and put her into the water slowly and gently, so that she has time to adjust to the new situation. And smile and talk to her during this routine—the more pleasant the routine becomes, the better. Third, do your best to avoid getting any soap or water into your baby's eyes. Some parents use a splash-guard shield that fits over the baby's head, allowing hair to be thoroughly washed without the risk of water and soap trickling into her eyes; but some babies find this appliance uncomfortable. Certainly, you should wash your baby's hair from the front of her head toward the back. Last, have bath toys with which you and your baby can play. She'll love playing with floating plastic toys as she sits in her bath.

If you find that your baby is agitated about bath time despite all your efforts to calm her, gently persist. Use very little water in the bath, minimize the possibility of splashing, and constantly reassure her. In addition, you may want to consider a very gradual introduction to bath time; for example, use a very small sink or even hold her in your arms and wash her with a damp sponge. Once your baby is more comfortable, you can then slowly move her to a bath with water.

See also Independence.

Bedtime It's not unusual for a child to resist going to bed at the end of the day: he would rather stay up and continue to have fun! The easiest way to ensure your child goes to bed in a timely fashion is to have a bedtime routine. Allow sufficient time for a gradual approach to bedtime. Often, your child finds "turning off" just as hard as you do. First, slow down the pace and turn off the television, or lower the volume, and subdue the overall noise and activity level in the house. Then, give your child attention as he washes up or has a bath, puts on his pajamas, brushes his hair and his teeth. Then, tuck him into bed along with his special animal or blanket, and read him a story, or poem, or talk quietly about the day's activities. Then, say good night, preferably with a special ritual cuddle and rhyme, or lullaby. Then, turn off the light, shut the door, and leave, saying "It's time for you to sleep now. I love you. Good night, and sweet dreams." You can put your child to bed in about twenty minutes, although you may enjoy more time with your child.

Of course, genuine reasons may underlie your child's reluctance to retire for the evening— insecurity, fear of the dark (he may be more secure with a night-light), sickness, hunger, thirst. But once you have ruled out these possibilities, you can reasonably assume that problems in getting your child to bed stem from his simple desire to be with you.

Now is the time for consistency, especially with a child around two or three years of age. First, talk to him about the importance of bedtime, about his need for sleep, and about the fact that you need your time, too. The best time for such a talk is probably any time other than bedtime. Remind your child that everyone in the family has set times for going to bed. Everybody in the family needs sleep because sleep helps the body stay healthy. After you go through your child's full bedtime routine, if he ignores you and refuses to stay in bed, repeat your final good night tuck-in ritual, and insist that he remains in his bedroom. Don't let him get up to be with you, no matter how hard he tries to persuade you. Should he leave his bedroom, take him back. This strategy will work after a few weeks, as long as you are consistent.

A child aged four or five may regularly resist bedtime because he feels he is old enough to stay up later, or because his older brother or sister has a later bedtime. Rather than blindly insisting that he adheres to the time you have set, ask your child what time he thinks he should go to bed. Then reach a compromise. Even if you concede only an extra fifteen minutes, this will make your child feel he has been involved in the decision-making process and, as a result, he'll be more inclined to keep his agreement.

If you and your child still become locked in bedtime battles, try an alternative method. Suppose you want him to go to bed at eight o'clock, but he struggles against this for hours and doesn't actually fall asleep until ten. Since you know that your child's going to stay up late anyway, tell him that for the next three nights he doesn't have to go to bed until 10:30 (i.e., half an hour after the time he is usually asleep). He will almost certainly cooperate with you now because you have removed the source of conflict between you and him. Praise your child for going to bed at the agreed time without a struggle. After three nights, bring his bedtime forward by fifteen minutes, and repeat this process every three nights, each time making bedtime fifteen minutes earlier. Within six weeks, you may find your child goes to bed at eight o'clock, without a struggle.

See also Fears; Nightmares; Routine; Sleep.

Bed-Wetting

Although bowel and bladder control at night is usually achieved around the age of three years, a number of children have difficulty with this stage of development (for example, at age seven, one child in five still wets her bed occasionally; at age ten, about one in fourteen does so; and by age fourteen or fifteen, one child in thirty-three has occasional accidents).

A child becomes dry at night after she becomes dry during the day. Having achieved daytime bladder control, your child knows what is required of her at night. The most common sign of readiness for night training is when your child's diaper is regularly dry upon waking in the morning. Girls frequently reach this stage earlier than boys.

Common-sense rules apply to nighttime toilet training. Your child should use the toilet before going to sleep, and should be able to reach the toilet easily if she wakes up. Have a potty close to her bed, if this is more convenient. Leave a light on in the bathroom all night, if necessary. No scientific evidence supports the theory that a child who wets at night is a very deep sleeper. Rather, research confirms that a child can pass urine at any stage in sleep—not always at the deepest moment—and most commonly when moving from a phase of deep sleep into lighter sleep.

Don't worry if your child takes months, rather than weeks, to become dry at night. She needs lots of encouragement, and lots of praise when her bed is dry in the morning. Be prepared to wash mounds of sheets during night training.

Before they go to bed, some parents lift their sleeping child and take her to the toilet. There is no proof that this actually stops bed-wetting. In fact, it can be counterproductive because the parents take the responsibility for dryness away from the child. Nor is there any proof that depriving a child of drinks in the evening will help her become dry at night. Even total deprivation will not stop her bladder from filling while she is asleep—and refusing to give your child something to drink when she is thirsty could be a source of conflict between you and your child.

Psychologists have identified two types of bed-wetting that occur in children beyond the age of five years—primary enuresis and secondary enuresis; primary enuresis applies to a child who has never achieved bladder control at night, and secondary enuresis applies to a child who has been dry at night consistently and then unexpectedly begins to wet the bed. Many factors can cause primary enuresis, including the following:

- *Heredity*. Research has found that parents who themselves were slow to achieve bladder control at night often have children who follow a similar pattern.
- *Maturation*. With some children, bed-wetting may be caused by a delay in the development of the part of the brain needed for bladder control.

- *Poor training.* Not all parents adopt a consistent approach to toilet training. Sometimes the situation develops into a battle. Inconsistent strategies only confuse the child, or make her anxious. Also, the child may pick up your anxiety to have this training finished.
- *Urinary problems.* Bed-wetting can be associated with physical abnormalities or urinary tract infection, which is why medical advice should always be sought.

The cause of secondary enuresis is virtually always stress. Although a child who starts to wet at night after she has been dry consistently for a long period may have an infection or other physical illness, the wetting is more likely due to an emotional difficulty (such as the birth of another child in the family; starting playgroup, nursery school, or grade school; worries about friends; or parental arguments).

Seek professional advice if bed-wetting—whether primary or secondary enuresis—continues much beyond the age of five. The type of treatment given to your child will depend on her individual circumstances; your child should always get help for any psychological or physical difficulties that might be underlying the condition. Even when these stresses have been removed, your child will probably need additional treatment for the wetting itself.

Some pediatricians favor the use of drugs to treat children who are enuretic. This method has been highly criticized by some doctors because any drug treatment has some inherent dangers, such as unpleasant and toxic side effects from the drugs, accidental poisoning, and even deliberate overdosing by an unhappy child. Such risks seem unnecessary when the problem can usually be resolved by psychological methods and consistency.

See also *Toilet Training; Unhappiness.*

Birth Order Were you the youngest child in your family, convinced you were always last in line for everything? Were you the oldest, fed up with being given responsibility for your

younger brothers and sisters? Or were you a middle child, who had to follow in the footsteps of a clever brother or sister? There is little doubt that a child's birth order—his position in the family—affects his personality.

Jealousy of younger brothers and sisters is common in first-born children. Having been the only child in the family for some time, a first-born may feel threatened when the next child arrives. It's hardly surprising that some first-born children react with anxiety rather than pleasure at the prospect of a new baby. These feelings of jealousy and insecurity can last well into adulthood. Ask any of your friends who are first-born children if they recall having felt any resentment toward their younger brothers or sisters. Chances are they did. You'll probably find this rivalry between them still exists today.

Research has also shown that the oldest child tends to achieve more at school than his younger brothers or sisters. And this higher level of attainment often extends beyond school. Oldest children usually have better jobs than other siblings in the family.

One explanation for the oldest child's greater success in life is that parents are more conscientious about "doing the right thing" when raising their first child than they are when raising their second and third. Parents are also able to give the first-born child attention whenever he wants. This gives the first-born a head start over his brothers and sisters. However, this explanation fails to take into account that we make most of our mistakes with our first-born child, and are more confident with the next. A more likely theory of the first-born child's high attainments is his fear of being surpassed by his brothers and sisters—which makes him try harder to succeed.

Middle-born children frequently complain they are worse off than other children in the family. While the oldest is allowed the most freedom, and the youngest may be "spoiled," the middle child falls somewhere in between. The rivalry between children that drives the oldest to be a high achiever has a different effect on middle children. They tend to be less conventional than their brothers and sisters; the typical middle-born child prefers nonacademic pastimes, such as music and art, and likes clothes that lead, rather than follow, fashion. As adults, they often have a relaxed and carefree manner.

Perhaps these characteristics develop because a middle child—walking in the shadow of a successful older brother or sister—decides not to compete. Parents and teachers may be greatly tempted to motivate a younger child by reminding him of how well his older sister did when she was in that class. Instead of acting as an incentive, however, this strategy may encourage the middle child to reject traditional goals.

The youngest in the family usually finds that he is the center of attention. Older brothers and sisters, especially those aged five or six years and older, often dote on a baby and make a big fuss of him. Parents often spoil their youngest child because he is the "baby of the family" or, conversely, give up and allow the youngest child earlier privileges. At other times, though, this same child may find himself pushed to the back of the line when candies are being given out, or when all the children want to tell their news to mom and dad at once.

Youngest children tend to be the most self-confident of all, capable of handling worries on their own, without relying on advice from others. This level of independence probably arises from necessity. By the time he arrives in family, the youngest has other siblings who also seek the parents' attention. Practical circumstances dictate that the youngest has to become independent or else get used to waiting for help.

Youngest children also tend to be more "streetwise" than others in the family, an attribute that develops from the daily experience of working to secure their fair share of family resources. Constant competition with older brothers and sisters hones the youngest child's survival skills, and strengthens his ability to manage the stresses of everyday life.

The effect of family position on an individual child depends on many factors, such as the age gap or gaps between children, and whether the children are all the same sex. But the most important factor determining how much your children are affected by their birth order is you, their parents. The way you interact with your children is the strongest influence on their personality development.

For instance, you can reduce potential rivalry between an older child and his younger brother or sister by preparing the older child for the birth of the new baby. When the new arrival is brought home, involve the older child in the baby's basic care as much as possible. A middle-born child should never be saddled with the achievements of the older child. Avoid the trap of using the oldest child's school performance as the standard by which your other children are judged.

A youngest child's need to achieve independence will be less intense if you ensure he doesn't have to fight for everything. Although it's tempting to distribute toys, attention, and clothes on the basis of the oldest child first, then the next oldest, with the youngest last of all, let your youngest come first once in a while. Let him be the one to have a new outfit occasionally, instead of having to wear hand-me-downs all the time. Each of your children should be respected for his own strengths and weaknesses, not judged solely in relation to how well he compares with everyone else in the family.

See also *Age Gap; First-Born Jealousy; Jealousy; Only Child; Sibling Rivalry; Twins.*

Boasting Everybody compares their characteristics, their achievements, and their possessions with those of other people. There are some children (and too many adults!) who make these judgements in a very public way and openly show off some object they have obtained or boast about some goal they have attained. Young children are particularly prone to this.

The act of boasting, of course, makes your child feel very important. But your child's friends are unlikely to be pleased with what she says. A child who constantly does this will eventually become unpopular. This is why you should discreetly discourage this type of behavior, perhaps by pointing out to your child that other children feel miserable when she boasts because it reminds them of the things they don't have, or that her boasting makes others jealous. You should also set a good example yourself (a boasting parent is likely to have a boasting child), which will discourage your child from developing this sort of behavior.

A child may regularly boast about herself as a result of a deep-rooted feeling of insecurity. Outwardly the child may appear very confident and successful, but inwardly she may feel miserable and inadequate. Boasting in these circumstances is the child's unconscious way of hiding from an unpleasant reality. Always look closely at a child who boasts regularly, in order to identify any underlying factors in her life that may be troubling her. Removal of these influences will decrease your child's need to rely on boasting to boost her self-esteem.

See also Lying; Self-Confidence.

Body Language Children communicate their ideas

and feelings in two ways—verbally, using words, and nonverbally, using body movements. Body language (also termed nonverbal communication) reveals as much as spoken language. What makes body language particularly fascinating is that we don't have as much control over it as we do over spoken language. Body language leaks out, without us realizing.

Sometimes a child's body language conveys the same message as the spoken language; at other times body language and spoken language appear to be in conflict. When this happens, always believe the body language rather than the spoken language. Remember the time you asked your son to tidy his room because he had said he wouldn't mind, but then he sulked silently for the rest of the morning? Or the time your child claimed not to be upset by another child's aggressive behavior toward him, and yet burst out crying a few moments later? Incidents like this—where a child's body language reveals feelings that contradict what he says—happen all the time.

Young babies have no choice over whether to use body language as a means of communication; they can't speak. Parents quickly learn to interpret their baby's nonverbal communication; they learn the difference between a cry that signifies hunger and one that signifies tiredness, or the difference between wriggling that represents playfulness and wriggling that represents discomfort. This sort of nonverbal communication goes on between parents and children in a very natural way.

Body language follows the same principles, whatever the age of the child, although the younger your child is, the less sophisticated his body language. A young baby's nonverbal communication will include the following:

- *Facial expressions.* A baby's smile tells you he is happy; his pursed lips tell you he is unhappy; and his pouting lip tells you he is so annoyed that he's probably going to cry or scream at any moment.

- *Leg movements.* If a baby's legs are gently kicking in the air, then you can be sure he's happy and playful. On the other hand, if his legs are drawn tightly up toward his tummy, the chances are that he is in pain.

- *Arm and hand movements.* A baby whose hands are tightly bunched and held close to his face is probably in some discomfort, while a baby whose hands are open and relaxed is almost certainly feeling contented. Similarly, gentle hand and arm movements suggest playfulness, while swinging, forceful arm movements suggest anger.

- *Noises.* At this stage of development, a baby also uses sounds to let people know what he is feeling and thinking, such as quiet gurgling when he's contented, loud screaming when he's irritable, and babbling when he's trying to catch an adult's attention. Respond: This is the beginning of your child's use of language.

- *Breathing.* When a baby's breathing is slow and deep, he's either in a state of sound sleep or else he is about to enter a state of sound sleep, whereas shallow breathing usually means he is upset.

Your ability to interpret your baby's body language is one of the factors that influence the extent to which you are able to form a two-way emotional bond with him.

Older children have a much wider repertoire of body language than babies because they have a more mature level of understanding, are mobile, and are able to use eye contact more effectively. These new dimensions greatly expand a child's non-verbal communication skills:

- *Social Understanding.* The gap we leave between ourselves and another person during conversation (social distance) is normally between eighteen and twenty-four inches (forty-five and sixty centimeters). A greater distance probably means bad feeling between the people (for example, when your child angrily shouts at you from the other side of the room), while a shorter distance can mean either temper (such as when you and your child have a disagreement), or closeness (such as when your child sits on your knee while you read him a story).

- *Mobility.* A child who is angry can express anger in a number of ways using body language. He can simply walk out of the room, or throw his toys all over the place, or even lie flat on his back and scream. Most of us have experienced this type of nonverbal communication from an irate child, and we don't have any problem interpreting the deeper meaning underlying it!

- *Eye Contact.* When a child is tense and nervous, or when he feels guilty about having done something he knows is wrong, then, chances are, he will not be able to make eye contact with you—he will look at the ground when talking to you. On the other hand, when he tells you something he is pleased about, he will probably look straight into your eyes as he talks to you.

See also Bonding; Postnatal Depression; Visual Difficulties.

Bonding The emotional attachment between parent and baby is known as bonding. Bonding is a gradual and ongoing process that sometimes starts before birth, or often at the time of birth, but for most parents is a longer process.

A newborn baby is biologically programmed to interact with her parents; she is born with a number of characteristics that enable bonding to take place. For instance, a newborn baby's

- *hearing* is already tuned to a specific frequency so that she hears human voices in preference to any other sounds in the environment.

- *vision* has the sharpest focus at a point somewhere between seven and nine inches (eighteen to twenty-three centimeters) away from her face, which is the distance she's usually held from her parent during feeding.

- *voice* has a broad range of tones, in order to let her parents know when she is hungry or in distress.

Psychologists place great importance on the bond between a child and her parents, because this emotional relationship has the greatest influence on the child's subsequent psychological development. The quality of this affectionate bond determines many of the child's emotional characteristics in later life.

You shouldn't worry if some time passes before you and your baby mesh. Whereas young animals can become emotionally attached, or imprint, to a caring adult figure (even to humans in some cases) only during a specific short period at the start of life, a human baby does not have to form an emotional connection with her parents during a fixed time span. A baby has to be able to differentiate her mother from every other adult before a unique connection can develop between them. Research has shown that while most babies can differentiate their mothers within hours after birth, some babies do not acquire this skill until around the age of six or seven months, so a genuinely reciprocal mother-infant attachment may not be formed until then, and it can take longer.

Children who have not formed a secure relationship with at least one adult before the age of four often have difficulty with relationships in later life. In extreme cases, failure to form an emotional connection can lead to psychological disturbance. Psychologists once thought that breastfeeding forges a closer bond between mother and baby than bottlefeeding does. But the specific method of feeding in itself has little to do with bonding. What matters is the emotional interaction between the mother and her baby. This interaction can take place either through a bottle or a breast. What matters is the caring way a mother holds her infant when feeding, and the soothing words she speaks. These factors are more important to bonding than whether the milk comes out of a human nipple or a latex nipple. A mother who is tense and anxious when breast-feeding is not putting her baby at risk psychologically by changing to bottlefeeding.

The following factors will help establish an emotional connection between you and your baby:

- *Your ability to soothe your baby when she is upset.* Bonds are strongest in families where a parent can calm an unhappy baby with his or her presence.

- *The amount of time you lovingly cuddle your baby when she is irritable and unsettled.* Your loving physical contact will draw you and your baby closer.

- *Your sensitivity to your baby's communication.* At first, you may be unable to interpret your baby's actions. Her crying could mean she is in pain, or it could mean she is bored. The more you understand and respond to your baby's signals, the stronger the emotional attachment between you.

Your child can form bonds with more than one person, not just with you; she is as likely to form an emotional attachment with her father as she is with her mother—or perhaps with her nanny or baby sitter. Nowadays, fathers play a much more active role in their child's life, and so the chances of bonding between a father and his baby are high.

See also Body Language; Fathers; Mothers.

Bottlefeeding Although breastfeeding undoubtedly has distinct physiological advantages over bottlefeeding for your baby, the same cannot be said about psychological advantages. The fact is that a bottle-fed baby will have the same satisfactory emotional development—and the same psychological attachment to his parents—as a breast-fed baby. What matters is the loving way your baby is held during feeding, the soothing words you say to him, and the degree to which his hunger is satisfied. He really doesn't care whether the milk comes out of a human nipple or a latex nipple, just as long as it is warm, tasty, and plentiful!

Psychological research has shown that bottle-fed babies tend to develop a more stable sleeping routine than breast-fed babies. This probably occurs because the schedule for bottle-feeding is determined by the parents and the amounts can be accurately monitored, whereas the breastfeeding schedule is usually determined by the baby and the amounts cannot be accurately assessed. Bottlefeeding also allows someone other than the mother to take a turn at night feeding, allowing the mother vital rest.

Bottlefeeding requires all the equipment to be sterilized and for the formula to be served at the right temperature. So follow the guidelines very closely, and don't take any chances. If in doubt about any particular bottle of formula you have prepared (for instance, because the milk is discolored, or it doesn't smell right, or you're not sure if you mixed it correctly) then throw it out and prepare another one. You may have to try a few different formulas before you find the right one for your baby. One of the dangers of bottlefeeding is that it provides an easy opportunity to thicken the formula as an early introduction to solid foods. Avoid this, as your baby may be physically unable to digest any type of solids at this age. Better to wait until your baby is about three or four months old before changing his diet in this way.

See also Bonding; Breastfeeding

Breastfeeding Your pediatrician will recommend that for the first year after birth, your baby be fed only breast milk or a commercially made infant formula. Mom's own milk is nature's answer to the feeding requirements for an infant. An infant formula is just that, a construction of ingredients that is a close approximation, but not an exact copy, of breast milk. Cow's milk should be introduced only after your baby reaches her first birthday.

Breastfeeding provides your baby with real physiological advantages. In the first days after birth, the mother's body produces a nutritious substance called colostrum, which also provides antibodies for the infant. These antibodies help your baby resist infection until her own immune system starts to function more efficiently.

Breastfeeding also prevents constipation, feeding problems, and possible allergic reactions to the ingredients in infant formula.

Infant formula is an expensive addition to the family grocery bill, requires heating, and has to be fetched from the refrigerator for middle-of-the-night feedings, while mom's milk is convenient and readily available.

Some types of formula have to be mixed with water. This can be a problem in areas where water is of dubious quality or where heavy metals or bacteria are present in the water supply. In third-world countries, many infant deaths are blamed on formula-feeding. Either the supply isn't constantly available and mom's milk has dried up, or the inadequate water quality causes infant diarrhea, and death.

One research study indicates that formula-fed babies are more at risk for adult obesity than breast-fed babies because mom or dad continues to feed the baby until the formula is gone, possibly because the formula is so expensive, although the baby may be full. The infant learns to disregard the cues to stop eating when she's full.

Breastfeeding also requires the new mother to slow down and relax with her baby while she feeds. The mother's milk will "let down" when she sits or lies down to feed her baby. Relaxing while she feeds her baby helps a mother to recover from the exhaustion she feels after the birth.

While breast is best, as the old saying goes, never feel guilty if you can't manage breastfeeding. Some women can't because of medical reasons. As well, not every woman desires to breastfeed. But do give it a try if at all possible, especially in those early days right after birth. Any is better than none for your baby. You can always introduce formula later.

See also Bonding.

Breath-Holding Your toddler is prone to tantrums from the age of eighteen months onwards, as he struggles to gain control over his temper. Your child's desire to do what he wants, when he wants, can be so overwhelming that he explodes into an uncontrollable rage. Tears, screams, and even physical aggression can result. However, some children express the fury of a tantrum in the form of breath-holding, when the child appears to swallow his tongue, stops breathing, and then faints. Breath-holding among young children is more common than you might think. There is no evidence that a breath-holding tantrum is caused by or results in any form of brain abnormality.

The sight of a breath-holding tantrum is terrifying and upsetting for parents; watching your child's face turn a shade of blue as he gasps for air that he himself is blocking is absolutely awful. Remember, though, that this happens involuntarily—it is definitely not a deliberate, manipulative act on the part of your child. He can't help himself, especially if he is three years old or younger. When your child recovers from the fainting episode, he'll probably burst into tears and desperately want a cuddle.

Your child cannot harm himself during a breath-holding attack (unless he knocks his head falling over). The moment your child faints, his tongue muscles relax, which in turn instantly clears his airway. However, try to stop these attacks if possible. If you know your child is likely to have a breath-holding tantrum when he loses his temper, then calm things down before the child reaches the explosion point. When he does begin to hold his breath, help him move his tongue forward, either by opening his mouth and *gently* hooking your finger round the back of the tongue so that you can manually ease it forward, or by opening his mouth and *gently* blowing to the back of his throat. These methods do not always work but they are worth trying. Catch your child before he falls, to prevent injury.

Your toddler will probably not remember what happened once he recovers, but talk to him about it anyway. As your child grows older, he will be more aware of the process and might be able to halt the episode before it occurs. Your child will grow out of this method of expressing his temper by the age of five years at the latest.

See also Tantrums.

Bullying Bullying is one of the worst forms of antisocial behavior because it involves exploiting someone else's personal weakness by frightening that person into acquiescence. Every child fears a bully. Some children are naturally adventurous and enjoy rough-and-tumble play—but this isn't bullying, because these children's behavior lacks a malicious or sinister dimension. Bullying involves a deliberate act of coercion.

A child bullies for many different reasons:

- *Identification with parents.* Children "identify" with their parents and copy their behavior. A child of parents who show concern for the feelings of others is more likely to be caring toward other children than she is to be uncaring. A child of parents who believe the best way to deal with others is to threaten them with violence is more likely to express aggression in her relationships than she is to express sensitivity and kindness. Identification means that bullying parents usually have bullying children.

- *Release of frustrations.* Like adults, children experience anger and frustration, which they should be allowed to release verbally rather than physically. However, some parents discourage their children from voicing negative feelings, preferring all unpleasant emotions to be concealed. A child in this situation can only express her anger outside the family, and this may manifest itself as bullying. The victim becomes the means through which the bully releases her tension. Remember, active play and lots of physical activity is a great release for repressed anger and frustrations in small children.

- *Extremes in family discipline.* Parents who are either too restrictive in the way they discipline their child (for example, they have very firm and narrow guidelines for acceptable behavior, and punish any infringement immediately) or too permissive (they avoid any rules and let their children do as they please) tend to have children who are aggressive and bullying. A more balanced discipline is preferable.

- *Feelings of inadequacy.* A child may compensate for poor performance at school or a lack of friends by trying to prove herself in other ways. Aggression toward her fellow pupils may be the one field in which she can come out on top. Unconsciously, this type of child bullies others in the hope of achieving some sort of recognition.

- *Unhappiness.* Any source of severe and long-term unhappiness (such as pressure at home, jealousy of brothers and sisters, or even sickness of a relative) can put a child under considerable stress. When stress of this sort is prolonged, the child may strike out against others.

What is bullying? It occurs when

- your child is verbally threatened, or physically attacked;
- your child is punched or kicked deliberately;
- your child's lunch is stolen, her homework destroyed, or her backpack dumped;
- your child is tripped or elbowed as she moves around the classroom;
- your child is the subject of verbal taunts and slurs because of who she is—perhaps she has special needs or belongs to a minority group or wears glasses or is short;
- your child is belittled in front of friends, peers, classmates;
- your child is pushed around.

Always treat complaints of bullying seriously. Remember that your child needs a great deal of courage to admit to you that she is being bullied. She may be terrified that you will approach the bully's parents or teacher and reveal to the bully that your child has lodged a complaint. Fear of retaliation makes most victims remain silent about bullying for a very long time. Reassure your child that you won't take any action without consulting her first. Try to persuade your child to let you discuss the situation with the other child's teacher or parent; often, this course of action successfully puts an end to the bullying very quickly.

However, you should also teach your child how to cope with bullying, using the following suggestions:

- *Persuade your child to walk away discreetly whenever the bully appears to be moving in her direction.* There is a pragmatic realism in the saying, "He who walks away lives to fight another day." Too often, this type of avoidance strategy is mistakenly construed by the victim as an act of cowardice. Safety is the first priority, and a child who keeps a low profile is less likely to be bullied.

- *Encourage your child to show as little reaction as possible to the bully's threats.* Generally, teasing and bullying will stop eventually if the victim displays indifference to the actions against her. Of course, ignoring verbal and physical threats is difficult, but it can be done successfully. One way to help your child achieve this is to role-play a bully situation with you at home. This will let your child develop skills to cope with the real event when it happens.

- *Increase your child's self-confidence.* Long-term bullying has the unpleasant side effect of reducing the victim's self-confidence. A child's realization that she cannot defend herself from attacks makes her feel inadequate. You can try to compensate for this by reminding your child of her achievements, whether these are in sports, school subjects, music, or in having many friends. Your positive remarks will increase your child's self-confidence and may indirectly increase her ability to cope with the bully.

- *Never tell your child to fight back.* Tempting as it may be to encourage your child to retaliate, this advice can have a number of drawbacks. First, your child may not have the necessary physical skills. With your encouragement, your child may go headlong into battle with the bully and actually end up worse off than before. Second, telling your child to fight back simply means that there will now be two violent children instead of one. Third, if your child thinks you believe in aggression—however justified the circumstances may be—she may think aggression is a suitable way to deal with any problem involving others. It isn't.

See also *Aggression; Discipline; Kindness; Modeling; Sociable Play; Streetproofing; Victim.*

C

Celebrations While our expectations are that birthdays, holidays, weddings, and other festive occasions are happy times for children, times for having fun or for giving and receiving presents, these occasions can also be a time of confrontation and stress between you and your child.

One source of conflict is the often unrealistic expectations that parents have of their child on such days. Most parents assume their child will be delighted with his presents (which he probably will be), that he'll play happily all day (which he probably won't, because the boredom factor soon sets in), and that he'll behave (which he probably won't, due to all the excitement). When the child doesn't fulfill these expectations, tempers become frayed.

Another source of conflict stems from the way parents can misuse their child's desire for a gift as a means of controlling his behavior. Parents sometimes use the promise of a present on Christmas Day, for example, as a "carrot" to encourage their child's good behavior, or they wield the threat of no present as a "stick" to discourage naughtiness. This method of discipline cannot work effectively. Make your child's gifts unconditional. Remember, the best way to ensure both you and your child enjoy any festive occasion is to have realistic expectations of his behavior on the day itself.

See also Discipline; Manners; Politeness.

Cerebral Palsy This is a general term that describes a range of serious coordination difficulties, including the following:

- *Spasticity,* in which the leg and arm muscles are very tight and contract very strongly when the child attempts any stretching movement. Spastic muscles often become shorter as the child grows older, resulting in limb deformities.

- *Athetosis,* in which the muscles move involuntarily and uncontrollably. The child can attempt to make a purposeful movement, but it often becomes distorted.

- *Tremor,* in which the arms and legs shake. Continuous tremors are rare—tremor usually only occurs when the child tries to use her limbs.

- *Ataxia,* in which balance is poor. The child walks with an unsteady gait, holding her legs and arms apart to help balance herself. An ataxic child often falls over.

Estimates suggest that approximately one child in four hundred has cerebral palsy. All forms of cerebral palsy are caused by specific damage to part of the brain. This can occur in the womb (such as when a mother becomes infected by German measles early in the pregnancy), during the birth process itself (when a baby is denied oxygen for a short time during labor), or after birth (possibly as a result of meningitis). The specific form of cerebral palsy depends on which part of the brain is affected and how widespread the damage is. Cerebral palsy is a nonprogressive (nonworsening) condition.

The brain damage that affects the child's motor coordination frequently affects other body mechanisms as well. A child with cerebral palsy may have difficulty swallowing. Nearly half of all children with cerebral palsy have some form of speech difficulty. Hearing and visual defects may occur, and in some instances of spasticity, the child may experience convulsions.

Unless the condition is extreme, diagnosis of cerebral palsy rarely takes place at birth. Several days or weeks may pass before the baby's mother and father begin to sense that their baby does not move her limbs in the ways that she should. Although there is no cure for the condition, the earlier it is diagnosed the better, since proper management of the child in the preschool years can make a significant difference in the way she manages her motor-coordination difficulties.

Once a child is identified as having cerebral palsy, a number of therapies—physiotherapy, occupational therapy, and speech therapy—will be made available to her if required. In every instance, the therapist will be actively involved with the child, and will give parents advice on activities suitable for the child at home. An occupational therapist may also arrange for the child to be supplied with specific aids, to enable her to sit at a table, to walk, and to eat independently. Surveys indicate that at least 50 percent of children with cerebral palsy have learning difficulties, and there is a higher incidence of severe learning difficulties among such children than there is among the general population. However, this does not mean that every child with cerebral palsy will inevitably be a slow learner. Each child must be treated individually, since the child's rate of development depends on the degree of brain damage.

A child with cerebral palsy should be encouraged to lead as normal, and as independent, a life as possible. This should begin in the preschool years. Encourage your child to cope with her coordination problems so that she can play with other children of her own age. While some children with cerebral palsy are so severely affected in their motor coordination, their intellectual development, and their speech that they require specialized schooling, many children with this condition can attend an integrated school.

In recent years, conductive education has become increasingly popular. This treatment aims at promoting the all-around development of a child with cerebral palsy. It combines physiotherapy, occupational therapy, and speech therapy in a multifaceted approach.

Conductive education prepares a child with cerebral palsy for school by developing her thought processes, language, communication, mobility, and hand control. This training can enable a child to participate more fully in the education offered in an integrated classroom. Advocates of this system claim that children are not taught how to use a wheelchair—they are taught to walk. They are not taught how to manage their incontinence—they are taught to be continent. They are not taught alternative means of communication because of their speech difficulties—they are taught to speak.

See also Clumsiness; Coordination; Hand-Eye Coordination.

Clinging
As your child develops during the early years, he gradually establishes his independence. For instance, he can do much more for himself at the age of four years than he could a year earlier. But your child still needs you for support no matter how independent he has become, and there will be times he clings tightly to you. Parents are often surprised to see their apparently independent child suddenly become clingy, usually when faced with a difficult or new situation. This clinginess is normal—it is a healthy sign of your child's strong relationship with you. Your child clings to you because he feels insecure and he knows that hugging you closely makes him feel safe.

Your child might be clingy in the following typical situations:

- *Meeting a stranger.* Even though you know this person very well, your child may be overcome with shyness and try to hide behind you.

- *Going to a party.* Despite your child's excitement, the moment of leaving you to enter the party can be daunting for him—as a result, he grips your hand.

- *Starting school.* This is a big step for a growing child, and he may be very clingy on the first day, even though he also looks forward to it.

- *Separating from you.* Any temporary separation (such as staying with a baby sitter, attending an activity class, or going to nursery school or playgroup) may be difficult for your child.

- *Experiencing something new.* Even a very confident child can crumble emotionally when faced with something new (such as a toy or a game), and he'll turn to you in his distress.
- *Fighting with a friend.* Friendships during the early years are volatile, frequently changing. This can make a child feel insecure and anxious, reluctant to let go of his parent.

Although it is normal for your child to be clingy at times, you should still encourage him to become independent. Your reassurance is very important—remember that he clings to you because he is insecure, so any reassurance you give will be helpful. Don't make fun of your child; suggesting that he is acting like a baby will decrease his confidence further. Instead, try to be supportive; encourage your child to persist with the event that is troubling him; remind him that he will manage; and make a big fuss over him when he does cope without being clingy. Of course, some children are by nature more clingy than others—these individual differences are perfectly normal.

You should be concerned, however, if your child's clinginess suddenly becomes very extreme (for instance, if your four-year-old clings to you desperately even though you simply want to go into another room for a moment to get a magazine). You should also be concerned when such behavior persists long after you have expected the clingy phase to have passed (for instance, when your child still sobs constantly for you while at preschool, even though all the other children have long since settled). In these circumstances, look closely at your child's life to identify something that could be troubling him. Once that is sorted, you'll probably find he is less clingy once again.

See also *Baby Sitters and Nannies; Friendships; Playgroup/Nursery School; Self-Confidence; Shyness.*

Clothes
Getting dressed in the morning is a skill that virtually every child masters. Before your child learns how to put clothes on, she'll learn how to take them off. It's a lot easier to take off a pair of socks or to slip out of a sweater than it is to put on a shirt or a pair of pants. The best age to start teaching your child to dress herself is about eighteen to twenty-four months,

when she has developed some coordination skills.

You will have to show your child how to get dressed, item by item. Pick an easy-to-put-on garment (such as a pair of sweatpants that can be pulled on without much effort). Put the garment on your child, then let her try by herself. Keep repeating this until she does it without your help. Point out clues that will help her: for instance, that labels go at the back of clothes; that the front of a T-shirt has a picture; that the pockets on a pair of pants are usually at the front. Give your child lots of time. First thing in the morning, when everyone is in a rush, is not the best time to start.

About the age of three or four, your child may be able to get partly dressed by herself. You can make dressing easier for her by laying out the clothes in a fixed order, on the floor. This way she knows with which garment to start. You might even put a small sticker on the front of each garment to help your child identify the way it should be worn. Pick clothes that don't involve complicated maneuvers during dressing—tops with loose necks are better than ones with buttons or zippers. Choose shoes with Velcro fastenings.

Your child will be more interested in getting dressed when she likes her clothes. Select items that are brightly colored, with attractive patterns. Young children particularly love clothes that they help choose. Let your child be involved in selecting which clothes she'll wear the following day; any child can be very fussy about what she wears. The more you involve your child in decisions about dressing, the more likely she is to cooperate with you.

By the time your child reaches school age, she should be able to put on most clothes by herself, without your help. However, even at this age zippers and buttons may still be too difficult. Likewise, your child may not be able to tie her shoelaces or fasten buckles on her sandals. Choose practical clothes that your child can manage independently, and iron on name labels for each garment. Give her lots of practice taking off her coat and hanging it on a hook and arranging her clothing neatly after she has been to the toilet. Your child will have to manage these tasks every day at school.

See also *Coordination; Hand-Eye Coordination; Independence.*

Clumsiness Children who are clumsy often grow up to dread physical activities because they see themselves as incompetent. These children develop a negative self-image about their coordination skills, and avoid any challenge that might test them.

Try the following tips to help a clumsy child acquire a more positive self-image:

- *Remind your child that he can do plenty of other things.* While admitting your child has physical limitations, stress his strong points: how many friends he has, how well he learns new skills, how well he sings. He won't forget his coordination difficulties, but emphasizing your child's positive qualities will strengthen his self-esteem.

- *Give your child physical challenges that are likely to lead to success.* Your child's self-confidence will be boosted every time he masters a physical task. Pick activities that are easy for him. Make the challenges appropriate to your child's level of motor coordination.

- *Accept your child's feelings if he gets upset.* Your child's tears after dropping his lunch tray in the cafeteria may seem silly to you because you know it's not a very important event in the grand scale of life. However, to a child, "blowing it" seems a catastrophe. Don't dismiss your child's emotions as babyish—let him know you know how miserable he feels.

- *Don't let your child avoid physical tasks.* For instance, when you want a breakable object brought to you from another part of the room, you might naturally tend to avoid asking your clumsy child. Although this strategy minimizes potential damage, it denies your child opportunities to learn how to improve his body movements. He needs these activities. Of course, you may want to keep *valuable* breakables out of your child's reach, be he clumsy or not.

The term "minimal brain damage" is often applied to an extremely clumsy child, suggesting that a small amount of brain damage is underlying the coordination difficulties. However, no clear dividing line separates a normal child who is clumsy from a clumsy child who has minimal brain damage. The main way to categorize a clumsy child is by looking at other areas of his development. While a normal clumsy child's development is adequate, apart from his coordination, a child with minimal brain damage frequently has additional problems, such as mild learning difficulties and confusion identifying left from right. These characteristics are found in many children who do not have minimal brain damage, but when a cluster of such attributes is present in a child, further medical examination is desirable.

See also Cerebral Palsy; Coordination; Hand-Eye Coordination.

Communication

You and your child communicate with each other in many different ways, depending on your child's age and stage of development. As a baby, your child's main form of communication is through body language, in which she uses smiles, tears, howls, and leg and arm movements to convey her emotions. You also use body language to communicate with your baby, as well as spoken language. The use of spoken language to communicate with each other increases in importance the older your child becomes.

Poor communication between parent and child can be a source of distress and unhappiness at home for all concerned. That's why it is vital to have effective and clear communication with your child. You may find the following suggestions helpful:

- *Talk to your child at an age-appropriate level.* There is no point, for instance, in telling an eighteen-month-old toddler that she must consider the feelings of others before snatching their toys—she won't grasp what you're saying. Likewise, a five-year-old child doesn't want to be spoken to as though she is a baby. Match your communication to your child's level of age, ability, and understanding.

- *Use actions as well, where appropriate.* By all means explain to a young child that you disapprove of the way she threw the jigsaw puzzle across the room in temper; but reinforce these words with action, perhaps by taking away the game until she calms down. Your young child will understand more clearly the message you are communicating when it is backed up by your behavior.

- *Make time to talk to your child.* Both you and your child have your own busy lives, and before you know it, you can find yourself spending more time taking your child from one place to the next than actually sitting beside her, communicating. Try to make at least a few minutes every day when you and your child chat to each other—she'll feel special, and this time provides you both with an opportunity to voice your feelings.

- *Criticize your child's behavior, **not** your child.* Being a parent can be very trying, especially with an uncooperative, demanding child who seems to be in trouble constantly. Of course, you have to discourage behavior of which you disapprove, but try to criticize your child's behavior (by saying, "Hitting other children is naughty") and not her ("You are naughty"). Your child needs to feel loved no matter what she does.

- *Pay games together.* Play is a child's natural form of communication and your child will love those moments when you play games with her, share a toy with her, or even read her a story. In these situations, your child will feel at ease and is more likely to reveal her emotions to you than at any other time. So join in with your child's play (though make sure you don't actually take over).

- *Respect your child.* The fact that your child is only three years old and has her whole life ahead of her does not reduce the significance of her experiences. Discovering that her favorite toy is broken will hardly make a headline in the local newspaper, but it might be a major catastrophe for your child. Treat her seriously and respect what she says to you even though it may seem trivial.

No matter what age your child, she also communicates through her behavior. Sometimes this is obvious (such as when she turns her back on you when she is in a huff or smiles when she is happy). But sometimes this communication can be more subtle (she might appear lethargic after fighting with her friend; or she might act aggressively because she is jealous of her younger sibling) and can be difficult to interpret. When you see your child behave in an uncharacteristic fashion, ask yourself what the cause of that behavior might be and what message she unconsciously might be conveying to you.

See also Body Language; Criticism; Language Development; Play; Quality Time.

Concentration No matter how eager your child is to
discover and explore his surroundings, he needs to concentrate on what he's doing. A focused attention span is important, particularly when your child nears school age and learns to travel around the neighborhood on his own.

Your child's attention skills change throughout the preschool years in the following ways:

- *From passive to active.* A new baby watches something only when it captures his attention by moving across his field of vision. An older infant actively searches and explores his world. His attention becomes more dynamic and controlled, more in line with his desire to discover.

- *From unsystematic to systematic discovery.* When you watch a young baby pick up and examine a rattle, you'll notice that he does it in a very haphazard way. An older child explores an object more systematically, so he discovers more about it.

- *From broad to selective attention.* Young babies can't filter out information very well—they try to attend to everything they see and hear. Older children are more able to focus their attention on one specific aspect of a situation—for example, they can see the "walk" signal at the cross-walk, even though there are hundreds of other objects around.

Some children have a very short attention span, long after others of the same age are able to concentrate for more than a few seconds. This can cause problems at school because such children may not listen carefully. A useful way to extend your child's attention span is to present him with a short activity (such as coloring) and observe how long he persists until his attention wanders (say, two minutes). The next night, encourage your child to color another picture and ask him to spend a little more time on it. Encourage him to persist with the activity for two minutes and fifteen seconds, and give him lots of praise when he achieves this. Then gradually increase the amount of time each night, until your child's attention span is longer. Depending on your child's reaction to gentle pressure, you may want to use a timer.

See also *Attention Deficit Disorder (ADD); Hyperactivity; Knowledge; Learning Difficulties; Learning Skills; Play.*

Coordination Your child's coordination skills—her ability to move and manage her legs, arms, hands, and fingers in a controlled and deliberate way—fall into two categories:

- *Gross motor coordination.* Your child's ability to control general body movements involving arms and legs (examples include kicking a ball, climbing over a fence, walking along a straight line, running quickly, catching a ball, and hopping).

- *Fine motor coordination.* Your child's ability to control hand and finger movements (examples include cutting with scissors, coloring, writing, picking up a small toy, making a model with toy blocks, tracing, and using eating utensils).

These skills are acquired at roughly the following ages. (Please note that these are approximate guidelines. Your baby may be ahead or behind these milestones.)

3 months   Your baby's head no longer flops about like a rag doll when she is lifted or when she lies in the crib; back firmness increases, and she shows signs of straightening her back when sitting on your knee; she will attempt to thrust out her hands when the breast or bottle comes toward her, but she will not be successful in touching it every time.

6 months

By this age, your baby will probably be able to sit up on the floor on her own without any support. Hand and finger control is more organized, allowing her to hold toys, shake them, and throw them when she is bored. She can also reach out deliberately to grab something that catches her interest.

9 months

Your baby's leg movements are not fully coordinated, but when put face down on the floor, she will try to propel herself along by crawling. She may even be able to stand up, using a low table or chair for support. Coordination between thumb and forefinger starts to show, and she begins to use them together, in a pincer movement, to pick up small objects.

12 months

Your baby can crawl without much difficulty, pulling and pushing with her arms and legs in unison; she may be able to walk rather unsteadily around the room, using furniture as support. Hand control may be developed to the point where she can use a pencil or crayon to make a mark on a piece of paper.

2 years

Your child can now walk confidently wherever she pleases; she can go up and down stairs on her own, although she still puts both feet on the same step before going to the next. She can kick a ball without falling over. Most toddlers of this age have established a definite preference for using one hand over the other.

3 years   Your child can jump up and down without overbalancing and can walk a few steps on her tiptoes. She can catch a large ball thrown gently to her, and she will attempt to tackle playground equipment in the local park. Pencil or crayon control is stronger, and she can make circular scribbling marks on paper. She will also have an idea of how to hold scissors, although she may not yet be able to cut with them.

4 years   Your child can use pedals to propel a tricycle along the ground. Throwing and catching is easier; she can run in specific directions and steer herself around obstacles without bumping into them. She makes a reasonable attempt to thread beads, and her pencil control is more mature. She can draw a person or a house.

5 years   Your child can now negotiate obstacles. She will show ability in ball games; she can also manage climbers, ladders, and other outdoor play equipment. She can hold scissors properly and cut paper with them. She may be able to write one or two letters that appear in her name.

Although some of these abilities develop naturally, your child probably acquires most motor-coordination skills through the process of learning—so your involvement in her play is crucial.

DO'S

- *Do give your child lots of practice.* Most activities for developing fine motor-coordination control can take place indoors. Activities such as coloring, painting, and cutting pictures out of old magazines are easily organized—and extremely beneficial.

- *Do take your child to the playground.* In recent years there has been a huge upsurge in the number of well-designed adventure playgrounds for young children. Climbing frames, balancing logs, and obstacle courses made out of smooth pieces of wood bound safely together with nuts and bolts are a child's dream. Your child's confidence in playing with these will increase with experience.

- *Do make play time fun.* Your child will learn more quickly in situations she enjoys. Laughing and joking together will make your child feel at ease and more willing to try to master new challenges.

- *Do break up each new challenge into small stages.* For example, when teaching your child to catch a ball, first teach her to watch the ball when it is thrown toward her. Next teach her to put her arms out toward the ball; then have her touch the ball with her hand when it is thrown toward her; and so on. Each successive stage helps your child move closer to the goal, until she eventually succeeds.

- *Do give lots of praise.* Each time your child makes progress—no matter how slight it may be—show her that you're pleased. Tell your child how well she's doing and how much she has improved.

DON'TS

- *Don't force your child to be too adventurous on play equipment.* You may be very frustrated watching a timid child tentatively explore the first step of a ladder when you want her to go to the top. A child should never be encouraged to go to limits she is unable to manage by herself.

- *Don't ever make fun of your child.* Your child will be unhappy enough when she realizes she can't propel her tricycle, especially when her friends do it with ease. She doesn't need you to make observations about her lack of skill. Sometimes cajoling is done with the best of intentions—but it seldom works.

- *Don't have unrealistic expectations.* Children mature at different rates. The fact that another child of the same age can kick a ball while running doesn't mean your child is inadequate because she can't. Nor is there much advantage in a child having coordination skills normally found only in older children.

See also Cerebral Palsy; Clumsiness; Hand-Eye Coordination.

Creativity
Psychologists have compiled a list of features that describe an object or idea that is creative:

- *It must have novelty.* It should be original and unusual (for example, inventing a skateboard was novel because no similar play object for children existed before the invention).
- *It must be appropriate.* It should be sensible and suitable (for example, the suggestion that we can travel to work by flying saucer isn't appropriate because we don't have access to flying saucers).
- *It must involve a transformation.* It should involve a change in perspective, a new way to look at an old problem (for example, the invention of the hovercraft was creative because it introduced a craft that could hover above water rather than move through it).
- *It must involve condensation.* It should incorporate many different characteristics (for example, the invention of the modern video recorder was creative because it allowed people to record programs, play programs others had recorded, and plan their leisure time more effectively).

Many famous figures in the world of art and music showed signs of creativity in childhood. Mozart composed symphonies before he was five years old, and Leonardo da Vinci early demonstrated his artistic ability. Creativity, like all human characteristics, is present in every one of us to some extent. Every child has the potential to be creative.

A "genius level" of intelligence is not needed. Most highly creative people are of at least average intelligence, but beyond that the intellectual levels of creative minds vary widely. Forgetfulness is not a requirement of creativity—no evidence supports the stereotype of the creative individual as the absent-minded professor. Research has shown that creative children tend to take more risks, be less frustrated by their mistakes, be self-confident, independent, successful at learning tasks, socially competent, unconventional, and eager to experiment with new ideas.

Tests for measuring creativity are open-ended (they have more than one right answer). The problem with these tests, though, is how to score the answers. Suppose two children are asked to take a blank piece of paper each and make as many different patterns on it as they can. One of the children might make five patterns, while the other might make six. Yet that does not necessarily mean that they differ in creativity levels—possibly, the first child's five patterns are all completely different, whereas the other child's six patterns are all similar. Such problems have made tests of creativity unpopular. Remember, too, that every child has his individual learning style. Some children simply don't enjoy open-ended challenges, which doesn't mean they lack creativity.

You can help your child develop his creativity:

- *Show respect when your child asks unusual questions.* You may have a busy enough day without answering such questions as "Why don't trains fly like airplanes so that they would arrive at the station quicker?" It's tempting to dismiss such inquiries as unnecessary interruptions, but that attitude will discourage your child from developing his creative thoughts. Treat unusual questions seriously, and take time to answer them. If you can't think of a suitable answer, then be honest and admit that. Arrange a trip to the library to find answers. Pay attention to your child's thoughts, and ask him what he thinks whenever he asks questions.

- *Allow your child to express his imaginative ideas freely.* Listen to your child when he suggests that cars should be made with engines that run on water because it's cheaper than gas. If you show interest, he will not be afraid to voice other imaginative ideas in the future. Never ridicule your child's ideas or be sarcastic about them.

- *Give your child opportunities to play in unstructured situations.* Resist the temptation to turn all play experiences into some form of directed learning. Your child needs to play freely at times, in order to unleash and develop his creative skills through play. Provide articles for play that can be used in a variety of ways—empty boxes, dress-up materials, blocks, and art materials.

- *Explain to your child the practical implications of his idea.* Research indicates that linking a child's creative idea to its practical consequences encourages further creativity (for example, you can tell your child that having cars that run on water would not only be cheaper, but also better for the environment).

- *Allow your child to solve problems for himself sometimes, instead of always showing him solutions.* One study of the problem-solving methods of children ages three to five involved each child determining how to reach a piece of chalk on the far side of the table at which he was seated. Each child had access to two short sticks and a clamp. Before each child was presented with the problem, he was either shown the long stick made out of two short ones or allowed free play with the sticks and the clamp. The investigators found that children who were allowed free play with the materials were much more innovative and creative in their solutions to the problem than were the other children.

See also Imagination; Intelligence.

Crib Death
The sudden death of a healthy baby is one of the worst tragedies any family can possibly experience. Yet the tragic fact is that every year approximately one baby in five hundred dies suddenly, without any apparent reason. Crib death—known medically as Sudden Infant Death Syndrome (SIDS)—affects babies between the ages of one and five months (the average age is four months). At least half of all babies who die in this way appear to be in perfectly good health before death, while the other half often have had a minor respiratory

infection. Frequently, parents only realize their baby has died when they try to wake her after she has apparently been asleep for a longer period than expected.

Despite a great deal of medical research, the cause of crib death is unknown. Medical consensus suggests that parents should be aware of the following factors:

- *Smoke-free environment.* Try to create a smoke-free atmosphere around your young baby. Never smoke in her bedroom, don't let others smoke in any room in the house that she uses, and don't take her into smoky places. A baby is at increased risk of crib death if her mother smoked during pregnancy.

- *Temperature.* Every parent wants to be sure their baby is comfortable and warm. However, the baby is at increased risk of crib death if she is too warm, so use lightweight blankets that you can add or remove depending on her body temperature; and maintain a comfortable and steady temperature in your baby's room.

- *Sleeping position.* Doctors advise parents to lay babies to sleep on their backs or on their side with the arm positioned slightly forward on the mattress to prevent them from rolling over onto the tummy. Although parents worry that their baby may be sick and then choke when she is asleep on her back, this does not appear to happen. Crib death is more frequent among babies who are allowed to sleep on their tummies. If you are uncertain about the best sleeping position for your baby, discuss it with your pediatrician.

Crib death is still a rare occurrence, and few families experience more than one. Aside from these basic general precautions, keep your baby close to you when you think she is unwell—this will enable you to watch her closely and to notice any abnormality in her breathing. If you are at all concerned about your baby during the early months, don't hesitate to visit or phone your pediatrician.

Criticism No child thrives on criticism, although every child benefits from helpful correction. While both these measures share the purpose of changing a child's behavior, criticism is nearly always negative. It tells the child what is wrong, without offering suggestions for positive change. A child who is constantly criticized will soon lack self-confidence and have little belief in his own abilities.

Your child cannot improve his behavior at home, or his performance in class, unless he is aware of his weaknesses and of ways to change them. This is part of the learning process. Don't be afraid to point out to your child that he has put his sweater on backwards. If you don't let him know his mistake, he's likely to repeat it. At the same time, help your child learn how to do it properly, perhaps by explaining that the buttons go in front. These two aspects should always be combined.

Parents can become trapped in a cycle of criticism when their child regularly misbehaves—a pattern that is hard to break. The more a child refuses to do as he's told, the more you reprimand him. This increases tension at home, which unsettles your child even further, resulting in more criticism. If you find yourself in the situation of constantly criticizing your child, try to determine why he has the need to misbehave. Perhaps he has had a fight with his best friend, or is worried about school. Perhaps your expectations of him are too high. Dealing with the factors that cause your child stress is a more effective way to improve his behavior than regularly criticizing him. Never blame your child for your own difficulties.

Of course every child reaches the point where he needs a reprimand for breaking the family rules. Always ensure your child understands the difference between rejection of his behavior and rejection of himself. You child has to learn that you can be angry with him for something he has done and yet, at the same time, still love him. If your child knows this, then your occasional criticism won't do him any harm. If he doesn't know this, then he will fear even a slight negative remark.

See also *Communication; Discipline; Scapegoat; Self-Confidence.*

Crying Baby If your baby cries constantly throughout the night and doesn't respond to your efforts to quiet her, consider the following possibilities:

- *Diaper change.* Your first step should always be to check whether your baby needs a change of diaper, or whether a diaper pin has become unfastened and is sticking into her. The chances of either of these causing regular crying throughout the night are remote.

- *Health check.* Ruling out any physical problems is always sensible. Although your baby may seem perfectly healthy, especially if she is very settled during the day, she might have a medical problem. A thorough examination by your pediatrician will reassure you.

- *Colic.* This is a term used by doctors to describe pain in the stomach caused by spasms of the tummy muscles. Colic is thought to occur only in infants of three months or younger. But not everyone is convinced about the existence of colic. The explanation sounds good, and it's a plausible way to account for a young baby's distress. But colic is impossible to verify—you can't be certain that your baby has stomach pains.

- *Gas.* Some people think that a baby's crying may be caused by an excess of gas in her stomach, since a baby who cries constantly releases enormous belches quite regularly. Yet this doesn't mean that it's the build-up of gas that caused her to cry. On the contrary, some argue that the very act of continuous crying makes a baby suck in vast amounts of air. A loud expulsion of gas can just as likely be the result of crying, not the cause of it.

- *Child's diet.* Some professionals claim a link exists between food additives—used as colorings and preservatives—and unsettled behavior in children, but the evidence on this point is unclear. Even so, it is possible that a crying baby may be allergic to milk formula, for example, so a change is worth trying.

- *Mother's diet.* If you are breast-feeding take a look at your own diet. Infants can be affected by mom's consumption of cabbage, broccoli, cauliflower, onions, spices, chocolate, alcohol, and other strong-tasting foods.

If you have ruled out these possibilities, but your baby still cries throughout the night, then you may have to broaden your perspective. Crying babies create anxiety in their parents, and this can become a vicious circle. Parents who automatically assume their baby will wake up crying will be tense and agitated at the prospect of another horrendous night. Your baby may sense this tension and react to it by becoming tense and tearful. Your own anxiety caused by anticipating your baby's crying could actually play a part in causing the behavior you dread most. That's why calmness is extremely important when managing a crying baby—make a big effort to stay relaxed at night, despite your knowledge of what almost certainly awaits you.

A possible explanation of your baby's regular crying at night is that it is attention-seeking behavior and that she wants to be with you. If this is the underlying explanation for your baby's crying, consider ignoring her. Of course, no parent feels comfortable leaving a baby alone when she is in tears, but you must use your own judgement. (If you do adopt this strategy, use a monitor so you can hear her, even though you don't go into her room to see her.) Stick to your plan for at least three weeks, rather than giving up after one or two nights. Ear plugs are a wonderful invention (just be sure that you can still hear your baby).

Some babies cry constantly for a completely different reason—perhaps because their emotional attachment to their mother (or mother-substitute) isn't as close as it might be. An infant who does not receive emotional warmth from her parents during the early part of her life will be very unhappy and cry frequently.

Getting short-term relief from a crying baby is always a valuable practical measure. Distancing yourself from your howling infant, if only for a short while, can make the world seem a brighter place. Never hesitate to use family or friends as temporary caregivers for your baby. A few hours away can have a very positive effect.

See also *Additives; Attention-Seeking Behavior; Bonding; Dreams; Ignoring; Nightmares; Sleep.*

Cystic Fibrosis Cystic fibrosis is genetically an inherited condition in which the mucus glands produce an abnormally thick, sticky mucus in the lungs, pancreas, and bowel. A scientific breakthrough gave hope to thousands of families with children suffering this disease when researchers identified the exact gene responsible. However, a cure is still distant. Cystic fibrosis affects approximately one person in 1,500 to 2,000. It is one of the most common genetic diseases in the western world.

While many people carry the gene responsible for cystic fibrosis, they are completely unaffected. Should their partner also be a carrier—and there is a 1 in 400 chance that pairing will occur—then the couple has a 1 in 4 chance of having a child with cystic fibrosis; a 2 in 4 chance of having a child who is a carrier, but who doesn't have the disease; and a 1 in 4 chance of having a child who is neither a carrier nor has the disease. The cystic fibrosis gene is not sex-linked, so boys and girls are equally affected.

Without treatment, cystic fibrosis can be a killer. The child's bronchial tubes become clogged, leaving him prone to pneumonia and other lung infections. Digestion is also affected, because the enzymes that normally flow from the pancreas into the small intestine are prevented from doing so. In the 1950s, when effective treatment wasn't available, most children with cystic fibrosis died before reaching adulthood. Medical advances in the past forty years mean that approximately 70 percent of children with the disease survive into adult life, and sustain relatively little damage to their lungs.

Treatment for the condition has two essential components:

- *Physiotherapy.* Treatment must be carried out regularly each day in order to keep the child's lungs clear of mucus. Although initially treatment is provided by a qualified physiotherapist, eventually it can be carried out by the parents and child working together at home.

- *Enzyme substitutes to compensate for the pancreas problem.* Often, the child takes a very large number of pills at mealtimes, in conjunction with vitamin supplements and a high-protein diet.

Parents vary in their reaction to the diagnosis of cystic fibrosis in their child. Some become overprotective and isolate their child from peers as a precaution against infection. Others encourage their child to lead a normal life. A child with cystic fibrosis is usually able to attend a day-care center or nursery school; the only difficulty may be that the child will need physiotherapy around lunchtime, carried out at home. School staff should be aware that a child with cystic fibrosis is not fragile, although they should exercise caution if the child becomes breathless and starts to wheeze.

See also Genes.

D

Daytime Wetting Most children gain bowel and bladder control around the age of three or four years and are able reliably to remain dry during the day. Of course, toilet "accidents" will still happen at times even up to the age of five or six years, when your child becomes so overexcited momentarily that she wets herself or when she simply gets so involved in a game that she doesn't realize her need to use the bathroom until it is too late. These accidents are normal and are part of the learning process—they will soon grow less frequent and fade altogether. For some children, however, daytime wetting is present long after it is expected to have ceased. First, have your child checked by your family doctor to ensure that there is no physical cause of the day wetting (such as an infection). Assuming medical checks reveal no problems, then consider the possibility that a psychological reason is underlying the wetting.

There are two types of day wetting. The first type, which is less worrying, occurs when a child who has never been reliably dry during the day continues to wet herself regularly when she is five years or older. Chances are that this happens because the child did not learn bladder control properly during the earlier years, and hasn't progressed since then. Appropriate help for this form of daytime wetting includes a well-planned training program with lots of rewards for those times of the day when she is dry. Such a direct strategy usually has a quick effect.

The second type of daytime wetting, which is more serious, occurs when a child who has been dry during the day for several months, even years, suddenly starts to wet herself. In most instances, this wetting is a sign of the child's unhappiness and insecurity. If your child does have this difficulty, talk to her about all aspects of her life until you can determine the source of her worry. Something at school could be troubling her, or something with her friends. Try to sort out the problem—once your child stops worrying, she will stop wetting herself during the day.

See also Bed-Wetting, Toilet Training.

Discipline
The style of discipline used in any family is defined by the parenting style. Extensive research shows that discipline follows three main styles:

- *Authoritarian.* In an authoritarian family, obedience is a virtue. The child has no verbal give and take. The child has little or no autonomy and often feels rejected. This is when "Father knows best," regardless. The parent uses control, fear, and manipulation to direct behavior. Punishing the wrong behavior is the primary method of encouraging the right behavior. The parent has the final word, the parent is always right, and it is up to the parent to enforce the rules. Preservation of all structures is essential. While the child of authoritarian parents toes the line at home, his actions often fall apart in school or out in the world. Children who grow up in authoritarian families often feel left out of the family or often serve as a scapegoat for whatever is going on. They often turn into bullies or victims. Teachers often describe them as "spacey," "going blank," or "absent-minded." Such children may also lack the ability to compete with others or be assertive. This type of discipline often involves hitting and spanking.

- *Authoritative.* In an authoritative family, the parents set reasonable rules and standards and enforce them firmly. They are gentle, flexible role models. This is a "do as I do" approach. Parents negotiate with the child and solicit the child's viewpoint, but the parent remains consistent, rational, and flexible. While the parent listens to the child, the family doesn't revolve around the child's desires. The parent uses reason, power, praise, and rewards to encourage positive behavior, and lets the child experience some of the consequences of unacceptable behavior. Authoritative parents realize that a child who is able to set some of the guidelines is less likely to break the rules.

- *Permissive.* In a permissive family, parents accept whatever behavior the children dish out. There are no rules, no consequences, and no consideration of the effects the child's behavior has on other people. This is a "children know best" or "I can't be bothered" approach. Parents are nondemanding and affirm whatever impulses the child has. There is no restraint at all. Children growing up in this type of family have no self-control or self-reliance.

The conclusions reached by these studies show that authoritative parents most encourage the qualities of social responsibility, independence, an orientation to achieve full potential, and a vigorous approach to life.

Defined standards of behavior help everyone in a family. Discipline is a framework from which to start and to which to return for help and guidance. Good discipline

- provides structure, consistency, and predictability;
- sets clear standards and expectations of how a child will behave toward himself and others;
- makes a child feel safe and secure (clear limits and expectations protect him);
- eventually leads to self-discipline.

Detailed investigations reveal that behavior problems and emotional disorders are less frequent in children raised in a warm, loving atmosphere, and delinquency rates are lower. Children raised in a very restrictive household tend to be submissive, overpolite, and dependent on others. Children raised in a home where "anything goes" find that things don't work that way in the real world. Extremes of discipline, or parenting style, rarely have a positive effect on a young child. A balanced approach—one with clear guidelines, standards, and expectations exercised within a framework of support and encouragement—is usually the best approach to discipline.

Discipline is the one aspect of child rearing where both parents must be consistent, or the child will receive a mixed message. Ensure that you and your partner have the same styles and expectations. Young children recognize inconsistency and are quick to play one parent against the other.

See also Attention-Seeking Behavior; Bedtime; Crying Baby; Illness; Self-Confidence; Spanking; Tantrums.

Down's Syndrome This condition was first described

by Dr. John Langdon Down in 1866. Although he couldn't identify the source of the problem, he was able to list a number of common physical and psychological features, and it became known as a "syndrome."

Almost a hundred years passed before scientists were able to demonstrate that the defect lies in a child's genetic structure. In 1959, research revealed that Down's syndrome originates in the baby's chromosomes, and that the condition can be diagnosed by analyzing a sample of the baby's blood. With Down's syndrome, each parent has normal chromosomes, but their baby has an extra chromosome in pair no. 21, making a total of 47 per cell, instead of the usual 46. This form of the condition is known as standard trisomy and accounts for 96 percent of all children with Down's syndrome. A small percentage of babies with Down's syndrome have either translocation, in which one of the no. 21 chromosomes becomes attached to another chromosome; or mosaicism, in which some of the cells have 46 chromosomes and some have 47. Since this latter form of the condition involves a mixture of affected and nonaffected cells, children with mosaic Down's syndrome may look less affected than other babies with Down's syndrome and may show better development.

Down's syndrome is present in approximately one in seven hundred babies, and occurs by chance. Research studies have shown that the likelihood of a baby being born with the condition increases significantly when the mother is thirty-five years of age or older at the time of conception. That's why prebirth screening techniques are targeted at this older age group.

The traditional screening technique for detecting Down's syndrome in the unborn baby is amniocentesis, in which a fine needle is inserted into the womb so that a small amount of amniotic fluid can be drawn off for analysis. There is a slight chance that this process may stimulate a miscarriage, so the test is restricted to those women in the high-risk category. Other types of screening tests are available, including chorionic villus sampling (CVS), fetal blood sampling, and maternal blood sampling. However, none of these techniques are as reliable as amniocentesis for accurately diagnosing Down's syndrome.

Children with Down's syndrome share certain physical characteristics, although not all features are present in every child. As a result, the condition can often be identified in the first few days of a baby's life. Common signs include floppy muscles and loose joints, an extra fold of skin at the inner corner of each eye, a low nose bridge, a protruding tongue, and a small, straight mouth. In the first week, a baby with Down's syndrome may not gain as much weight as would normally be expected.

Health difficulties are associated with the condition. A child with Down's syndrome is prone to chest and sinus infections. Cardiac problems may occur—varying from a minor murmur to a more serious defect. Therefore, medical specialists always pay close attention to the child's heart development, especially during the first year. Difficulties with eyes and ears are common. Speech may be unclear because of poor muscle tone in the child's mouth. The average life span of someone with Down's syndrome is shorter than normal, but some people do live beyond the age of seventy.

Virtually all children with Down's syndrome have some form of learning difficulty, ranging from mild to severe. They need a stimulating environment in the preschool years. Language development is frequently delayed, though useful speech is often acquired eventually. Speech therapy may be helpful, and many attain a purposeful degree of independence that extends into adult life.

At one time it was assumed that children with Down's syndrome, whatever their level of development, had such severe problems that they could not benefit from regular primary classroom education. Most pupils with the condition automatically attended segregated special schools with smaller classes and specially trained teachers. Education experts have begun to question the value of segregated special schooling. Many local school boards are ready to accept the principle of integration and are increasingly willing to support pupils with Down's syndrome in local primary schools. Some local authorities start the process of integration in kindergarten, which makes it easier at the primary school stage. Provision does vary from school board to school board.

Parents may fear that, while integration is acceptable in principle, it doesn't work. A study that compared the development of eighteen pupils with Down's syndrome who attended ordinary schools against the development of eighteen pupils with Down's syndrome who attended segregated special schools for children with moderate learning difficulties found that the children who were mainstreamed made significantly more progress than those who were segregated, in terms of numerical ability, comprehension, and mental age.

Decisions about schooling of any child with special needs should only be made after detailed consideration of the individual child's educational, social, medical, and psychological needs, and of the educational facilities and opportunities provided by the local school board. At least, now more parents are offered a choice.

Not every parent wants their child with Down's syndrome to attend a local primary school. The attractiveness of a child moving at her own pace, the confidence that special equipment and learning materials are readily available whenever needed, and the knowledge that the child can get the teacher's individual attention when necessary make many parents still favor segregated special schooling.

See also Integration, Educational; Special Needs.

Dreams Ask your child what he dreamed about last night. Can he remember? Chances are he can't, but chances are he did dream. Virtually everybody dreams, even though they often forget the content of their dreams when they wake up.

Dreams occur during REM sleep—that phase of sleep in which the eyes move about very rapidly while still shut, as if scanning a picture beneath the unopened eyelids. Experiments have revealed that 80 percent of people report having dreams when woken during REM sleep, while less than 10 percent do when woken at other times. The length of the dreamer's description of a dream is directly related to the length of time he has been allowed to have an uninterrupted period of REM sleep.

Research by American psychologists suggests the following:

- Three-year-olds give short accounts of dreams, with very little action and feeling in them. Dreams in this age group are often about play sequences that take place in familiar settings, or about animals.

- Six-year-olds produce much longer accounts of their dreams, with a lot more movement and activity. Their dreams usually feature friends or members of the immediate family. The dreamers themselves play a passive role.

- Six-year-old girls tend to dream about about friendly people, and often have happy endings. Six-year-old boys' dreams contain more conflict and aggression. This gender difference disappears when children reach age seven or eight.

- Ten- to twelve-year-olds usually have dreams that focus on their home, the play area immediately outside home, or school. Mostly, the people appearing in these dreams are friends or members of the child's family, although boys of this age often dream about male strangers. Children's dreams mainly center on play and other leisure activities. The majority of dreams experienced by young children are not frightening or distressing.

REM sleep is found not only in adults, children, and young babies—even a fetus has REM sleep. Ultrasonography has shown that a fetus begins to have REM sleep as early as the twenty-third week of pregnancy. Amazing to think that a being so young—some seventeen weeks before leaving the womb — could actually be dreaming. Of course, precisely what is going on in the mind of the fetus is unknown at this point. But we do know, from close electronic monitoring of newborns, that during periods of REM sleep babies experience intense stimulation through their central nervous system. Almost 50 percent of a new-baby's sleep is REM sleep.

During a baby's first year of life, total sleep time drops from about sixteen hours per day to about thirteen hours per day. Since the amount of non-REM sleep stays the same, this means that the amount of REM sleep is considerably reduced between birth and twelve months. This pattern continues until adulthood, by which time approximately 20 to 25 percent of total sleep is REM sleep.

Freud maintained that the only way to fully understand a child is to understand his unconscious mind, and that the best way to do this is through interpretation of the child's dreams. He reached two major conclusions about children's dreams. First, the purpose of a child's dream is to allow a hidden wish to come true: a wish that can never become a reality in the child's real world—or that would get the child into trouble if he did try to make it come true—can become a reality in the child's dream world. Second, a child's dream is usually triggered by something that has happened in the previous twenty-four hours—for example, a fight with a friend, a reprimand from parents, an incident involving a particular toy, or a comment from another child.

Analyzing the dreams of very young children, from eighteen months upwards, is very easy, claimed Freud, since a young child always dreams of the fulfillment of wishes that were aroused the previous day but were not satisfied. So in order to understand the child's dreams, simply ask the child about his previous day's experiences.

Some dreams, though, require more interpretation than this because they use symbols to represent people and objects in the child's life. For instance, parents are often symbolized by figures of authority, particularly royalty. Other common symbols that appear in children's dreams include falling into, or coming out of, water (representing birth); houses (representing people); and rodents or other small animals (representing brothers or sisters). Very young children rarely use symbolism in their dreams.

To interpret the meaning of your child's dreams, use these principles—you may not get it right every time, but you'll have some fun trying.

- *Wait until your child is fully awake before you ask him about his dreams,* because young children can have difficulty knowing when they are awake and when they are asleep.

- *Use a relaxed, casual voice when asking your child about his dreams.* If you seem too interested, he may become concerned and not want to tell you.

- *Be satisfied with a short answer.* Don't expect a long description. Most young children will give only a sentence, two at most, about their dreams.

- *Look for symbolism.* Pay particular attention to the people and objects mentioned in the dream, even if you don't recognize them. These objects may be dream symbols that represent something else in the child's life.

- *Look for a central theme running through the dream* that may signify the fulfillment of your child's hidden desire.

- *Try to make a link between the content of the dream and an incident involving your child that has taken place in the past day or so.*

- *Bear in mind related emotions.* Once your child has told you about his dream, ask him how he felt during it. The feeling accompanying a dream can be a good clue about its meaning because it can reveal whether the dream is happy or sad, worrying or relaxing, and so on.

- *Have patience.* If you have difficulty analyzing your child's dreams, don't worry—despite what Freud said, some psychologists spend years in training before they are able to interpret children's dreams accurately.

See also Bedtime; Crying Baby; Nightmares; Sleep.

Dyslexia When a child has dyslexia, you might notice a surprising disparity between her apparently good ability and her low educational progress. The effects of dyslexia vary from mild difficulties with reading, writing, and spelling to complete illiteracy. Some dyslexic children also have problems learning mathematics. Early identification is vital in order to provide appropriate help.

Nobody knows the cause of dyslexia, although most psychologists now accept that it is related to the brain's neurological structure. There is no cure for it. Dyslexic children can be helped to deal with their difficulties through the provision of multisensory teaching methods, which combine sound, sight, touch, and movement. Dyslexic children have problems processing information through at least one of these senses. Effective multisensory teaching must be highly structured, moving one small step at a time, so that a pupil can build up her reading, writing, and spelling skills in a systematic way. Many school boards provide specialist teachers who have been trained in these methods. Basic exercises to improve memory skills are also useful.

With proper professional help, a dyslexic child can progress successfully through primary and secondary school, and even through higher education. A child's special educational needs call for close consideration at every stage. This can only be achieved through adequate assessment, appropriate teaching methods, and sensitive understanding from all the adults involved.

See also *Attention Deficit Disorder (ADD); Hyperactivity; Intelligence; Learning Difficulties; Learning Skills; Memory; Self-Confidence.*

E

Eating Sometimes a meal can be unattractive to a child, even though his parents find it very appetizing. That's because eating isn't just about the quality of food—it's also about the way the child perceives the eating experience. Pause for a moment to consider how the meal looks from your child's side of the table or high chair. The world looks different when you are only three years old and thirty inches high. Ask yourself the following questions:

Q. *Is my child seated comfortably?*
A. Most children can find a comfortable sitting position in a high chair because it has been specifically designed for their body length, bottom size, and length of reach. When your toddler makes the transition to the family dinner table, the chairs are designed for an adult's bottom size, height, and length of reach. Place a small cushion (or telephone directory) on your child's chair to raise his height; and bring his plate nearer to the edge of the table so that he can reach it easily.

Q. *Are my child's eating utensils the right size?*
A. Try eating a main course using a garden fork and trowel instead of a regular fork and a spoon. Difficult, isn't it? That's the struggle facing a young child who is expected to use adult-sized eating utensils. Using inconveniently sized knife, fork,

and spoon won't speed up the rate at which your child learns to use those utensils—if anything, it will slow him down.

Q. *What sized portions am I giving my child?*
A. Your child has a smaller stomach than an adult, and therefore, he doesn't eat as much. An adult's portion of mashed potatoes can seem like Mount Everest to him, and a bowl of stew like the Atlantic Ocean. Putting too much on the plate may put your child off his food before he even lifts his fork. Small portions are best—you can always give your child seconds if he clears the first plateful.

Q. *Is the food at the right temperature?*
A. Most adults like food to be piping hot. They are capable of managing such temperatures. They blow on the food, or take a very small amount to start, or simply wait until it cools down. Your child may not be as confident and may be afraid of burning himself. He prefers warm food that can be placed into his mouth without concern about possible injury.

Q. *What does it taste like?*
A. Everybody is sensitive to five kinds of taste—sweet, sour, bitter, salty, and spicy. Our sensitivity to each of these varies with age. While most adults enjoy the sharp taste of olives and pickles, children rarely do. The flavoring that you enjoy may not suit your child. So, cook the food first, and then add spices, seasonings, salt, and pepper to each portion individually.

Q. *Is the texture pleasant?*
A. Children vomit more easily than adults. Food that is too dry can stick to a child's upper palate and make him sick. This action is involuntary. It's not a trick to avoid eating. Greasy food can have the same effect, and chewy meat can be very unpalatable. Avoid textures that your child doesn't like.

Taking these factors into account will give you insight into the way your child views eating. Remember, the more palatable the meal is from your child's perspective (not yours), the more likely he is to eat healthfully.

See also *Additives; Eating Out; Fussy Eaters; Healthy Eating; Manners; Overfeeding; Overweight; Snacks.*

Eating Out Going to a restaurant can be fun. Someone else does the cooking—and the dishes—which allows you to relax and give your child your full attention. Your child gets to choose her own meal, which means she is more likely to eat. You probably relax the rules about her choices, too. All of these factors should make for a happy experience. But it doesn't always turn out that way.

For a successful family meal in a restaurant consider the following basic principles:

- *Let your child see the children's menu before you enter the restaurant.* This way you can be certain the restaurant has something your child likes. Give her plenty of time to look at the menu. If she can't read, tell her the choices and ask what appeals to her.

- *Explain to your child that the food may be served differently than at home.* Advanced warning will help your child accept a food presentation she has not experienced before.

- *If there isn't a children's menu, check whether child-sized portions are served.* Most restaurants provide children's meals. If not, ask for an extra plate so that you can give your child some of your own meal. Ask the waiter how your child's meal will be presented. If the sight of tomatoes completely kills your child's appetite, when you place your child's order request that tomatoes be left off her plate.

Don't expect your child to behave perfectly, or to eat everything she ordered. Eating out is a thrill for a young child, and she may accidentally spill her drink or drop her fork on the floor. Ironically, excitement may also deaden her appetite. If so, ignore her lack of appetite and enjoy her enjoyment.

***See also** Eating; Fussy Eaters; Healthy Eating; Manners; Overfeeding; Overweight; Snacks.*

Emotional Deprivation In 1953, Dr. John Bowlby wrote that every baby must have "a warm, intimate and continuous relationship with his mother," or else he will not thrive. Although this theory of emotional deprivation has been heavily criticized for its assumption that a mother-child relationship must be continuous (there is no proof whatsoever that a child must be in his mother's company all the time), Bowlby's two other major assumptions have stood the test of time, namely:

- A close emotional attachment between mother (or equivalent) and baby is essential for satisfactory childhood development.

- A baby deprived of such an attachment will show adverse effects throughout later life.

A wealth of evidence supports this view. Your child can become distressed even when separated from you only briefly. Extreme reactions have been observed in children admitted to the hospital without a parent present. These children usually show an initial period of protest, followed by a period of despair and apathy, which in turn is followed by detachment from others around them.

The effects of this type of short-term emotional deprivation are often temporary. This was confirmed by one study that focused on a group of young children who experienced maternal separation when their mothers went into the hospital for the birth of another baby. The infants' actions were recorded on video during play episodes before, during, and after the mother's stay in the hospital; the children's activity level and heart rate were recorded at night. Mothers also commented on their infants' behavior. The researchers found that the brief separation did have a marked effect. For instance, while the mother was in the hospital, her child was likely to have an increase in night wakings, heart rate, crying, and fussiness. He was also likely to be more aggressive, more clingy, and less cooperative at mealtimes. Fortunately, all of these adverse effects eased when the mother returned home.

Given this background of research findings, parents often ask the following three questions:

Q. *Will emotional deprivation be avoided if I spend every minute of the day with my child?*
A. Not necessarily. What matters is the quality of the parent-child relationship, not the quantity. The amount of time you spend with your child does not, by itself, indicate whether he will be emotionally deprived. Some parents are with their child all the time, and yet don't have a close and caring relationship with him, while others work all day, rarely see their child, and yet have a very strong relationship with him.

Q. *Should I stay at home and not return to work, in case my young child becomes emotionally deprived?*
A. Not necessarily. A British survey of preschool children looked at the link between their mothers' working habits and their mothers' mental health. Those who had given up work were most likely to be depressed—and a child looked after by a depressed mother who feels trapped in the house by her parental responsibilities may experience emotional deprivation even though his mother hasn't returned to work. This doesn't mean that you should automatically go back to work when your baby is young. Decisions of this sort are very personal and depend greatly on individual circumstances. But it does mean that you should not instantly feel guilty about resuming your career early in your infant's life.

Q. *Will my child be emotionally deprived if I send him to a day-care center instead of looking after him myself during the day?*
A. No, although the quality of the day-care arrangement is crucial. Children who have quality day care tend to be more sociable, engage in less solitary play, are less attention-seeking, and are more cooperative with other children and adults. Quality day care can add to a child's emotional stability and can even compensate for poor parent-child relationships at home.

See also *Bonding; Hospital; Quality Time; Separation and Divorce; Working Mothers.*

Epilepsy A child with epilepsy tends to have recurrent seizures that are caused by abnormal bursts of electrical activity in the brain. The condition has several different variations, resulting in more than twenty types of seizures. Certain types of epilepsy don't result in seizures but affect the child in other, milder ways. A single seizure is not normally a sign of epilepsy. Some isolated childhood seizures are caused simply by a high body temperature. Medical investigation is the only way to identify the condition. Epilepsy affects about one in two hundred of the population, and one in fifty may have an epileptic seizure at some stage in life. These seizures are neither infectious nor a sign of mental illness.

Epilepsy has many different causes, including brain damage as a result of a birth injury or accidental injury, infection (such as meningitis or encephalitis), tumors, and hormonal problems. In many instances, the specific cause cannot be accurately pinpointed. Epilepsy can start at any age, but it frequently starts in the preschool years. Most commonly, the first seizure occurs before the age of twenty. The frequency of seizures varies from once in a lifetime to several in an hour.

Seizures can be triggered by many factors, depending on the particular child. Common triggers include flashing lights, sudden loud noises, lack of food or sleep, stress, anxiety, and infection. Following are two main types of seizures:

- *Petit mal.* This mild seizure occurs only for a second or so. Although the child loses consciousness momentarily, she remains standing (or seated). During the episode, the child will look blank and stare into space; she may also blink or twitch slightly. As soon as the petit mal seizure is over, the child will continue as though nothing has happened. Some children have several in one day.

- *Grand mal.* With this major type of seizure, the child will lose consciousness, her body will stiffen and jerk, her lips may develop a blue color, and she will fall to the ground. She may also wet and soil herself. The most important thing you can do is protect your child from injury. Cushion her head, don't put anything in her mouth, don't try to pry open her mouth if her teeth are clenched, turn her on her side in order to help her breathing. Stay with your child until she has fully recovered, quietly reassuring her all the time, although she may want to go to sleep immediately after the seizure.

Medication can control—but not cure—epilepsy. Almost 80 percent of people with the condition use drugs to control or greatly reduce the seizures. The choice of drug depends on the child and the type of seizure she experiences. Doctors prefer to use one drug only, where possible, rather than a combination, and most children do not experience side effects if they take the medication in the way it is prescribed. Also, some research in neural feedback indicates that some seizure types can be avoided using this technique.

Equality
Each child is an individual, with his own particular emotional needs and his own particular likes and dislikes; each needs love and attention in varying amounts and in different ways. Therefore, treating each of your children equally is not the same as treating them fairly.

The idea that the best way to raise children is to treat them identically—by giving them all the same toys, activities, or opportunities—is a mistake and will not satisfy anyone.

You may be tempted to buy each of your children identical toys because that way they can't complain about one getting something better than the others. If one gets to go to skating lessons, they all must go to skating lessons. This tactic does not take into account each child's individuality and means that one or more of them will get something they don't like or want! Treating your children fairly means taking each child's individual needs into account. For example, if one takes swimming lessons, another might be allowed to join a drama club.

Even if parents adopt a policy of equal treatment, the children will find that the outside world takes a different approach. Schools encourage children to progress at their own pace. Clubs, whether sports organizations or scouting, encourage each member to develop mastery in different areas, depending on his skills. Individual differences make life interesting. A child who lives in an environment that tries to create equality in everything will receive an abrupt jolt when he ventures beyond the family home. Try to strive for a family structure in which every member has equal opportunities to develop his full potential, even though this may result in different activities and lifestyles for different family members.

See also Sibling Rivalry.

Eyes A baby's eyes are large in relation to the size of her head, when compared with an adult. In fact, a baby's eyes are almost 65 percent the size of adult eyes. This is why some adults find babies so attractive—their disproportionately large eyes seem very appealing.

The visible part of the eye is covered with a thin, delicate transparent membrane—the conjunctiva—that extends to line the inside of the eyelid. Fluid produced by the tear gland washes the eyeball and keeps it well lubricated.

Underneath the conjunctiva, at the front of the eye, lies the cornea, a disc-shaped section that bends the light rays and brings them to focus as they enter. The cornea also protects the parts of the eye lying directly behind it and is extremely sensitive, with a built-in ability to remove any bits of dirt that land on it.

The eye itself is filled with fluid, known as vitreous humor. The iris—the colored portion of the eye—lies behind the cornea. This has a dark hole in the middle (the pupil), which is controlled by lots of very small muscles, and light enters the eye through it. Just like the aperture of a camera, the pupil adjusts constantly in relation to the degree of light—in bright sunlight, it becomes smaller, and in dim light it becomes larger.

Immediately behind the iris is the transparent and solid lens whose muscles adjust its shape in order to focus light rays on the retina at the back of the eye. When cells in the retina are activated, visual impulses are transmitted along the optic nerve to the brain. At this point, they are transformed into an image. Damage to any part of the eye, or to any part of the nervous system linking the eye to the brain, will result in visual difficulties.

See also Genes; Vision; Visual Difficulties.

F

Family Structure What has historically been regarded as the "traditional" or "nuclear" family, with mother, father, and baby makes three, is not necessarily today's reality. Dad may no longer go out to work, mom may no longer stay home, and baby may not have two parents living in the household.

The traditional family is now defined (by Statistics Canada) as being

- a male worker and a female homemaker with or without children;
- a male worker and a female worker with or without children;
- a single parent with children;
- a parent with children and a stepparent.

Other family configurations are regarded as nontraditional. Here are some modern realities in family structure:

- More families than ever have experienced divorce, remarriage, or children with stepbrothers and stepsisters, or half-siblings.
- Single mothers make up 27 percent of new mothers.
- More grandparents bring up children than ever before, often because the mother is young and single.
- More and more people leave unsatisfactory relationships.
- More women give their ex-husbands custody of their children than ever before.
- One survey suggests that as a result of either death or divorce, at least 1.5 million single fathers in the United States care for about 3.5 million children. One in three marriages ends in divorce. More and more fathers get custody of their children. In Canada, in 1991, of 954,710 single-parent families, 168,240 were headed by males.

- More than 50 percent of new mothers will be in the labor force before the child reaches school.

- More partners in same-sex relationships have children than ever before. Often a partner will assume a parenting role to a child of a partner. Sometimes a partner will adopt as a single parent. Sometimes a partner may choose to have a biological child independently.

- Parenting is a bisexual word that indicates the parent-like activities performed in a family that has children. Parents perform the expected legal and cultural responsibilities of raising children. Parenting can be done by parents of either sex, or by others in that role.

- More men now leave the labor force to become "house-husbands." This may be the result of downsizing, unemployment, self-employment, or a mother's successful career. Dad may not be the primary breadwinner, either by choice or by economic necessity. Many formerly middle-class men have experienced a downward employment spiral. More and more families struggle financially.

- United States has the highest rate of child poverty in the industrialized world, and Canada has the second-highest rate.

These are all major stressors. As well, modern families often come under stress from outside as others try to come to grips with the new realities. Institutions such as schools, other parents, and cultural variables within a community—such as different religious and ethnic backgrounds—can put pressure on all members of a family. It is important to focus on the positive aspects of family life, no matter how the structure is defined, where children are raised in the spirit of love, caring, nurturing, mutual support, and devotion, which add to life's joy and purpose.

See also Mothers; Fathers; Working Mothers.

Fathers Over the years, research findings have consistently showed that for most men, family is a greater source of both involvement and satisfaction than is work.

As the roles of mothers have changed in recent years, so too have the roles of fathers. More and more men report that their greatest satisfaction in life comes through their relationship with their children. The typical father of Victorian times would be surprised, and possibly perturbed, by today's typical father. No longer is a father's role rigidly confined to earning money, making decisions about how the money should be spent, or kissing the children good night after they have been fed, washed, and changed by others. The biggest change to have taken place is the degree to which the father is expected to become involved in matters of child care. A contemporary father is asked to share in every aspect of his children's lives.

This increased involvement starts even before a baby is born. The number of soon-to-be fathers who attend prenatal sessions with their partners has increased tremendously. Attend the prenatal classes at your local hospital with your partner and you will see large numbers of men helping their partners through the regimen of relaxation exercises and participating enthusiastically in the discussions of "how to change a diaper" and "postnatal depression."

This very early interest in family life signals a pattern that will probably persist throughout the child's life. Both partners benefit. For a mother-to-be (who may be understandably apprehensive about pregnancy and childbirth), her partner's presence during the prenatal phase can be reassuring. For a father-to-be (whose apprehension probably equals that of his partner), participation in the prenatal preparation stops potential feelings of isolation and detachment. Many men are extremely enthusiastic about this change in their role, and take advantage of the opportunities it affords.

Fathers are now routinely present at the birth of their child. This has become so firmly institutionalized that people show surprise when a man admits he wasn't there. Fathers are expected to take a more active parental role. From buying disposable diapers to taking baby for a walk in the infant carrier, the fact of the matter is—family roles have changed.

The very significant change in a father's role and involvement with the family runs alongside his role in the outside world. In a high percentage of the population, the father is still the primary breadwinner, particularly when the children are in the preschool years. This means the man has to accommodate the demands of both these roles, which may not be easy. Some men reject the new role.

Many observers anticipate that the trend for fathers to play an increasing role in raising children will become even stronger in future years. Following are several reasons for this trend:

- Couples realize the benefits a father's increased involvement brings the children.

- Many men find themselves enriched by relationships with their children beyond the traditional disciplinarian role.

- Women welcome the sharing of household tasks that a father's new role brings.

- Sharing the care of the children is a fairer way to manage family relationships.

Fathers can offer a unique and special contribution to their child's life; the father-child relationship is distinctive, not secondary. Psychological research has revealed significant differences in the way moms and dads interact with their growing children, for instance:

- A young baby tends to gaze when she sees her mother's face and tends to smile and laugh more when she sees her father's face.

- Moms tend to play with their babies using nurturing and soothing activities, while dads prefer more stimulating and challenging activities.

- Dads worry less than moms about leaving their children at a playgroup; 35 percent of dads expect their child to cry in that situation, compared to 75 percent of moms.

- Moms encourage their partner to share care of the child because of worries about loss of identity, whereas dads encourage shared care in the hope of becoming closer to their child.

- For moms, the biggest impact of the new baby is the increased daily chores, while for dads, the biggest impact is adjusting to the baby's personality and need for attention.

These differences influence the way a father and a mother interact with their child, and so each parent makes an individual contribution to their child's development. Remember that children who are raised without a father do not necessarily suffer psychologically, but if the father is present at home, the family interactions are different.

See also Family Structure; Mothers; Older Parents; Parents; Quality Time; Single-Parent Family; Working Mothers; Young Parents.

Fears Childhood fears are a normal part of early development. Almost 90 percent of young children experience a mild fear at some point. These fears may be real, such as a fear of lightning, or they may be imaginary, such as a fear of ghosts.

Children can develop fears about the strangest of things, even though there doesn't appear to be any obvious explanation. Childhood fears—just like adult fears—do not have to be rational. Many adults are afraid of the dentist, even though modern dentistry techniques ensure virtually pain-free treatment. Few adults can logically explain what it is about a visit to a dentist that frightens them so much. Similarly, few children can explain what quality of darkness makes them feel uneasy.

Fears usually emerge around the age of two years. A child of this age has a greater understanding and awareness of the world around him. However, his understanding is not so great that he can fully explain everything that happens. A toddler knows that birds fly because he sees it happening quite regularly, but he does not know that a bird will not pick him up and fly off with him, or that a bird will not eat him. Therefore, he may be afraid. If your child is worried by something that is apparently irrational, he needs your reassurance and explanation.

Parents can arouse fears in young children by talking carelessly in front of them. Of course, your child must be made aware of the routine hazards of domestic life. Hot stoves can cause burns, people can fall down stairs, burglars can break into a house, and children can drown in a few inches of bathwater. These very real dangers have to be kept in perspective.

Continual reminders of what could happen may make your child afraid rather than cautious, and that is not the aim of safety warnings. Sometimes fears are used as a threat to a child, as a way to make him mind. Parents are often tempted to resort to this strategy when all else fails. Dad takes his four-year-old son to a children's party, but when they arrive the child will not let go of dad's hand. He pleads with his father to stay a few moments longer, and in a fit of embarrassed rage—because somehow every other child is settled—Dad warns: "If you don't shut up, I'm going to leave you right now." This only increases the child's anxiety. Threats of this nature, which play on a young child's weakness, are only likely to make the child's fears worse.

Always take your child's fear seriously, no matter how ridiculous it may appear. What may seem a minor obstacle to you, may seem like Mount Everest through your child's eyes. Never try to bully your child out of his fear. Comments such as, "Act your age" or, "You're behaving like a little baby" will only increase the child's agitation. Take a planned approach to help your child.

First, ascertain exactly what your child fears. A child who becomes anxious when he approaches the bathroom may be apprehensive about any one of a number of things. Is he afraid he will fall into the toilet bowl? Is he afraid of the smell? Is he afraid that he cannot reach the taps to wash his hands afterwards? Is he afraid of the flush? Ask your child what frightens him. You may not get a direct answer, but by breaking down the frightening event into small components, you should be able to establish the precise area of concern.

Second, show your child that he can manage, that he doesn't really have any cause to be afraid. For instance, your child may be afraid of thunder because he thinks it will make the house fall down. You can reassure him that the house cannot be damaged by noise; demonstrate this by turning your television, radio, and stereo system on full volume for a few seconds. Once your child sees that the house is still standing, even though that was louder than any noise thunder might make, he will probably be less afraid.

Third, give your child lots of encouragement when he takes a step toward overcoming whatever it is that scares him. Constant praise from you, coupled with your frequent reassurance that he is safe, is a very effective way to boost your child's self-confidence. Some storybooks are written specially to help children overcome fears. You may find that reading some of these books to your child is an effective way to help him tackle his fears.

See also *Hazards; Phobias; Road Safety.*

Fighting Minor fights are common in childhood. Your child may become involved in a fight for a variety of reasons (for example, she feels threatened; someone has taken one of her possessions; she can't get her own way). You should try to teach your child other ways to solve conflicts, ways that don't involve physical assault on others.

Since fights often start because two children want to play with the same toy, an effective way to avoid conflict is for both parties to reach a compromise. You can help your child develop this skill. When you see your child disagreeing with a friend over what game to play, suggest that they play one game first, then the other. Emphasize that this type of compromise is not the same as giving in, because both of them will get what they want. Tell your child this is a more sensible way to settle disputes. The best time for compromise is before the disagreement has escalated into a full-scale conflict.

Fights can also be avoided by discussion (this doesn't always work, but it is certainly worth a try). Children who are unable to explain their feelings are frequently the same children who get into fights. The more a child is able to tell someone what is troubling her, then the less likely she is to fight. A child who is able to talk her way out of trouble may never have to fight her way out.

Another way your child can avoid a fight is to distract the

child who threatens her. Focus the hostile child's attention else-where. Say, "Here comes the teacher," or, "Look at this." This can be a very effective way to break tension. Teach your child to leave situations where she is threatened by another child. Say, "You don't have to stick around."

Before you suggest these alternatives to your child, however, you must first clarify your own beliefs. Some parents feel quite strongly that their child should be able to stand up for herself and retaliate when struck by others. Although this may appear to be a reasonable point of view, your young child will have a problem differentiating between fighting to protect herself and fighting to get her own way, and your older child may find her-self branded as a bully. If you do encourage your child to defend herself physically, make sure she knows when fighting is accept-able (such as when she is in danger from another child) and when it is not acceptable, such as when it is merely a way to achieve what she wants).

See also Aggression; Sibling Rivalry.

First-Born Jealousy Nothing can unsettle a first-born child like the impending arrival of a new baby. Until this moment he's had mom and dad all to himself and he expects this way of life to continue forever. No wonder that the thought of a new brother or sister fills him with anxiety.

Look at it from the child's point of view. You and your part-ner spend all your time with him when you are at home; he is the only child you spend your money on; he gets lots of clothes and presents; and his aunts, uncles, and grandparents shower him with love. Then, just when everything is ticking along nicely, the adults start talking about a new baby. He may have thoughts like, "Why do mom and dad need another baby? Am I not good enough for them?" "What have I done wrong to make them want another child?" or even, "Will the new baby take my room so that I'll have nowhere to sleep?" We, as adults, know without a shadow of a doubt that loving a second baby doesn't decrease our love for the first. However, your first-born doesn't know that. He has to learn by experience, and that takes time. In the meantime, feelings of jealousy toward the new baby may dominate.

Tell your child in advance that he's going to have a new brother or sister. Don't wait until the last moment when the contractions are coming every couple of minutes. But don't tell him about the new baby when you are only a few weeks into your pregnancy either. A child's sense of time is different from that of an adult; he may see no difference between a week and a month, or between one month and six months. He may become bored with the long wait.

Start introducing the idea of the new baby when your tummy is so large that even an inexperienced toddler would notice it, probably around the seventh month or so. Tell your child calmly and openly. Conduct the conversation at a level suitable for his age and understanding, and avoid giving too many bits of information at one time. Whatever you do, don't beat the topic to death.

Your child may react with indifference, or he may seem very interested and want to talk about it further. Or he may simply burst into tears. Be prepared to let your child ask you questions, either at the time you tell him or later, and always reply honestly. Let your child express any anxieties he has, without reacting in a way that makes him wish he hadn't opened his mouth.

When your first-born sees his new brother or sister for the first time, make sure the baby has a present for him (one that you had ready beforehand) and let your first-born have one to give the new arrival. Of course, this exchange of gifts is artificial, but it can help forge an emotional connection between the two children right from the start.

Expect your first-born to feel jealous. He may show signs of this by becoming aggressive toward you, or by being clingy and not letting you out of his sight, or even by regressing and becoming babyish himself. These reactions are natural. Try not to get angry with your child when he behaves this way, no matter how irritating and attention-seeking he is. Any anger and rejection at your child's behavior will only confirm his worst fears that you love him less than the new baby.

The following strategies will help ease your first-born's jealousy:

- *Get your child involved in the practicalities of baby care.* Let him fetch diapers from the cupboard, or pass the baby powder. Even a toddler is able to do something to help.

- *Encourage visitors to spend a few moments with your first-born before they go in to see the baby.* The steady stream of visitors to your house has come for one purpose only, namely, to set eyes on the new arrival. Discreetly ask them to give your older child some attention as well.

- *Let your child help you show the baby to visitors.* The baby is a new member of his family too. He can take the adults into the baby's room and can explain to them all about his little brother or sister.

- *Acknowledge your child's maturity.* If your child is upset by the presence of the new arrival, an extra ten minutes of television before bedtime because he is "a big brother now" will provide some recognition of the fact. Any positive change that acknowledges he is older than the baby will help. Let your child spend more time with adults instead of being sent out to play; read a special book together; allow your child to choose what cookie he eats with his juice.

- *Be honest with your child.* Nothing is wrong in admitting to your first-born child that caring for a young baby makes you tired, and that at times you get exhausted from all the chores you have to do (though don't overdo it in case he thinks you dislike the baby).

See also Age Gap; Birth Order; Jealousy; Only Child; Sibling Rivalry.

Friendships Children form friendships for many reasons. At times it is difficult for parents to understand why two particular children enjoy each other's company so much. Friendships provide psychological benefits, such as giving a child self-confidence, giving her someone to share her secrets with, teaching her about loyalty and sharing, providing someone to compare herself with, and offering emotional support when she feels unhappy. Friendships also provide practical benefits, such as allowing a child to play with her friend's new bicycle. In fact, many friendships in early childhood are motivated more by this type óf self-interest than by feelings of personal attraction.

Genuine friendships don't usually start until the age of three, because only then is a child able to play cooperatively with others. At this age, children tend to pick friends who have the same interests and are happy to play with children of the opposite sex. Most friendships among three-year-olds fluctuate from week to week because at this age a child is very self-centered. From the age of five or six onwards, children tend to mix more with others of the same sex, and during the next three or four years their friendships become more stable. Usually, not until a child is nine or ten does she begin to form long-lasting friendships. An inability to acquire friends may be an indication that a child has emotional problems.

Most parents would like their child to be popular, to have lots of friends, and to be invited out to play. You feel good when you see your child surrounded by friends of her own age. Popularity, however, partly depends on characteristics over which a child has no control. For instance, popular children tend to be quite bright at school. A child who is physically attractive, as well as sporty, is also likely to be popular.

Popularity also depends on characteristics over which a child does have some control, such as social skills. Being able to take turns, to follow rules in games, and to share, will help your child socially. She has a better chance of being popular if she isn't aggressive and is prepared to listen to other children's points of view. Encourage your child to develop these characteristics.

Problems arise when parents disapprove of their child's friend because the friend behaves in ways that are not acceptable by their standards. This requires delicate and tactful handling:

- *Try to avoid banning your child from playing with a particular friend.* This will only make the friendship more desirable. Instead, tell your child why you don't like her friend (for example, the friend swears, takes toys that aren't hers, hits other children). Don't overdo it or your child will think you are being totally unfair. Occasionally, a straightforward ban on a friendship may be your only option—use this strategy only as a last resort.

- *Tell your child why she should not play with her friend.* Give practical reasons: for instance, because the friend gets into trouble for hurting other people. Say something like, "People will think you are just like your friend, so you will get into trouble too."

- *Remind your child that although she likes her friend, she doesn't have to behave the same way.* If you find that your child plays with the friend you dislike, despite all your efforts, suggest to her that although they play together, they don't have to act like each other.

- *Encourage your child to be friends with different children.* This is a more positive approach, and is especially successful with children under the age of six or seven. Invite to your house children with whom you want your child to play, and do your best to give them an enjoyable time. This strategy may allow the friendship of which you don't approve to fade into the background.

See also Sociable Play; Social Development.

Fussy Eaters Every child is a picky eater occasionally.
From an early age, your child will have particular food preferences. This phase may pass within a few days, or it may be more long-lasting. Surveys have found that

- while only 10 percent of parents worry about their child's eating habits when he is one year old, this figure leaps to 42 percent by the time the child is four;

- 10 percent of three-year-olds are described by their parents as "finicky about their food";

- 31 percent of children who have poor appetites at the age of three still have poor appetites when they are eight.

You're not alone in having a child who is a fussy eater, who sits and picks at his food as though he's afraid harm will befall him if he swallows it. A picky eater can spoil mealtimes—in fact, if your child is one, you may find it easier to serve his meal first, allowing the rest of you to sit down peacefully when he is finished. To change your child's eating habits, try these suggestions:

DO'S

- *Do serve meals at regular times.* Routine is especially important with a fussy eater. Having meals at reasonably fixed intervals means that your child doesn't get too hungry or overtired, both of which upset his appetite.

- *Do keep meals simple.* The more time and effort you invest in a meal, the more upset you'll be when your child doesn't wolf it down—so don't slave over a hot stove for hours.

- *Do make the food attractive.* Some parents expect their child to eat food that they wouldn't touch themselves. Bear in mind that if the sight of a particular meal makes you turn up your nose, then it may have the same effect on your child.

- *Do let your child finger-feed.* Table manners are important, but your child will acquire these later. What matters is that the food gets inside his tummy; it has the same nutritional value whether it arrives at his mouth by hand or by fork.

- *Do end the meal when your child has had enough.* Keeping a toddler trapped in his high chair in the hope he'll eat more is pointless. When your child has stopped eating, lift him down. The same applies to an older child who asks to leave the table. There is no harm in some gentle persuasion at that stage, but don't let it build up into a confrontation.

- *Do allow your child choice.* Your child will approach mealtimes with enthusiasm if he has a choice over what to eat. This doesn't mean you should run your house like a restaurant, but it does mean you could let him choose from two items for lunch (for example, scrambled eggs on toast, or yogurt followed by fresh fruit).

- *Do be flexible.* The order in which food is served isn't fixed by law! Young children love to experiment with everything, including food. You may not find the thought of soup mixed with salad attractive, but your child may. If he wants to experiment this way, let him.

- *Do set a good example yourself.* Your child will copy your bad eating habits. If you come home munching a bag of greasy fries, you can hardly expect your child to behave differently.

DON'TS

- *Never, ever force-feed your child.* No matter how desperately you want him to finish his meal, you can't force him to eat it—try and you'll end up feeling drained, while he'll end up being sick.

- *Don't hover during mealtimes.* Nothing is more likely to make your child anxious about eating than seeing you hover about while you study every mouthful he takes. You don't like someone peering intently at you during meals—neither does your child.

- *Don't exclude your child during preparations.* One way to encourage your child to eat a meal is to involve him in its preparation. Of course, you're not going to ask a young child to cook a hot dish, but a two-year-old can put a cup on the table and wash the potatoes, and a four-year-old can help set out the silverware, cut out cookies, and stir.

- *Don't stay silent.* Just as you enjoy a good chat while eating, so does your child. Sit down beside him and talk. This way, eating becomes a social occasion.

- *Don't be negative.* Work on the assumption that your child isn't going to starve, no matter how little he eats. The more you worry, the more tense he'll be every time you put a plate of food in front of him.

- *Don't use threats.* Out of sheer frustration, you may be tempted to cajole your child with promises and threats such as, "You can have some dessert if you eat your spinach" or, "Your dad will be furious when he hears you've not eaten your spinach." This rarely works, because your child may well think to himself, "The spinach must be really awful or mom wouldn't try so hard to persuade me to eat it."

- *Don't concede defeat when your child rejects a new food.* Children take time to acquire tastes for unfamiliar foods. When you do try to introduce a new item into your child's diet, persevere a couple of times a week, for at least a month. He may gradually develop a taste for it.
- *Don't rush through meals.* Mealtime is a social occasion, not just a time to fuel the body as quickly as possible. Food is more easily digested in a calm, unhurried atmosphere. A fussy eater is usually also a slow eater, and he needs lots of time to work his way through a meal. This will be particularly noticeable at breakfast, so wake him up in plenty of time.

See also *Additives; Eating; Eating Out; Healthy Eating; Overfeeding; Overweight; Snacks.*

G

Gender Play Try this: Make a list of play activities and toys you think are suitable for young boys, and another list of play activities and toys you think are suitable for young girls. To make this task slightly easier, consider your own children or a particular boy and a particular girl you know, and think of the games and toys with which you would want them to play. Allow yourself about ten minutes to compile the lists.

Having done this, consider the following questions:

- *Did you find this easy to do?* Most people have no problem making up these separate lists because they know that boys seem fascinated by one set of play activities (such as soccer, play-fighting, toy cars) and girls by different ones (such as brushing a doll's hair, dressing-up, preparing pretend tea parties).
- *Do any activities or toys appear on both lists?* Chances are that you identified a number of pastimes—perhaps art and craft

activities, reading books, and doing jigsaw puzzles—that you thought suitable for either sex. Most adults agree that these types of activities are acceptable for all children.

- *Are you able to find any common theme running through the boys' play activities and a different theme running through the girls' play activities?* Most likely, many of the suggestions on your list for boys are action-based, suitable for releasing aggressive emotions (such as toy weapons, toy soldiers, sports), and that many on your list for girls are sedate activities that encourage domestic behavior (such as dress-up activities, toy dishes, dolls).

- *How do you think the parents of a young boy would react if you bought him one of the girl's toys or vice versa?* You would probably find that they would be very concerned if you gave their son a Barbie doll as a present, or their daughter a Transformer.

Those are the easy questions. Now for the difficult ones. Where do these differences in toy and game preferences begin? Are children born with them? Are such preferences created by the media? Do they come from ads on television? Does the play at nursery school or day care have an impact? Do parents inadvertently encourage their child to play with specific toys? Or is it just chance that boys tend to like different toys from those favored by girls?

Psychologists have considered these vexing issues in detail, but conclusive answers have yet to be found. A number of theories attempt to explain sex differences in play preferences. Some theorists claim that males are born with a biological instinct to be aggressive and that females are born with a biological instinct to be domesticated, to have children, and to raise a family. These instincts are reflected in children's play preferences, these theorists continue, which is why some boys enjoy aggressive play activities, while some girls enjoy more placid ones. However, this idea fails to explain why some girls' dislike domestic-based play activities and instead prefer to play more active games traditionally associated with boys.

A more popular view is that sex differences in play stem from social pressures and from the media. You only need to watch commercials for children's toys to see this. Commercials for dolls never show boys playing with them, and commercials for sports equipment rarely use girls. This inflexible presentation influences the views of adults and children alike.

A more covert social pressure on play choices stems from the language that adults use to describe children. For instance, the term "tomboy," which is still in common usage today, describes a girl who shows a preference for rough-and-tumble activities. The assumption underlying this term is that these activities are the sole province of boys, and that a girl loses some of her feminine characteristics by playing this way. It's not surprising, then, that such social pressures on children to play in predetermined ways have their effect.

As your child's parent, you have the greatest impact on her play, because usually you choose her toys. You make these choices partly on the basis of her own interests, but mainly on the basis of your own views about suitable toys. Selection of toys is one of the ways in which stereotyped play preferences are passed down from generation to generation.

Nothing is inherently wrong with girls playing with dolls or boys playing with cars and trucks—or vice versa. Children should be allowed to participate in a wide range of play opportunities, and they shouldn't be limited to preconceived notions of what constitutes "boy's play" and "girl's play."

See also Learning through Play; Play; Sexism; Sociable Play.

Genes Every human body is made up of millions of tiny cells, and usually each cell contains twenty-three pairs of chromosomes, those parts of the cell that contain the blueprint for the growth and development of the body. Each chromosome has thousands of smaller particles, called genes, which carry instructions for physical development. The genes determine the child's sex; body size; color of eyes, skin, and hair; and blood group.

Genes interact to form complementary pairs. However, some genes are "dominant" (their instructions are recognized by the body in preference to those of the other gene in the pair) and some genes are "recessive" (their instructions are not recognized by the body unless both genes in the pair are recessive). For instance, the gene responsible for brown eyes is dominant and the gene responsible for blue eyes is recessive. At conception, if the gene pair has two "brown" genes, or has one of each color, then the child will have brown eyes. On the other hand, if the gene pair has two "blue" genes then the child will have blue eyes. In this way, two brown-eyed parents can also have a blue-eyed child (having inherited a recessive "blue" gene from each parent), but two blue-eyed parents cannot have a brown-eyed child (since if either parent had a dominant "brown" gene then they themselves would not be blue-eyed).

The way in which genes act depends on the characteristics they control. While certain genes show their effect in early life, such as in blood type and skin color, others act only at specific periods in the child's development. These age-linked genes contain plans for sequences of events, such as the age teeth will appear in the child's mouth, when the child will walk, or when menstruation will begin. There is no evidence that genes carry plans for personality development.

See also Down's Syndrome.

Giftedness
The distinction between a "very clever" child and a "gifted" child is unclear. Some psychologists regard a child as gifted when she has an IQ of above 130, whereas others require an IQ of at least 140. Estimates suggest that about one or two children in 200 are gifted.

The stereotype of a gifted child is a humorless, precocious, and bespectacled young person who is more concerned with knowledge and worldly matters than she is with typical childhood interests. Not all gifted children conform to this pattern. They have the same psychological needs as any other children—the need to be loved, to feel secure, and to fulfill their potential. What does differentiate a gifted child is her exceptional thirst for learning.

A gifted child usually shows her ability in the preschool years, often in the following ways:

- *Early developmental milestones.* The child may attain bowel and bladder control early, and may walk and talk at a younger age than would normally be expected.

- *More energy than usual.* The child may need less sleep at night than other children of her age. (However, this is also a common characteristic of hyperactive children, and therefore should not be used as the sole criterion for assessing giftedness.)

- *An insatiable curiosity.* The child may show great interest in the world around her, asking lots of questions about abstract issues—for example, about life and death.

- *Well-developed language.* The gifted child often has an an extensive vocabulary, and she is probably able to talk fluently about a wide range of topics, long before other children of her age are able to do so.

- *Keen powers of observation and reasoning.* The child may be able to see relationships between events, and to understand general principles on the basis of a few examples. A gifted child's memory is often quick and retentive, and her imagination may be unusually vivid.

- *A preference for the company of older children.* Chances are that the child enjoys spending some of her time with older children and adults because they are better matched to her intellectual level.

Bear in mind that a gifted child may not be good at everything. Her handwriting skills can lag behind her reading ability. Some gifted children are better at seeing and doing than they are at talking and listening; they may have difficulty expressing themselves in words, yet show exceptional mechanical ability.

Never push your gifted child too far, or become concerned only with her educational achievements while ignoring her personal and social development. A six-year-old who has the intelligence of a fifteen-year-old is unlikely to feel at ease in the company of teenagers.

A Canadian study found that most gifted children have no

social difficulties. The results showed that the typical gifted child is a well-adjusted individual, able to manage the social and emotional demands of childhood. Much depends on the attitude of the child's parents. Parents who attend to all aspects of their child's development, and who don't simply focus on her intellectual needs, are less likely to create psychological hazards for her than are parents who place their child's intellectual skills above everything else.

Following are three approaches to the education of gifted children:

- *Segregation,* which involves the child attending separate classes (or even separate schools) for children of exceptional ability, where every child in the class is categorized as gifted. The drawbacks with an approach based on segregation is that the child loses contact with most others of her age and has little contact with children of other levels of ability.

- *Acceleration,* which involves a gifted child progressing through the ordinary school curriculum at a faster rate than the other pupils. She may even skip one grade entirely. Like segregation, this approach carries with it the danger that the child will be thrust into situations that she can deal with intellectually, but not emotionally or socially.

- *Enrichment,* in which the child has mainstream schooling for most of the week, but in addition attends enrichment classes to increase knowledge and understanding. The advantage of enrichment classes is that the child's intellectual ability is stretched, and yet she is still able to spend most of her time with her peer group.

See also Creativity; Intelligence.

Grandparents
Becoming a grandparent means that one's own child has become a parent. This point might seem obvious, except that the combined effect of these two wonderful but emotionally charged events can be explosive.

For the new grandparents, the birth rekindles their own

memories of early parenthood and is an opportunity to relive many of those moments. For the new parents, the birth is the start of the next phase in their life, a phase usually anticipated eagerly. The baby is the parents' child first, and the grandparents' grandchild second. The prime responsibility for decision-making rests with the parents. Many couples complain that in the first few days and weeks of their baby's life the new grandparents act as though the baby were their own. This undermines the parents' self-confidence and frequently results in increased family tension. Grandparents should take a back seat at this stage and allow the couple to gain confidence in their new role as parents.

The relationship between parents and their own parents changes as the grandchild grows older. In the early years of the infant's life, the parents may rely on the grandparents for occasional advice. But as the child develops, the grandparents may be asked for more practical help—such as looking after the child so that the parents can go out. The grandparents may begin to take on the role of trustworthy baby sitters rather than advisers. However, looking after the grandchild in this way helps strengthen the bond between grandparent and grandchild and keeps that relationship special.

Grandparents often overindulge their grandchild. This may cause resentment. Grandparents' rules may be far more lenient than the parents' discipline. Most children are well able to handle two such sets of standards. Difficulties can arise, though, when grandparents undermine the parents' authority by disagreeing with them in front of the grandchild. For example: The whole family gathers together for a big occasion, the child is excited, his parents tell him to behave. Then the grandparents announce that the child should be left alone as he is not doing anyone any harm. At this point, the relationship between parents and grandparents becomes strained. In-law relationships can become especially tense, as family values and beliefs sometimes conflict.

Grandparents must remember that they are exactly that—namely, the child's grandparents, and not his parents. Matters of discipline are best left to the child's mother and father. This doesn't mean that everything the parents say and do is correct—nobody is infallible when it comes to looking after children. It does mean that if grandparents are concerned about their grandchild's development, they should raise any concerns they may have when the grandchild isn't present. The grandparents should also be prepared to accept that their advice and opinions may not be heeded.

The grandchild-grandparent relationship should be maintained, both in intact and divorced families. Sadly, one of the common, though not inevitable, side effects of divorce is that a child may lose touch with one set of grandparents. This can add psychological stress to a child already distressed by the loss of one parent at home. If the child already has a close relationship with his grandparents, it is best to maintain this relationship, irrespective of the parental separation.

See also Family Structure; Parents; Separation and Divorce.

Grief

Few adults come to terms with the concept of death, and so it is not surprising that children can have difficulties coping with their own grief following the death of a relative or friend, or even a pet. One problem a child frequently faces after a bereavement is that her feelings are ignored. Adults are usually too busy trying to manage their own distress to consider the feelings of a young child, but that child will be grieving all the same.

A child under the age of eight or nine does not fully understand death in the rational way that adults do. Her reaction to bereavement is unpredictable. One minute she may tell you that she knows her grandmother has died and that she has gone forever, and the next minute she may ask you when grandma's coming back home. Don't get annoyed when your child poses this question; a young child simply can't understand that death is irreversible.

Children (same as adults) show a wide range of grief reactions when faced with the death of a friend or relative:

- *Shock*. The overwhelming sensation that arises the moment a child is informed of the death. She may become very quiet, or even angry and hostile. It's an instant response to the burst of sadness and confusion that overwhelms her. At this time, your child needs your comfort and reassurance.

- *Denial.* This reaction usually passes within a few days. Until it does, a child acts as though the death hasn't occurred at all. For instance, she may buy a chocolate bar for her grandmother, just as she did before her grandmother died. Denial is a psychological mechanism that allows the news to filter through slowly. If your child behaves this way, don't continually confront her with the facts. She will face them eventually, when she is psychologically ready to do so.

- *Searching.* In this grief reaction, a child may literally look for the deceased person—in the rooms she used, and even in the chairs she sat on—in the hope of finding her. This searching stems from the child's deep desire for the death never to have happened. As with denial, this phase will pass within a few weeks.

- *Guilt.* Amid the confusion and despair associated with bereavement, a child may develop a sense of guilt about the death. She may believe that the loss occurred as a punishment because she was naughty earlier that morning, or because she didn't tidy up her room the previous night when she was asked. The child may even blame herself because once, in a temper, she wished that person would die. Guilt isn't rational. However, it still hurts, and can stay with a child for years.

- *Fear.* A child's fear arising from bereavement can take many forms. The child may fear that she is going to die very soon, or fear that someone close to her will die. As a result, she may be afraid to leave her house or to let you out of her sight. In time, she will regain her confidence, but this sort of fear can last for several weeks.

The most common bereavement children experience is that of the death of an elderly relative, although, sadly, some children do have to cope with the death of a sibling, parent, or friend. The closer the child's relationship with the dead person, the stronger her grief will be. Adults frequently make the mistake of assuming that children can't experience genuine grief, and consequently don't pay enough attention to them at this time. Your child's grief reaction will probably be as strong as your own, even though she can't voice her feelings as clearly as you. So keep an eye on your child's behavior in the days following a family bereavement. She may show her distress in unexpected ways—for instance, poor concentration in school, fighting with friends, bed-wetting, or unusual reliance on a security object. Be careful not to misinterpret this behavior; your child's reaction is a sign of grief, not a deliberate attempt to upset you.

Following are some ways to help your child come to terms with her feelings about bereavement:

- *Encourage your child to talk about her emotions.* Pick a reasonably quiet time when you and she are together, and ask her how she is feeling. She will probably say, "Fine," but then you might say that you are feeling upset and you are sure she is too. Sharing your emotions with your child will let her know that it's permissible for her to describe her own feelings. Whatever she says, listen respectfully.

- *Give your child support.* There is nothing like a supportive cuddle from mom or dad to lift the gloom from a troubled child. It won't bring the dead person back, but it will ease some of the pain, no matter what age your child is.

- *Let your child express her feelings through play.* Encourage your child to play with modeling clay, paints, dolls, and building blocks. These provide a vehicle for her to release her inner emotions nonverbally. In addition, your local library probably has books about bereavement, written especially for young children.

- *Talk about the good times and the memories that you will have forever.* These won't disappear.

A child may have had to consider death before any family bereavement, if she has looked after a pet. Small pets that are popular with young children (such as goldfish, hamsters, rab-

bits, gerbils) often have a short life span. The passing of a pet can be used as an opportunity to discuss the concept of death.
See also Play; Unhappiness.

Guilt A child's feelings of guilt stem from his conscience, the part of his mind that tells him that he has broken a rule and that he should feel bad about it.

Conscience is not present at birth. A newborn baby has no sense of what is right and what is wrong, and doesn't have guilt feelings. As far as a baby is concerned, if he wants something then he should get it. When he is hungry and desires more milk, he cries. He doesn't care that he was fed just a few minutes ago, or that his parents are tired and need a rest. A baby only thinks of himself.

Parents are the prime influence on the development of their child's conscience. From birth onwards, an infant begins to identify with his mother and father. Quite simply, he wants to be like them and he begins to behave like them. Identification goes further than this. As well as behaving like his parents, a child begins to think like them. He begins to adopt their attitudes and values, their feelings, and their moral views.

By the age of three, a child begins to experience guilt feelings when he does something wrong, because by then he is able to make elementary decisions about minor moral issues. For instance, should he play with a fragile glass ornament when he has been warned not to? He feels bad when he realizes he has broken a rule. Of course, breaking a rule is not good, but the child's awareness of right and wrong—and the accompanying feeling of guilt—is a sign of satisfactory psychological development.

Within a few years, your child will have internalized many of your attitudes about right and wrong. This means that he knows how to behave even when you are not with him telling him what to do. Your conscience has become his. One indication of this is that he experiences guilt when he breaks rules.

Psychologists have studied guilt feelings in young children by placing them in situations that tempt them to break a rule. One classic investigation of this type used a large room that had a rabbit in a hutch in one corner and a pile of toys, comics, and candy in the opposite corner. One child at a time was taken into the room and was asked to watch the rabbit while the experimenter left for a few moments.

On no account, the child was strictly warned, should he leave the rabbit to go over to the "goodies" in the other corner. After several minutes, the inevitable happened—the lure of the toys and candy became too much. The child abandoned his assigned task of looking after the rabbit and instead wandered over to the goodies. As soon as he did that, the experimenter (who observed the child through a one-way mirror) pressed a switch that made the rabbit disappear down a concealed trapdoor.

When the child eventually returned to the corner with the hutch in it, he saw the rabbit was gone. At that precise moment, the experimenter burst into the room demanding to know what had happened to his rabbit. The children's responses varied from total denial to reluctant admission and tears.

Through studies like this—along with detailed observations of children in a variety of natural settings—psychologists have identified a number of techniques to encourage the development of a healthy conscience:

- *Explain rules to your child in terms he can understand.* Simply telling him what the rules are will not encourage him to feel guilty when he breaks them; he should also be told why his action is wrong—for instance, because it upsets you, or because he might hurt someone.

- *Make moral rules clear and specific.* Instead of saying to a child who has just smashed his best friend's toy car, "It's not nice to upset people," it would be more effective to say, "Don't break someone else's toys because she will cry and might break your toy in return." Start with specific rules. As your child matures, he will be able to extend them himself to cover more general situations.

- *React reasonably when your child misbehaves.* The most effective type of punishment is that which is balanced against the seriousness of the offense. A punishment that is too extreme is likely to fuel your child's resentment, rather than his guilt feelings.

- *Never spank your child when he breaks moral rules.* Research confirms that spanking a child for his wrongdoings doesn't change his behavior. It simply encourages him to be more secretive in order to avoid punishment. It also reduces his feelings of guilt.
- *Don't put your child into situations that you know will tempt him.* That only puts your child under unnecessary pressure. If you see that your child is about to do something wrong, step in and stop him before he does it.

See also *Discipline; Lying; Scapegoat; Spanking; Stealing; Swearing.*

H

Hand-Eye Coordination
Watch your young child try to close a zipper on her jacket and you'll soon realize how very difficult this task is for small, uncoordinated hands. Such a task requires a great deal of hand-eye control, a skill your child may not have fully acquired by the time she reaches school. Your child improves with practice, so make sure to give her plenty of opportunities. However, your child will be limited by her stage of physical development.

The acquisition of hand-eye (visual-motor) coordination occurs gradually, in the following sequence:

3 months   Control over hand movements is basic and only begins to emerge. Your child may bring her hands together very suddenly, almost as though she doesn't know how she did it.

6 months   Rather than put toys straight into her mouth as she did when she was younger, your child can now manipulate them more purposefully. She may shake them, throw them, or even bang them against the side of her crib to make noise.

9 months   Your child exhibits the first signs of mature finger control. When your child is sitting in her high chair, put a small piece of cereal on her tray, so that she can clearly see it. You'll notice that she uses her thumb and forefinger together in a pincer movement to lift the item to her mouth.

12 months   Your child's thumb and forefinger pincer movement is better coordinated. She may even be able to hold a crayon firmly enough to make a mark on a piece of paper.

18 months   Place a pile of small (about one-inch) building blocks in front of your child, and start to build a small tower, one block on top of the other. Your child will imitate you and may be able to build a tower of up to three blocks before it topples.

2 years   Your child's hand-eye coordination has developed to the point where she can build a tower of at least six or seven blocks, before it topples. Hand preference has probably been established by this age, and your child can pick up small objects with ease.

3 years   Your child can grip a pair of child's scissors, with their specially shaped handles, but may have a problem cutting with them. She will also have improved pencil control and can make a good attempt at copying a circle.

4 years   Hand-eye coordination has developed to the
                         extent that your child can use a pair of scis-
                         sors capably to cut paper and can manage to
                         thread some small beads onto a thread.

5 years   By this age, your child is probably able to
                         manage large-sized plastic zippers, with
                         your help. However, a couple more years
                         will probably pass before she is completely
                         confident with them.

See also Coordination.

Hazards Fear of potentially hazardous events is a healthy
reaction. A child who does not want to hurt himself avoids dangerous obstacles, such as holes in the pavement, boiling water,
and fast-moving cars.

Some children are fearless and lack the common sense that
tells them to go no further. They go as high as they can on the
climber, even though they cannot get down by themselves, and
they ride around so fast on their tricycles that they often fall off.
A child like this has to learn that there must be limits to his
death-defying feats; that even though he came through
unscathed this time, he may not be so lucky tomorrow. Never
applaud your child for dangerous actions. Continually remind
him that he is behaving dangerously. By associating reckless
performances with your disapproval, your child will eventually
realize that his bravado is unacceptable. Hopefully, he will learn
this before any serious injury occurs.

Other children are accident-prone, not because they fail to
recognize common hazards, but because they are preoccupied.
A young child who is troubled or unhappy about something
may be too distracted to observe basic standards of safety. Some
children are accident-prone because of their unconscious desire
for attention. Injury is one way to guarantee mom's and dad's
interest, since a child's injury always ensures a strong parental
reaction. So if your child is a "walking disaster," spend some

time ascertaining whether he has any deeper worries making him accident-prone.

See also Road Safety; Streetproofing.

Health

Health and behavior are strongly connected in childhood. A chronically ill child is more likely to have an emotional disturbance than a healthy child. A link also exists between minor illness and unsettled behavior. Many children experience a loss of appetite, seem listless, or become uncharacteristically irritable before the onset of a cold or flu.

A research project followed the lives of nine hundred children from birth to age five. The investigators compared each child's record of upper-respiratory infections (coughs, colds, sore throats, bronchitis, or ear infections) with the child's record of behavioral problems. The researchers found that frequent upper-respiratory infections during childhood were closely associated with night waking (defined as waking at least four nights a week), poor appetite (especially at the toddler stage), severe temper tantrums, and management difficulties, due to lack of cooperation on the child's part.

One explanation for this finding is that many children are allergic to certain chemicals found in particular medicines; a child who has a cough may be given a drug to which she is allergic, which may cause the child to behave disruptively. You should discuss all medications with your doctor.

A more likely explanation of the association between health and behavior is that a child who is physically unwell is more vulnerable to stress and less able to take everyday problems in stride. Minor events that the child can handle easily while in full health (such as losing her favorite toy, tidying her room) become major hurdles. The illness weakens your child's ability to cope, making her grumpy and unsettled. Fortunately, a return to good health is usually accompanied by an improvement in the child's behavior.

See also Additives; Crying Baby; Illness.

Healthy Eating The best way to ensure good eating habits in your child is to have good habits yourself. Several studies show that young children will, over a period of several weeks, eat a satisfactory diet—as long as they are offered a broad range of nutritious foods.

One research project presented toddlers with an array of milk, cheese, eggs, vegetables, fruit, and so on. The children could eat what they wanted, using their fingers, and they received no advice or interference from any adult. Three amazing findings emerged:

- The children tried everything eventually, and only rarely did they eat a large amount of any one particular food—quite incredible, given a toddler's almost predictable rejection of vegetables when they are given to him by his parents.
- Not one child had a stomachache, even though the project lasted for several weeks.
- Analysis of the contents of over 35,000 meals revealed that the children had all eaten a perfectly balanced diet, almost as though a dietician had planned their meals in detail.

However, these young children were allowed to eat only from a range of wholesome foods. Nobody appears to have repeated the experiment using potato chips, candy, and cakes! So, you should know the sorts of foods your child should eat. You may well find, when you actually make a note of your child's food intake over a two-week period, that his eating habits aren't as bleak as you first thought. Everything your child eats contains at least one of these substances:

protein   Helps the body grow and keeps it in good repair. Children need more proteins than adults because basic body tissue—the brain, muscles, blood, skin—is growing quickly. Animal protein is obtained from meat, fish, eggs, and dairy products, while vegetable protein is obtained from cereals, nuts, legumes, and root vegetables.

carbohydrates   Provide essential energy, but when too many are consumed, the excess is changed into body fat and stored until needed. The main carbohydrates are sugar, starch, and cellulose. Carbohydrates are present in sweet foods (such as jam, cakes, candy, cookies, chocolate) and in starchy foods (such as bread, potatoes, rice, lentils, flour).

fat   Another source of energy; some fats include vitamins (see below). Fat is present in meat, fish oil, and some vegetables, and can also be in solid form (such as butter, lard, margarine) or in prepared foods (such as French fries, potato chips, sausages, cream, mayonnaise). Excess fats are converted into body fat. Current studies show that all fats, especially animal fats, should be reduced. Don't eliminate them entirely, though. The best fats are unsaturated (vegetable) and unhydrogenated (cold-pressed) monounsaturated fats (olive oil is a great example).

fiber   Encourages good digestion and discourages constipation. Fiber (roughage) is found in fruit and vegetables, whole-grain flour, breads, and cereals, as well as nuts and legumes. Breakfast cereals that contain oats, wheat, or bran contain fiber.

vitamins   Our bodies cannot manufacture most vitamins, so they have to be obtained from food. The main vitamins are

- vitamin A: for healthy skin and night vision (found in fish, cheese, eggs, butter, chicken, spinach, carrots);

- vitamin B: allows the body to obtain energy from food (found in milk, liver, cheese, whole-grain bread, oats);

- vitamin C: for bone development and healing (found in fresh vegetables and fruit, especially citrus fruits);
- vitamin D: builds strong bones and good teeth (found in fish oil, liver, dairy produce, and sunlight);
- vitamin E: strengthens blood cells (found in oats, brown rice, liver, nuts, legumes, and whole-grain cereals).

minerals Occur naturally in the earth, and are present in most foods. The main minerals are

- calcium: forms bones and teeth (found in milk, cheese, yogurt, canned salmon and sardines, green vegetables);
- iron: prevents anemia by building red blood cells (found in red meat, eggs, bread, cereals, green vegetables);
- salt: maintains the body's water balance (and already present in many foods);
- fluoride: important for teeth formation (now found in some water supplies, infant vitamin supplements, toothpaste).

Your child needs a variety of foods every day so that he will grow fit and healthy. The amount your child should eat at mealtimes depends on his particular body size, height, age, daily routine, and metabolism. Episodic growth spurts often cause a temporary surge in appetite, which returns to its previous level following the growth spurt. Give your child portions that you know he can eat. If your child struggles with dinner, serve the meal as finger-food.

See also *Additives; Eating; Eating Out; Fussy Eaters; Manners; Overfeeding; Overweight; Snacks.*

Hearing Assessment Research into hearing loss has
revealed that, in most cases, the child's parents first suspect the
difficulty.

If you suspect that your child has a hearing problem, accurate hearing assessment is vital, because a hearing-impaired
baby faces specific problems:

- The child can't hear what is said by others. Hearing difficulties impair the child's ability to interact with others and
  can cause a sense of isolation.

- The child gets no feedback from her own speech because
  she can't hear the sounds she makes. A deaf baby starts to
  make sounds about the same age as a hearing baby, but the
  lack of feedback means the child has less encouragement to
  practice and extend those sounds.

- The child may develop balance and motor-development
  problems as a result of her hearing loss or ear abnormalities.

Since babbling and listening to sounds provide the foundation for later speech development, a child who misses these
early experiences will find learning to speak harder than will a
child with normal hearing. A hearing-impaired child may be
slower to speak, may not use her first words until long after the
age she is expected to, and may be slower to understand the
meaning of words. The sooner a hearing loss is identified and
assessed, the sooner action can be taken to help the child

Your pediatrician will give your baby a routine hearing check
soon after birth. These checks are repeated when a baby is about
six months and again at regular intervals throughout the
preschool years. If this very basic screening suggests a child has
some hearing loss, the child will be referred for more detailed
assessment by an audiologist, who has specialized equipment
available. The audiologist will present the child with sounds at
varying, but finely controlled, frequencies. Children referred for
speech therapy always undergo a full audiological assessment.

Once an initial assessment leads to the diagnosis of a hearing
difficulty, the professionals involved will establish the full extent
of the child's residual hearing, which hearing aids would be most

suitable for the child, and how well the child understands and uses language. This analysis enables the hearing loss to be seen within the wider context of the child's general development.

Children who have been assessed as having a hearing problem may become involved with a number of professionals, all of whom have an important role to play:

- *Otologist:* an ENT (ear, nose, and throat) consultant, specializing in diseases affecting the ear, who will be in charge of medical treatment for the child's condition.

- *Audiometrician:* a specialist who measures hearing levels, and who may be involved in fitting hearing aids.

- *Teacher of the deaf:* a specially trained teacher who works with hearing-impaired children and their families and advises on the child's educational needs.

- *Educational psychologist:* a psychologist who is trained in child development, and who is also a qualified teacher, who will assess the child's progress regularly throughout schooling.

Hearing assessment categorizes a child's hearing capacity in two main ways:

- *In terms of the loudness of sounds that the child can hear.* With this system, a mild loss has occurred when a child can't hear a whisper; a moderate loss has occurred when the child can't hear a normal voice from three feet away; a severe loss has occurred when the child can't hear a human voice at all; a profound hearing loss has occurred when the child does not react to any sound whatsoever.

- *In terms of the sound frequencies that the child can hear.* With this system, a hearing deficiency may be in the high range of tones, or in the low range, and will impair the child's ability to hear human voices clearly.

See also Hearing Loss; Language Development; Language Difficulties; Language Learning; Language Stimulation.

Hearing Loss Whether total or partial, hearing loss is the single most common reason underlying a child's failure to develop normal speech. A hearing-impaired child may be slower to speak, and slower to understand the meaning of words. Approximately one child in ten has a mild hearing loss, and approximately one per one thousand has a severe hearing loss or total deafness. Almost 90 percent of deaf children have parents with normal hearing.

With normal hearing, sound gets picked up by the outer ear, then passes to the eardrum through the ear canal. This activates the small bones in the middle ear, passing the sound on to the cochlea, where it changes into electrical impulses. These electrical impulses are rather like messages that pass along the hearing nerve to the brain. Problems can arise in any part of this system, and in many instances the cause of hearing defects cannot be traced. Hearing loss can be either conductive or perceptive:

- *Conductive.* In this condition, sound is prevented from reaching the inner ear from the outer and middle ear, perhaps because of a blockage of wax. "Swimmer's ear"—resulting from bacteria and water trapped by ear wax—is another cause of conductive hearing loss, as is middle-ear infection, which often arises from the common cold. Medical treatment usually resolves conductive hearing loss.

- *Perceptive.* This condition is much more serious because it usually cannot be cured. It arises from damage to the inner ear, to the hearing nerve, or to that part of the brain responsible for hearing. Perceptive hearing loss is often congenital. Fortunately, the majority of children with this type of impairment have some residual hearing and are likely to benefit from using a hearing aid. Cochlear implants help some children with perceptive hearing deficits.

Hearing loss in a baby is difficult for parents to detect, but some of the signs to watch for include the following:

- *Lacks response to your voice.* Your baby should show an almost immediate reaction when you speak to him, either by turning his head toward you or by showing some change in his behavior. Failure or slowness to react could signify a hearing loss.

- *Unsoothed by your voice, unless you are in his line of vision.* Most unhappy babies will be soothed by a familiar voice. A hearing-impaired baby may be soothed only when he can actually see you.

- *Startled when someone comes into his line of vision.* Babies with normal hearing soon learn to anticipate the arrival of another person by the sound they make, such as footsteps coming closer or the noise of the door opening. A baby with hearing problems doesn't have this early-warning system and may be startled when he suddenly sees you.

- *Produces restricted sounds after the age of six months.* After this age, a deaf baby's speech fails to develop, whereas a hearing baby's babble continues to increase.

- *Unable to locate the sound source.* By the age of two months, a baby with normal hearing will react to a sound by turning his eyes or head toward it. A baby with a hearing loss may seem confused because he can't tell where the sound originates.

- *Turns the same ear toward a sound source irrespective of the direction of the noise.* A baby with normal hearing will turn the left or right side of his head toward a sound, depending on the sound's direction.

Numerous signals make it easier for parents to detect a hearing loss in an older child:

- *Fails to respond to a simple request.* Of course, the child may pretend not to hear you. If the child fails to respond consistently, then he may have a hearing difficulty.

- *Fails to stop an activity when he is told to stop.* Again, this behavior may be a result of the child's unwillingness to cooperate with you, but repeated instances may be a sign of hearing loss.

- *Needs to have questions repeated before he responds.* A child with partial hearing frequently becomes confused when asked a question, because he can't hear it properly.

- *Watches the speaker's face and mouth closely during conversation.* A child with hearing loss may rely on lip-reading and other facial clues to help him understand what is said.

- *Has delayed speech development.* Several characteristics are more common in the speech of children with partial hearing than in the speech of children with normal hearing. For instance, the ends of words are missing, vocabulary is poorer, letters are mixed up (t and k, or d and g), and sh and s may sound the same.

None of these indicators necessarily mean that your child has a hearing loss. However, if your child repeats the above patterns of behavior every day, seek a professional hearing assessment. Techniques for stimulating language development in a child with normal hearing apply equally to a child with a hearing loss.

You should also think carefully about suitable toys. For a young baby, choose a rattle that is brightly colored and lets him feel vibrations when it is shaken. At six months, a baby will feel beat and rhythm when you hold a toy music box or portable radio close to him. When the child is twelve to eighteen months old, games that present different sounds in different places (such as peek-a-boo using musical instruments) will be useful. For a child aged two or three years and older, most toy shops carry a range of games that stimulate language and listening experiences.

Make sure your child wears a hearing aid if it has been prescribed. Hearing aids can make sounds louder for the user, though a deaf child will still not hear words exactly as a child with normal hearing does. The child may not be comfortable wearing the aid and may feel embarrassed by it, but the aid should be worn continually at the correct volume setting. Modern hearing aids are extremely powerful and can offer substantial help to a child with hearing loss.

See also *Hearing Assessment; Language Development; Language Difficulties; Language Learning; Language Stimulation.*

Home Schooling
Although the majority of children receive their education at a school, more and more parents now teach their children at home. Parents choose home schooling for many and varied reasons. Some parents are unhappy about the quality of teaching in schools today. Some are concerned about the level of bullying and intimidation their child experiences in school. Some embark on a program of home education because they think they can do the job better than anyone else.

Home schooling can be very successful, providing an environment in which a child thrives academically and personally. But it isn't a commitment to be taken on lightly. Preparation, short-term and long-term planning, identification of resource materials, and a positive attitude from parent and child are all prerequisites of a successful home schooling program. In addition, the child should be provided with plenty of opportunities to mix with other children of her own age.

Several self-help organizations are run by parents who educate their children at home. Such organizations are good resources if you are considering home schooling for your child.

See also Creativity; Giftedness; Integration, Educational.

Hospital
Going into the hospital isn't something that happens just to other people's children—half of all children are admitted to a hospital before they reach the age of seven. Sometimes the admissions are planned. At other times they are the result of an accident. Whatever the circumstances, hospitalization can be a traumatic emotional experience for a young child. Look at it from your child's point of view. Hospitals are large, noisy places, where people wear green and white clothes. Some of them even wear masks. The food is different from home, not what mom usually makes. Hospitals may already be associated with the death of a relative. Yet all this pales in comparison with what actually goes on inside the hospital: injections, pills, and possibly unpleasant examinations—no wonder children are often apprehensive. And this apprehension can affect their rate of recovery.

Most pediatricians accept that a child's return to good health depends very much on the way he's managed in the hospital—and this management must include due attention to the child's psychological welfare as well as to his physical welfare. There are very good reasons for this: if a child is unhappy in the hospital, he may not eat properly and will feel stressed. When this happens, the child will not recover as quickly as he would if he felt comfortable and at ease.

The foundations for coping with hospitalization should be laid long before your child has a health problem. You are happy to discuss fire stations, the library, and the supermarket with your child—so include hospitals. Lots of children's books about being in the hospital are available, which you can read to your child at home in a relaxed setting. You can point out your local hospital when passing by; there may even be an opportunity to take your child with you when you visit a hospitalized friend.

If your child has a planned hospital admission, talk to him about it several days in advance. This will give him plenty of time to ask questions—to which you should give direct answers, according to your child's level of understanding. Emphasize how kind the doctors and nurses will be, and reassure your child that he will be there for only a few days. Many children's hospitals plan a preadmission visit to show children the routine and answer their questions.

Be calm on admission day. Let your child take a couple of his favorite toys with him. Ask ward staff to introduce your child to some of the other patients. Don't be afraid to tell the nurses about your child's individual habits, for instance, that he always has warm milk in the morning or that he watches a particular television program each day. The more the hospital routine resembles your child's home routine, the happier he'll be.

Actually being with your child while he is in the hospital is the most effective way to ease his psychological stress. Children should be allowed unrestricted visiting when in the hospital, and mothers should be allowed to stay with their hospitalized child. These elementary facts of child psychology have not been universally implemented. The problem is that not every child is admitted to an all-children hospital. A high percentage is admitted either to a children's ward within a large general hospital, or

to an adult ward with designated children's beds, where staff
have not been specially trained to deal with young patients. Such
institutions are unlikely to have residential facilities for parents,
and visiting hours for children are likely to be restricted.

If you want to be with your child throughout his stay in the
hospital, even though he's in a ward with restricted visiting, do
the following:

- *Remember you have a right to be there.* Most doctors realize
  that it's in your child's best interest for you to be with him
  when he's in the hospital. You are not eccentric when you
  exercise this right.

- *Don't be put off by the excuse, "There's no room."* A chair by
  your child's bed will not take up much space, nor will it
  inconvenience any of the other patients.

- *Challenge staff who say that they can't work while you're in the
  room watching them.* There's no justification for this sort of
  claim.

- *Speak to the head nurse—or hospital administrator, if necessary—
  if you are consistently told you can't stay.* Ward routines can be
  flexible, if the goodwill is there. So stick to your guns.

See also Illness; X-Ray.

Hydrocephalus Most babies born with spina bifida

also have hydrocephalus. In this condition, cerebrospinal
fluid—a naturally occurring watery substance in the brain that
serves to bathe the brain's surfaces and to carry essential nutrients—is unable to drain into the bloodstream. Consequently,
this fluid begins to build up in the brain, causing it to enlarge.
The effects of hydrocephalus vary, but often include visual and
learning difficulties, seizures, and coordination problems.

The signs of hydrocephalus do not usually manifest themselves until an infant is a few weeks old, or even a few months
old. This is one reason why doctors measure the circumference
of a new baby's head as a matter of routine. Very often these
measurements lead to the early identification of the difficulty.

The most common treatment for hydrocephalus is a surgical procedure that implants a shunt to divert the built-up cerebrospinal fluid back into the bloodstream. The shunt has a system of tubes with a valve to control the rate of drainage. Although the device may become blocked, or infection may develop, these difficulties can usually be resolved. Before the development of this treatment, the majority of children with hydrocephalus died.

See also Spina Bifida.

Hygiene
Personal hygiene is important for everyone. Encourage your child to take an interest in his level of cleanliness from an early age. Following are three main benefits of good personal hygiene:

- *Health.* A child who isn't bathed regularly is prone to infections and irritations, particularly in the genital area and where he has folds of skin. He may ingest germs and bacteria when he brings his unwashed hands into contact with food.

- *Sociability.* Nobody likes a smelly child! Everyone loves to hold a clean, sweet-smelling baby. Nobody wants to hold one that smells of feces, urine, or vomit. A child who has a strong, unpleasant body odor soon finds that he is alone in a crowd. The only way these problems can be avoided is by regular baths.

- *Comfort.* Poor personal hygiene leads to discomfort. A baby becomes distressed when its diaper gets dirty. An older child is uncomfortable wearing dirty clothes that feel stiff and scratchy. Everybody likes the sensations of well-being that arise from putting on fresh, clean clothes after a warm, soapy bath.

Bath time is the first opportunity for your child to become involved in his own cleanliness. Even a baby as young as six months can learn to associate cleanliness with pleasure—as long as bath time is fun. Try not to rush your infant in and out of his bath; let him play with bath toys and splash around. He'll learn to enjoy being in the water, especially when you have fun too. If a child associates bathing with something unpleasant, bath time can become a source of conflict. Shampooing, in particular, can cause tears. Ask your child what upsets him. He may have fear of soap getting in his eyes, or of slipping under the water while his hair is being shampooed. He may even be afraid that he will slide down the drain when the plug is removed. Once you have identified the cause of your child's anxiety, reassure him and offer a solution—for example, fear of shampoo getting into his eyes can be eased by stroking his hair toward the back of his head when washing it, or by using a mild baby shampoo, or by covering his eyes with a facecloth. These measures will make bath time more fun.

The issue of personal hygiene arises again once your child starts toilet training. Teach your child to wash his hands after he sits on the potty. This becomes even more important around the age of three or four, when he is able to wipe his bottom without help. Girls must be reminded to wipe from front to back, to avoid infections. Make hand washing standard practice when your child uses the toilet so that it becomes a habit. From the age of three, your child should be expected to wash his hands on his own before mealtimes—although be prepared to remind him each time.

Your child will feel better when he starts the day clean. He will also feel good when he ends the day that way. Develop a bedtime routine that involves him washing his hands and face on the nights he doesn't have a bath, and brushing his teeth. Until your child is five or six, you may find that he needs encouragement to wash up at night; most young children would rather climb into bed when they are tired than get themselves clean and fresh. Point out how nice he is to cuddle when he's clean and fresh from his bath, or how pleasant his breath smells after he brushes his teeth.

Good standards of personal hygiene can be established in the preschool years. A child who has an interest in his own cleanliness at that age will probably maintain it throughout his life.

See also Bath Time; Independence.

Hyperactivity

A hyperactive child shows an abnormally high level of activity, combined with a short attention span, a low level of concentration, and a superabundance of impulsive and reckless behavior.

Perception of the child's behavior is a major factor to be considered in the identification of hyperactivity. Parents who are themselves quiet, withdrawn, and bookish may describe their child as hyperactive if she doesn't sit down peacefully to play with her building blocks for thirty minutes at a time. Outgoing parents who believe children should be allowed to express themselves freely and energetically are likely to be more tolerant of their child's very active behavior.

One of the difficulties in identifying hyperactivity is that young children vary considerably in their activity levels. Even during pregnancy, one woman may find her baby moves infrequently, while another at the same stage of pregnancy may find that hers kicks and wriggles most of the time. These differences in activity rates continue after birth. Babies who are genuinely hyperactive are noticeably different from other children in terms of their general day-to-day behavior. For instance, a hyperactive baby often doesn't like being cuddled, and will struggle in its mother's arms. These babies seem uncomfortable and miserable, as though nothing is right for them. Often these babies are poor sleepers and fussy eaters, and they are very difficult and demanding to care for. Researchers have also found other features associated with hyperactivity. For instance, during pregnancy, the mother is more likely to have had high blood pressure and to have experienced vaginal bleeding. Whereas premature delivery occurs in up to 15 percent of the population, up to 25 percent of hyperactive children are premature. In the period immediately following delivery, a hyperactive child is more likely to have a breathing difficulty.

Whatever the complicating factors in identifying hyperactivity, a significant number of very active children do cause serious problems for their parents. It doesn't really matter whether these children are called "hyperactive." Several possible causes of hyperactivity have been suggested (each with its own form of treatment):

- *Diet.* One suggestion is that hyperactivity is caused by a child's diet, and that if an overactive, disruptive child eats only natural foods, without any additives, then her behavior will improve. Some parents find this works. Others do not. Your pediatrician will supply you with an additive-free diet sheet.

- *Discipline.* Another theory is that hyperactivity is caused by the way parents behave toward their child. Every child needs structure and predictability in her home life, and this is usually achieved by having consistent discipline. Parents of a hyperactive child often let her break rules without reprimand, simply because they are too tired to challenge her. The child does need a structured form of discipline.

- *Brain damage.* Some doctors claim that hyperactivity is caused by "minimal brain damage," which interferes with the child's behavior. This explanation derives from the medical discovery that a few hyperactive children do have identifiable brain damage. However, the existence of minimal brain damage is impossible to verify using contemporary neurological tests, and consequently many professionals reject it completely.

- *Drug abuse during pregnancy.* Children born to cocaine- or crack-addicted mothers show a higher level of hyperactivity.

Explanations that attribute hyperactivity to a physical cause have led to the development of drug treatment. A number of stimulant drugs can have a temporary calming effect on a hyperactive child, but they often have worrying side effects, including lethargy and appetite loss. Few parents are happy at the thought of their young child taking drugs. This type of treatment remains controversial.

Research also suggests that high lead levels in the atmosphere—from gasoline fumes—could cause hyperactivity. Investigators claim to have found a link between blood lead level and hyperactive behavior, and conclude that lead at low levels of exposure probably has a small but harmful effect on a child's behavior.

Parents of hyperactive children have a tough time, and

should be offered support wherever possible. A psychological approach—such as providing a structured and consistent form of discipline at home—gives parents an active role in managing their child's behavior, and is usually the first suggestion offered. Such a management system is not guaranteed to alter the behavior of every hyperactive child, but it can have a positive effect. It offers the added benefit of making parents feel that they are beginning to have some control over their child again. This in itself can raise their self-confidence, and consequently decrease family tension. It's encouraging to know that whatever causes hyperactivity, the problem tends to fade as a child reaches adolescence. In most instances, a previously unmanageable child becomes more settled during the teenage years.

See also Additives; Attention Deficit Disorder (ADD); Discipline; Learning Difficulties.

I

Ignoring Giving attention to your child when he misbehaves can often add fuel to the fire by actually increasing the frequency of misbehavior—your child might learn that misbehavior is an effective way to gain your attention. Therefore, sometimes the best action to take to discourage your child's misbehavior is simply to ignore it.

Ignoring can be very difficult, however. You may find that you can ignore your child's behavior only up to a point, and then you explode with anger; this reinforces your child's actions because he would rather have an angry reaction from you rather than no reaction at all. Or you might find that you start off by trying to ignore your child's behavior but give in after a few minutes because you can't tolerate his nagging any more; again, this simply teaches your child that if he nags long enough, he will get what he wants. Before you decide to use the tactic of ignoring, weigh your own ability to follow it through. You may decide that this technique doesn't suit you.

If you do decide to ignore your child the next time he does something annoying, then have a plan of action to follow. For instance, you could ignore him by

- looking busy with something,
- reading a book or a magazine,
- watching television,
- talking on the telephone,
- listening to music.

Whatever the course of action you take when ignoring your child, stay calm at all times, and show no reaction to him, even when his misbehavior intensifies. Keep a neutral expression on your face, seem interested in your own activity, and say nothing about your child's behavior.

Ignoring doesn't always work because its effectiveness rests on the assumption that your child can control his behavior—and sometimes he can't. For instance, ignoring a mild tantrum might stop it from escalating into a full-blown outburst, but ignoring a full-blown outburst might have no effect at all because your child has lost all control at that point. Judge each situation individually before deciding to ignore it.

At first, you may discover your child's behavior actually gets worse once he realizes you are ignoring him. It's only natural that he'll try harder to attract your attention. Keep your temper and remain calm. Accept that this deterioration in his actions is an inevitable initial reaction to your management strategy, and remind yourself that it will get better eventually. Make a note of how long your child keeps up his misbehavior when you first ignore him, and compare this with the length of time on subsequent occasions—you'll be delighted to discover that the episodes become shorter and shorter as time goes by.

See also *Attention-Seeking Behavior; Crying Baby; Discipline; Spanking; Tantrums; Whining.*

Illness Dealing with a sick child is difficult at the best of times. There are so many things to worry about, ranging from the trivial (who will do the car pool instead of me?) to the more serious (I wonder what's wrong with my child?). After a few days, your child is usually on the way to a full recovery, and normality is once again restored to your household. Unfortunately, not all childhood illnesses follow such a brief and predictable course. Some children develop illnesses such as cancer or kidney disease that can take an exceptionally long time to respond to treatment, and chronic ill health of this sort dominates a family. A child with long-term ill health has an instinctive desire to get better, and the more emotionally secure the child is, the speedier her physical recovery will be.

A chronically sick child has the same psychological needs as a healthy one. True, an ill child has additional requirements, such as the need to be reassured that she is going to get well eventually, the need for appropriate medical treatment, and the need for lots of rest. Your child's basic emotional needs remain the same (though perhaps a little stronger) as they would have been had ill health not loomed on the horizon. Every child thrives best in a family in which she feels cared for and in which she experiences structure and consistency. Without these qualities, your child will feel insecure.

You may ease your standards of discipline when your child is ill. After all, she is less active and far less likely to break the rules.

Although it is perfectly understandable when parents "spoil" their sick child—and we are all guilty of this at times—abandoning family routine altogether has a number of potential dangers. First, a sudden change in the rules may confirm the child's worry that something is terribly wrong and increase her unconscious fears that her illness is serious. Second, abandoning family routines may cause relationship difficulties: within a short time you may find yourself coping not only with a chronically sick child, but with a chronically sick child who thinks she can do as she pleases. Your other children might also be confused about this relaxation of family rules.

Adjustment from ill health to normality can be difficult

enough (with such tasks as restoring self-confidence, becoming independent once again), without the added task of relearning the guidelines.

You must be flexible. There will be occasions when you "turn a blind eye" to your chronically sick child's behavior. Of course, you should fuss over her and do everything you can to make her feel comfortable and happy. Of course, you should spend as much time with her as you can, to keep her from feeling lonely and miserable. But this is quite different from abandoning structure altogether.

Another way to help your chronically ill child is to establish some form of routine in her daily activities. To a child confined to bed all day, time can seem to drag. She may begin to focus on negative aspects of life—the boredom, missing her friends, worrying about school work. Make it a matter of routine that, if at all possible, your child gets up from bed for meals, that at a specific time of the day she reads a book, and that she has a bath every evening. Incorporating these routine events into her life may seem rather tedious from your point of view, but from hers, regularity of this nature can be welcome. It enables your child to anticipate the day's events, just as she would during a normal day when she is in good health.

Give your child occasional surprises. A surprise visit by one of her friends can prove memorable; the unexpected present of a book or game can perk up a dull day.

See also Discipline; Health; Hospital; Routine; Spoiling.

Imaginary Friend
Many young children have an imaginary friend, someone who exists only in their mind. Although others go through their preschool years without using their imagination in this particular way, it is a normal part of early child development and an extension of symbolic play. The advantage of having an imaginary friend is that a child has full control over play situations. The child decides when to play with his friend and what they will play at together. Freed from relying on other children to be cooperative and pleasant to him, your child can do as he pleases with his imaginary friend, and

no one can interfere with their game. This makes the imaginary friend all the more desirable.

Your child knows that this friend is not real. Children have usually passed through the imaginary-friend phase by the time they begin school; the peak age for this phenomenon is around four years. Imaginary friends can serve a number of purposes, including the following:

- *Security.* An imaginary friend provides comfort and security in times of stress. When a child is under pressure, he can turn to this friend for support, and the friend will say what the child needs to hear. For instance, a child who is afraid to visit the dentist may be reassured when his imaginary friend tells him that he'll be fine. And once he leaves the dental office, the friend can disappear until next time.

- *Company.* Only children, or children with few friends of their own age, or children who live in an isolated area have a greater tendency to play with imaginary friends. The reason is obvious. what a lonely child cannot create in reality, he can create in fantasy. It is far better for a young child to engage in this sort of symbolic play activity than to sit around doing nothing at all, moping because he has no friends.

- *Communication.* A child can be very subtle in communicating information to adults, and the imaginary friend can be a useful mechanism to do this, especially when the child wants to say something that his parents may not want to hear. Telling his imaginary friend (within earshot of his parents) that he's worried mom and dad will be angry when they discover his new toy is lost is one way to break the news gently to them!

In some instances, the friend may start to play too dominant a role in the child's life, or the child retains this form of symbolic play long after other children of his age have grown out of it. When it gets to the point that the child's day-to-day life is impaired by the presence of the "friend," then it probably indicates that the child has a deeper emotional difficulty, of which the need for the imaginary friend is a symptom—for instance, if the child won't go anywhere without his friend, if he absolutely insists an empty chair is left beside him at every meal so that his friend can sit down, if he says he is crying because his friend is unhappy. If this kind of thing happens with your child, look more closely at his life to see what could be troubling him.

See also Imagination; Play.

Imagination Imaginative play does not emerge until a child is about one year old, and continues to develop throughout the preschool years. This form of play has two features that distinguish it from earlier exploratory play. First, a toddler is now able to use one object to represent another. A block can represent a car, a cuddly toy can represent mom or dad. The child can also use herself to represent someone else—for instance, she can pretend to be her mother or a truck driver. The range of potential play situations is infinitely extended. Second, symbolic play frees a child from the here-and-now. The child is not tied to what she can see in front of her: objects, people, and experiences are present in her memory, for her to utilize.

Symbolic or imaginative play develops in progressive stages, although the ages at which children pass from one stage to another vary greatly. The first stage occurs at about one year and involves a toddler using a familiar behavior in a different context—such as when she pretends to feed herself out of a toy cup. The second stage comes at about eighteen months, when she herself is no longer the focus of her pretend play: she will act out imaginary sequences with a doll, or another person, instead of always making herself the center of attention. The third stage of symbolic play comes at about three years, when the child is able to adopt roles in play. Children at this stage like pretending to be other people, whether it is the milkman, their mother, their father, or the doctor. Elaborately designed clothes are not necessary. The dress-up box at home requires only a modest collection of old clothes, a few hats and scarves, some cheap jewelry, a couple of shopping bags—that's enough for a child to create any character she wants. Young children love to imagine they are someone else.

Symbolic role-play serves different psychological purposes. It provides your child with an opportunity to test out roles she may anticipate playing in later life. Your child may wonder what it would be like to be an adult, or to be one of her friends, or to be a television character. Role-play lets your child experience this for herself. You may be surprised when you observe your child playing like this, especially when you see her act out the role of "mom" or "dad." Your child may take great delight in strutting around, pretending to be a complaining parent, bossing everyone else around. Frightening to think that this is how our children sometimes perceive us!

Role-play also allows your child to release her deeper emotions in a socially acceptable way. A young child would normally be reprimanded for being aggressive and shouting at other children. However, when she delves into the dress-up box, puts on a policeman's hat and starts issuing orders, nobody bothers. Symbolic role-play lets your child release her aggressive impulses without fear of punishment.

This type of play can be called "imaginative" because the child is able to distinguish it from reality. When she is engaged in imaginary play, the child knows that what she is doing is only make-believe. She does know the difference. You probably have seen your child have a raging argument with her friend, and when you have gone over to separate them, they will have greeted you with the reassuring remark, "It's all right. We're not really fighting. We're only playing."

See also *Aggression; Creativity; Imaginary Friend; Learning through Play; Play.*

Immunization Although babies who are breast-fed tend to have fewer health problems in the first year of life than babies who are bottle-fed, all children are susceptible to disease. Fortunately, immunization can protect against the major childhood diseases that can be fatal, including polio, diphtheria, tetanus, and whooping cough. Medical specialists claim that a fully implemented program of immunizations could eliminate these childhood hazards completely.

Modern techniques now mean that childhood immunizations are less complicated. The vaccines providing immunization against diphtheria, whooping cough, and tetanus are combined into a triple vaccine (DPT); this is administered as an injection at the ages of two, four, and six months (that is, three times). Infants are now given the polio vaccine in the form of drops in the mouth, usually when they receive the DPT. And the vaccines against measles, mumps, and rubella (German measles) are combined into one injection (MMR), administered at the age of twelve to fifteen months. The last stage in the preschool immunization program is between the ages of three and five years, when a child receives booster vaccines against diphtheria, tetanus, and polio in order to give added protection for starting school. There is also a vaccine (Hib) that offers protection against meningitis, and one for hepatitis B.

Serious side effects to vaccines are rare, while minor reactions (such as temporary irritability) are common. However, the vaccine for whooping cough has come under particular criticism in recent years because some parents have claimed it has caused brain damage. Evidence supporting these claims is not clear-cut, but it has shaken parental confidence in the vaccine's safety. Yet whooping cough remains a very dangerous disease that can itself result in brain damage, and most doctors agree this is a greater risk than possible serious side effects from the immunization itself.

Certainly, if you have fears about side effects, discuss them with your pediatrician before the immunization; the pediatrician is fully aware of your baby's health record and will be able to provide you with reassurance. There are some medical reasons for delaying immunization, or for cancelling it altogether: for example, if your baby is unwell, if he has ever had any convulsions or a severe allergic reaction, or if he has had a bad reaction to previous immunizations. Some children are allergic to eggs. Because the serum for rubella is based on an egg protein, albumin, do not introduce eggs into your toddler's diet until after he receives his German measles inoculation.

Independence

One minute your child is determined to prove that she can undress herself without your help. The next she desperately wants you to cuddle her because she's afraid to go upstairs in the dark. The early years are characterized by these two conflicting trends—your child's increasing dependence on you for love and security, which gives her a strong psychological foundation for later life, and her inborn desire to be independent.

There is no specific age when your child should be independent, when she should be able to do things without your help. True, some milestones of independence are important for all children, such as walking, talking, and having bladder and bowel control. Apart from these obvious skills, much depends on your own view as a parent.

Encouraging your child to be independent is hard work because of the demands that it makes on you. Don't leave the development of your child's independence to chance; take a planned approach. Have specific goals that you want your child to achieve. For instance, putting on a sweater by herself is a clearer goal than getting dressed by herself. Explain each goal to her. Your child will have more success in increasing her independence if she takes small steps rather than large jumps. Whatever you want your child to achieve, break it down into small tasks and then tackle them one at a time. Give your child lots of praise when she succeeds, and lots of reassurance when she doesn't.

Parents sometimes inadvertently instill in their child conflicting sets of expectations about self-reliance. For instance, a child who learns to tidy her room may want to extend her independence to choosing what clothes she should wear, and what television program she should watch. During the process of becoming independent, most children have difficulty knowing when to assert their individuality and when not to. Be prepared to explain carefully what is acceptable to you and what is not.

Children often take a step backwards in their stride for independence precisely at the time when they should move forward. For example, a four-year-old who is learning to eat with a knife and fork may seem awkward all of a sudden. These moments of regression are normal and allow your child to gather the emotional strength needed to move on to the next stage of independence, rather like an athlete who turns away from the high-jump moments before she takes a run at it. When your child does seem to be going backwards instead of forward, be patient with her. Her behavior is natural and happens at all ages and stages.

Developing independence can be inconvenient for the whole family. Your morning household routine is probably hectic, when everyone is rushing to get out to work or to school. A young child struggling valiantly to dress herself may slow down everyone. Temptation to assist her can be strong. So if you are trying to encourage your child's competence at a particular task, make sure you give her plenty of time. The atmosphere must be relaxed, or her desire for success will evaporate. A balance between overreliance on you and total independence must be struck. Your expectations should be realistic—just as it is inadvisable to "baby" a child, so it is inadvisable to expect too much from her. Don't push your child to attain a level more advanced than normal for a child her age. There is no advantage in a five-year-old being able to do some things that only eight-year-olds usually do.

Breaking away from a state of total dependence begins early and continues throughout a child's life. Often a painful process, it is a necessary aspect of every parent-child relationship, and it benefits the child. The confidence that your child gains from controlling her world is a tremendous boost to your child's self-esteem; that wonderful moment when she bursts into the room, telling you excitedly, "I put my sweater on all by myself; I did it myself," says it all.

See also *Playgroup/Nursery School; Self-Confidence.*

Integration, Educational Until recently, it was
assumed that the best way to help a child with special needs was to place him in a "special" school, where he would mix with other children at the same level of development and with the same sorts of difficulties. The theory underlying this outlook is that the child's needs can best be met in that type of establishment because it has small classes, is staffed by specially trained

teachers, and has additional services (for instance, speech therapy) available on site. Yet the wisdom of placing children into segregated special schools, separate from their "normal" peers, has been challenged. Now, the drive is away from segregation toward integration, also known as mainstreaming.

Integration is not an all-or-none phenomenon: it develops along a continuum. Integration has three levels:

- *Locational integration.* Occurs when a child with special needs attends an ordinary school, but where the child has very little social contact between him and the rest of the pupils. Some parents are satisfied with this type of provision because it means that their child attends his local school, albeit in a restricted way. Other parents reject locational integration on the grounds that it is no better than segregated provision.

- *Social integration.* Occurs when a child with special needs attends an ordinary school where the child has planned opportunities to mix with the others (such as during breaks). Most parents of children with special needs view social integration positively.

- *Functional integration.* The fullest level of integration, which occurs when a child with special needs is not only located in an ordinary school and mixes with the pupils, but also attends the same classes. Functional integration means that a child with special needs participates fully in school life. This type of integration is often the most conducive to the child's overall development, although it does not meet the needs of every child.

Integration has gained prominence as an educational policy through the increased awareness that segregated special schools do not always benefit all the children who attend them. Evidence shows that these children do not necessarily make greater educational gains than children with special needs who attend their local school. Many parents of children who have attended segregated special schools admit at the end of their child's schooling that, while they have been delighted with the care and professionalism of the school, they are deeply concerned about the child's inability to deal with the outside world. The child is so accustomed to daily living in a sheltered environment that he has problems managing independently in society.

Remember, integration can go wrong. A child may be rejected by the other children, which is likely to make him unhappy and resentful. Even if the child does not meet such peer-group barriers, he may find that working at activities that are vastly different from those of his classmates is stressful. He may regard this as a constant daily reminder of his differences. Not all classroom parents are sympathetic to the aims of integration. They may be concerned that their own children will lose out because of all the individual attention focused on a child with special needs. They might also be worried that their own children will imitate a special needs child's less-mature behavior. These potential problems can usually be overcome through sensitive management by school staff. Integration means attending to the needs of all the children, not just to those of the child with special needs.

See also Cerebral Palsy; Down's Syndrome; Giftedness; Physical Disability; Special Needs.

Intelligence Many people think of intelligence only in terms of school performance, and judge a child's intellectual ability on the basis of her scores in educational tests and exams. This is a very narrow perspective because some intelligent children don't do well at school. From a broader viewpoint, intelligence is a child's ability to make sense of what goes on around her; her ability to adapt to, and cope with, new experiences; and her ability to find solutions to novel problems.

There is heated debate over whether intelligence is inherited, or whether it is affected by the environment. Those who adopt the former view maintain that every individual has a fixed level of intelligence, and therefore should be taught in a school with pupils of the same level of ability. Those who think intelligence can be affected by the environment advocate an educational system that gives every pupil as much stimulation and encouragement as possible, in order to develop potential to the fullest level.

A psychologist may use an intelligence test to assess a child's intellectual functioning. The test consists of a number of different items that measure various intellectual skills, such as language, auditory memory, visual memory, comprehension, and speed of information processing. Once one of these tests has been administered (usually taking one to two hours), an IQ (intelligence quotient) score can be calculated. The average IQ is 100, and approximately 70 percent of all children have an IQ between 85 and 110. One criticism of intelligence tests is that they don't actually indicate how a child will perform in a real-life situation. Another criticism is that the results of an intelligence test don't lead to practical suggestions for helping a child with learning difficulties.

See also Creativity; Giftedness; Knowledge; Learning Difficulties; Learning Skills.

Interrupting Young children are, by nature, egocentric. In other words, they tend to think only of themselves, only of their feelings, only of their wants. As they develop in understanding and sensitivity, children begin to consider the perspective of others—this process starts during the first year of life and continues throughout childhood. One of the effects of a child's egocentricity is that he expects to come first in everything. Your three-year-old doesn't like to wait his turn in line, for instance, and so he barges to the front or gets upset. Nor does he like to wait his turn to say something, and so he interrupts you in the middle of a sentence.

These interruptions are not malicious or naughty—they are a genuine reflection of the way your child perceives his world at that time. Your child will become more aware of social responsibility by the time he's about five years old; in the meantime, though, interruptions may be a typical part of his behavior. The following techniques will help you encourage your growing child to interrupt less, either behaviorally or verbally:

- *Accept that interruptions are normal in young children.* Of course, you will be annoyed when your child tries to talk to you in the middle of your conversation with someone else, especially if he does this regularly. But you can at least take comfort in the fact that this is a reflection of your child's developmental stage, not his difficult personality.

- *Explain turn-taking to your child.* Tell your child explicitly about taking turns. Explain this in terms he can understand, giving examples of how turn-taking will benefit him; for example, waiting in line means that others can't barge in front of him. Your message will get through to him eventually.

- *Take a consistent approach.* The most effective way to discourage interruptions is to be consistent. When your child interrupts, finish whatever you were doing before you respond to him. Naturally, you have to be flexible—sometimes your child's interruptions are a sign of a genuine problem that requires your immediate attention—but in most instances, wait before you respond to him.

- *Practice turn-taking at home.* The more experience your child gets waiting to say something, or waiting to take his turn, the better. Turn-taking can be practiced at home while playing games, or while having normal discussions at family mealtimes. When your child does interrupt, remind him that he has to wait.

- *Have realistic expectations.* Interruptions will become less frequent only when your child has matured to a developmental stage in which he recognizes the importance of other's feelings. So it is unrealistic to expect a two- or three-year-old child never to interrupt. Your child only develop this perspective when he has reached the age of four or five years.

Occasionally, your child's interruptions may be attention-seeking, with the sole aim of making him the center of your attention. Since most interruptions are for the purpose of stating an opinion or asking a question, one sign that interruptions may be attention-seeking is when they are repetitive. In addition, your child won't be particularly interested in the answers you give him. The most effective way to tackle those sorts of interruptions is to ignore them. However, if you find that your child does interrupt constantly, consider why he has an emotional need to do so. Maybe, your child feels unable to gain attention from you unless he interrupts. Think about the way you and he relate to each other, in order to satisfy yourself that your child is able to get your attention and interest without pushing his way into your conversation with others.

See also Attention-Seeking Behavior; Body Language; Communication; Ignoring; Social Development; Questions.

J

Jealousy Jealousy is a mixture of resentment, fear, insecurity, possessiveness, and suspicion—feelings to which we would not willingly admit. At best, jealousy makes a child unhappy and dissatisfied with what she's got. At worst, it makes her behave in a hurtful way toward others. Sometimes feelings of jealousy between children in the same family can be so strong that they last throughout life. Many psychologists take the view that children are instinctively selfish and possessive, so jealousy is shown by every child to some extent, and that development in the preschool years involves the child moving away from thinking only about herself to thinking and caring about others. Jealousy begins when your baby first realizes, usually around the age of six months, that she doesn't have you all to herself. You may find that she becomes upset when she sees you cuddling another baby, even if you do so for only a few seconds. The brief instant of sharing your attention with another child is enough to make your child feel a surge of jealousy. At six months your child will make no attempt to hide this fact from you—she will cry and cry until you put the other baby down and pick her up.

Your child becomes more able to handle these feelings as time passes. A growing child learns to manage this type of jealousy when she realizes through experience that your attention toward someone else doesn't detract from your love for her. By two or three, your child probably won't become upset when she sees you with her peers.

Your child will inevitably feel jealous at some points in her life, and the following tips will help you and her manage her feeling:

- *Never make your child feel ashamed of being jealous.* If you make your child feel badly about her feelings, she'll hide her true feelings from you.

- *Let your child know that you've been jealous.* There's no harm in admitting to your child that occasionally you are jealous of others. Ensure you add that you never let these feelings upset you or spoil your fun. Once your child knows that you understand how she feels, she won't be so upset.

- *Accept that jealousy varies from child to child.* Just because your older child is not the jealous type and is prepared to share her possessions with others, doesn't mean your younger child will be the same. Avoid comparing your child with others. That will only make her even more jealous.

- *Very intense jealousy can be a sign of a child's deeper anxieties.* Constant jealousy may be a symptom of deep-rooted insecurity and a lack of confidence. If your child feels this way, try to identify the underlying cause, and deal with it.

See also *Age Gap; Birth Order; Equality; First-Born Jealousy; Sibling Rivalry.*

Jokes Listen to some children's jokes—such as "What did the salad say to the potatoes?" "Shut your eyes, I'm dressing "—and you'll probably find it hard to believe that these are the early signs of a more sophisticated adult sense of humor. The foundation of the ability to see the funny side of things is laid down in the preschool years. A sense of humor is, after all, one of the characteristics that differentiate humans from animals.

Your baby will probably show his first smile when he is about six weeks old. This smile, usually in response to a familiar face smiling at him, is the first sign of the psychological mechanism by which a child can derive amusement from his environment. As the child matures, different types of jokes make him laugh. What amuses one young child may not amuse another, as anyone who tries to make a living as a clown at birthday parties will confirm!

Children around the age of eighteen to twenty-four months typically enjoy jokes that involve familiar objects used in an unusual way: for example, when dad sticks teddy up his sweater. The incongruity of the situation is what makes the child laugh. By the age of three or four years, a child's greater use of language means that he now prefers jokes that involve words rather than objects, although an adult might not always know what exactly the child finds amusing. The child will chuckle merrily at the sight of a custard pie being thrown in someone's face.

The more subtle the joke, the harder it is for a child to identify the humor, even though his ability to laugh at jokes is not directly connected to his level of intelligence. Every child is capable of laughter, irrespective of his intelligence.

See also Intelligence.

K

Kindness Human beings have an inborn tendency to be kind to others. You only need to look at very young children to see the evidence. Sometimes when a new baby hears another baby cry, she bursts out crying himself (and psychologists have also proved that she cries more in response to a human cry than to a computer-generated cry). This suggests that babies, even at a very early stage of their development, are sufficiently concerned about other people's distress to become upset themselves.

This inclination to be considerate becomes clearer as the preschool years unfold. By the age of twelve months, an infant no longer cries when she hears someone else cry, but instead will have a troubled look on her face. By the age of fifteen months she will probably go over to a crying child or adult, to offer a comforting cuddle. A typical three-year-old will take positive action to help someone in distress, for example, by giving her crying friend a teddy to cuddle.

So what happens in the years between childhood and adulthood to transform us into the inconsiderate individuals we see all around us each day? Perhaps this change occurs as parents and schools encourage children to carve a niche for themselves and to compete against each other. Often, success can only be achieved at the expense of others. In such an atmosphere, a child's innate tendency to show kindness and consideration is gradually pushed into second place in preference to self-interest. It's almost as though children are taught how not to be caring.

Teaching a child how to be kind to others is just as easy as teaching her how to think only of herself. All you need is a little bit of careful thought, preparation, and self-awareness. Your child models herself on you. That's why she shares your attitudes, behavior, and mannerisms. Stop for a minute, and consider your own actions. You can't expect your child to care for other people if you don't. This does not mean that you should gush lovingly all the time, but it does mean you should treat people with respect. Your individual acts of consideration will motivate your child to behave in a caring manner toward others.

Aside from scrutinizing your own attitudes and behavior, you can use direct strategies to teach children to be more caring. One simple method is based on the elementary principle that children learn to be helpful by being helpful. Practical involvement in helping others increases a child's tendency to be caring. Your child can be given caring responsibility at home in many different ways. Assigning your child a few daily chores, such as helping to clear the dishes after a snack, or putting away her crayons, gently directs her toward caring behavior. Even though your child may not be eager to do these tasks, she will probably do them willingly, eventually.

Some children are unwilling to become involved with any helping task because they tend to be selfish. Role-play is an effective way to overcome this barrier. A small group of children, even as young as three years, can create a play in which some of them pretend to need help, while the others pretend to come to their rescue. Then they can reverse the roles. The effect of this type of role-play is more intense when children are encouraged to talk about what happened during the play, and to talk about the feelings they experienced when they played the different roles. Role-play can also be used to help children understand what it is like to experience bullying. This may encourage positive behavior in the playground and in other unsupervised play.

Another useful way to teach kindness and consideration to a young child is to ask the child to explain how to be caring to another child her age or younger. This task of "tutor" benefits both the learner and the tutor, probably because it forces them both to think about the reasoning underlying their actions.

See also Bullying; Modeling; Sociable Play.

Knowledge A young child is like a scientist. He gathers knowledge as he explores the world around him, making one new discovery after another. This process, which starts at birth and continues endlessly throughout childhood, is a constant source of excitement for your child. He actively uses movement, vision, hearing, taste, and touch in an increasingly sophisticated way to explore his surroundings. Through this process, your child gains knowledge about himself, his skills and abilities, and the world.

Your baby is preprogrammed to gain knowledge through discovery. Research shows that babies are born with an impressive range of sensory and perceptual skills that enable them to interact with their environment through their senses:

- *Vision.* Within hours of birth, a baby can differentiate his mother's face from that of a stranger. When a baby as young as nine minutes is shown a picture of a normal face and a picture of a mixed-up face (where the eyes and the nose are interchanged), the baby looks more closely at the normal face, indicating his preference for it. A newborn can also discriminate red, green, yellow, and blue, and can see the difference between drawings of a triangle, cross, circle, and square.

- *Grasping.* Place your finger in the palm of your newborn baby's hand. You'll find that his fingers encircle your finger in a grasp that is so tight that you may be able to pull him to a sitting or standing position.

- *Reaching.* A newborn reaches purposefully for objects placed in front of him, although his hand may be closed by the time it makes contact with the object. In one study, young babies wore special goggles that presented the illusion of a reachable object. The investigators found that the babies reached for the illusion and then cried when they discovered they couldn't grab it.

- *Touch and balance.* Soon after birth, a baby reacts differently to the touch of brush hairs of different thicknesses. The baby will also respond to puffs of air that an adult has difficulty detecting. Although the baby doesn't have a well-developed sense of balance, he will become sick if spun around rapidly. He'll try to right his head if placed in an awkward position.

- *Taste and smell.* New babies make distinct facial expressions when they experience sweet, sour, and bitter tastes. These expressions match those of adults experiencing the same tastes. A sense of smell is also present soon after birth; a baby makes a positive expression when smelling fruity odors, and a disgusted expression when smelling fishy odors. Research also shows that a newborn will turn toward the smell of his own mother's breast pad, but not toward the smell of someone else's.

- *Hearing.* A newborn baby cries at the sound of another baby's cries, but stops when he hears a tape-recording of his own cries. This suggests the newborn can tell one cry from another. Newborns also prefers the sound of a human voice to any other type of sound, and they have a particular preference for their mother's voice. A newborn baby can also discriminate between the noise of a buzzer and the noise of a rattle.

These innate skills enable your young baby to start immediately on his never-ending quest for knowledge. Although many of your baby's reactions are automatic at first, within a few months he will explore toys and other objects more purposefully.

Your child's strategies for discovery change with age and experience. For instance, your child will develop different forms of hand grasp once he has had the opportunity to handle different shapes; he will learn to look at different parts of an object rather than look at the whole thing; and his hand-eye movements will become better coordinated. The more your child tries to extend his knowledge, the more sophisticated and elaborate his discovery skills become. Jean Piaget, a Swiss psychologist, was the first to propose a comprehensive theory about the way children acquire knowledge of the world around them. His theory is based on four stages of development:

- *Sensorimotor period (birth to eighteen months).* In this early phase, an infant uses overt behavior—such as sucking, licking, touching, grasping, smelling—to learn about objects with which he comes into contact. This is a time of continual exploration and discovery.

- *Preoperational period (two to seven years).* A child at this stage has the ability to use one object to represent another, and this means he can engage in symbolic play; he can also use language, which is simply a system of shared symbols that allows people to communicate knowledge and ideas to each other. Drawings become possible because your child can represent his ideas on paper.

- *Concrete operational period (seven to eleven years).* Now a child is able to organize his thoughts, ideas, and information in a more logical way. He can cope with more complex numerical operations, such as addition, subtraction, multiplication, and division, and he uses these to gain a deeper knowledge of the way things work. A child of this age can also reason out general principles from specific incidents in his own experience.

- *Formal operational period (twelve years+).* At this stage of development, a child can extend his reasoning skills to objects and situations that he hasn't seen or experienced firsthand. Problem-solving skills are more advanced, and he is more able to take another person's perspective.

See also *Concentration; Imagination; Intelligence; Language Development; Learning Skills; Play.*

L

Language Development It's amazing that every child develops language in the same way, progressing through the same stages in the same order. Bear in mind that the following suggested ages are only approximate, and that wide individual variations are normal between children. At each stage, the child uses language in a new and more-sophisticated format:

- *Cooing.* Cooing usually begins around the age of eight weeks, and then disappears about twelve weeks later. Although at times a baby's cooing sounds like words, it has no meaning whatsoever.

- *Babbling (random).* By the age of five months, an infant's vocal chords have matured to the point where she can begin to experiment with pitch, vocal range, and breathing, in order to produce a range of sounds. Every child has her own distinctive patterns of noises at this age, and she uses them to communicate with any adult who pays attention to her. Psychologists have found that infants tend to produce the same kinds of babbling sounds, irrespective of their parents' native language.

- *Babbling (controlled).* In the next couple of months, an infant gains more control over her sounds. Babbling becomes more conversational. Her sounds become related to the language used by her parents. She may repeat strings of sounds (such as bababababababa), and may have a favorite sound that she uses consistently in the same situation.

- *Early speech.* Toward the end of her first year, a baby begins to use her sounds as though she is engaging in conversation. She may have an earnest expression on her face and make sounds using tones and emphasis found in adult speech.

- *First word.* By the age of twelve to fifteen months your child will probably have used her first word—she regularly uses a particular sound structure to refer to the same object or person. She may generalize this word to include anything that pleases her. Very often this first word is intelligible only to people who know her, but it is her first word all the same.

- *Vocabulary growth.* From the age of fifteen months onwards, an infant's vocabulary increases spectacularly. Many two-year-olds are able to use more than two hundred words, although they understand many more.

- *Sentences.* By eighteen to twenty months, a typical toddler begins to combine two words together to make a short phrase or sentence—for example, "Dada gone" or "More juice." From this moment on, throughout the remaining childhood years, your child's ability to use sentences with more words and more-complex meanings continues to develop.

This similarity in terms of stages in the growth of language has enabled psychologists to plot key "milestones" of language development—significant points that most children pass at approximately the same age. The following milestones should serve as a guide to help you judge your child's progress:

1 month	A one-month-old baby will respond to words directed at her by turning to the source. She will try to synchronize her sounds with those of an adult talking to her. She is able to make a range of cries, each of which indicates something different.
3 months	Your baby begins to listen more closely when she hears noises; for instance, when a bell gently rings, she will become quiet and pay attention to it. She can probably make at least two distinct sounds, such as "ba" and "da." She enjoys music.
6 months	Your baby's babbling sounds are consistent. She can produce at least four different sounds and can accurately turn her head toward the source of sound. Listening to music may change her mood.
9 months	Place a ticking watch beside your child's ear and she will immediately turn to look at it. She will use two-syllable babbles, such as "ah ba" or "da ba"; her first word may appear at this age (usually "mama" or "dada").
1 year	Your child may be able to use up to three clear words. She will be able to follow very basic directions. Hearing is usually clear at this age. Your child will babble to herself when she plays on her own or when she concentrates on a game or toy.
15 months	Although your child can't say her own name, she'll recognize it when someone else uses it. She will respond to basic commands, such as "Come to Mommy." She will try to join in familiar songs and rhymes.
18 months	Your child's vocabulary will be about a dozen words (though possibly a lot more), which

she uses properly. She understands more words than she can say. She is able to use language to communicate her basic desires.

21 months

Your child now uses an increased range of single words, and may begin to combine them to form such two-word phrases or sentences as "Mommy car" or "want go." She can also identify familiar objects in a picture book.

2 years

A child of this age is fascinated with people's names, and constantly asks what someone is called. She can use many more words now (possibly even hundreds). When asked to identify certain body parts, she can reliably show hair, eyes, nose, mouth, and feet.

3 years

Your child talks confidently in three- or four-word sentences, and may even use adjectives in her speech. She loves having her favorite story read to her. The number of who, what, when, how, and why questions increases.

4 years

Your child now has a broad vocabulary, which includes pronouns and adjectives. Nursery rhymes are popular and fun. She may be able to identify several basic colors, she may count, and she may know the alphabet. She will also be able to give a reasonably accurate account of a recent experience.

5 years

Your child is able to speak clearly and has little difficulty making herself understood. Most five-year-olds can give their first name, last name, address, and telephone number. Make sure your child knows hers.

See also *Hearing Assessment; Hearing Loss; Language Difficulties; Language Learning; Language Stimulation; Questions.*

Language Difficulties Children acquire speech at such various rates that slow progress in language growth at the toddler stage is often within the limits of normal development. The situation becomes worrying if the gap in language skills between one child and others of his own age persists beyond the age of three years. If you suspect your child's use of language is delayed, and you have had his hearing tested, ask your pediatrician to refer him to an educational psychologist or to a speech and language therapist.

Speech and language therapists are trained in human communication skills and are able to identify and treat problems with speech and language. At the initial visit, the therapist will assess many aspects of a child's language development (such as articulation, use of grammar, listening ability, concentration), using both observation and formal assessment techniques. Having diagnosed the difficulty, the therapist will decide on a suitable course of treatment. For a younger child, this might mean a series of language games that can be integrated into his play routines. Older children may be seen regularly for speech therapy, either in a small group or in individual treatment. Parents are expected to give full support to the treatment plan.

A child with a language disorder, particularly in the preschool years, is prone to tantrums. This occurs because the child's inability to communicate his feelings and wishes gives him a strong sense of frustration, which he can only release through temper. He has no other way to express his annoyance. Parents often find that their previously frustrated child becomes more settled once he can use language more effectively.

A child may have a speech difficulty, even though all other areas of his development are satisfactory. In such cases, the speech difficulty is the child's sole problem and it either clears up spontaneously, or else responds to help from a speech therapist. Minor speech difficulties include the following:

- *Lisping.* A child often develops a lisp in the early years. He begins to make letter substitutes, such as "th" for "s," "f" for "th," and so on. These speech patterns usually pass as the child reaches school age. A child may acquire a temporary lisp when his first teeth begin to fall out. A lisp can also be caused by misuse of the tongue or by a cleft palate. Speech therapy can help this condition.

- *Mispronunciation.* Learning to speak takes time, and mistakes are part of the process. Many children have difficulty with certain sounds, causing their speech to become unclear. This defect usually disappears spontaneously. If your child's speech is still unclear by the time he nears school age, then speech therapy may be required.

- *Inadequate stimulation.* Speech development partly depends on a child's interaction with others in his family. By listening to others talk to him, the child develops an interest in language. Some children lack this essential stimulation. The remedy for this is lots of individual attention using discussions, stories, songs, and poems.

- *Stammering/stuttering.* With this defect, a child talks very hesitantly, perhaps repeating the first letter or first part of a word several times. Many children in the early stages of language acquisition develop some form of stutter, probably because they want to say so much. This temporary form of speech impediment clears up as a child becomes more confident in his use of language. Never make fun of a stuttering child. Never imitate him, and never become impatient with him. Speech therapy can help stutterers gain more control over their speech.

More-serious speech and language difficulties can involve the following:

- *General developmental delay.* With this problem, a child will also be slow in other aspects of development, such as learning to walk, learning bladder control, becoming independent, and learning to socialize with other children. The earlier this type of difficulty is detected, the sooner the child will be able to receive help.

- *Hearing loss.* This is the most frequent cause of serious language difficulties. Adequate hearing is crucial for a child to learn language. If he can't hear the sounds of speech, then he won't be able to reproduce them. A child referred to a speech and language therapist will always undergo a hearing assessment as well.

- *Autism.* An autistic child uses language in a bizarre way, making normal communication with him impossible. In addition to social and emotional difficulties, an autistic child has delayed language development and impaired comprehension. Treatment for this condition is usually a multiprofessional approach in a special-school setting.

- *Brain damage.* Specific areas of the brain are responsible for specific functions. If the areas responsible for language are damaged, then the child will have a language difficulty. The seriousness and extent of the problem depends on the degree of brain damage that has occurred.

- *Severe articulation disorders.* A child may have problems actually producing speech sounds, even though he may know what he wants to say and how it should sound. Mild articulation errors are a normal part of development: for example, many young children miss out parts of words (saying "at" for "cat"), or may substitute one sound for another (saying "toat" for "coat"). Severe articulation disorders lasting beyond the age of five may render an older child's language totally incomprehensible. Speech and language therapy is necessary in this instance.

See also *Autism; Cerebral Palsy; Hearing Assessment; Hearing Loss; Language Development; Language Learning; Language Stimulation; Learning Difficulties (LD).*

Language Learning
Spoken language is a child's main means of communication. A baby is able to communicate her feelings and desires nonverbally long before she can speak. When a new baby cries, her parents know something is troubling her, and when she smiles, they know she is happy. When your baby is about two months old, her desire to communicate verbally emerges—when she starts cooing (happy, gurgling

sounds)—and it continues throughout childhood.

One of the most remarkable features of language development in the preschool years is that it takes place at all! Think about it for a moment. Suppose you were a native French speaker and you had to learn English. You would need to remember thousands of words, seemingly endless grammatical rules (which have so many exceptions), and a long list of words with more than one meaning. Then there are words that sound the same but have different spelling patterns (such as their/there), and words that have similar spelling patterns, yet sound different (such as cough/bough). You would probably think it an impossible task, yet most young children manage to learn without any special help.

That's why most psychologists claim that the ability to learn language is innate, that babies are preprogrammed to recognize certain types of words and grammatical structures when they hear them. This does not mean, of course, that the child's environment is unimportant: on the contrary, a child who is raised in a family with a low level of language stimulation will probably have a limited range of speech herself. A child who is raised by English-speaking parents learns to speak English, while a child raised by French-speaking parents learns to speak French. Environment plays a part in language development. The best way to view the growth of language skills is in terms of an interaction between a child's inborn ability and the environment in which she is raised. Each affects the other. The combined effects determine the level and quality of a child's speech.

See also *Body Language; Hearing Assessment; Hearing Loss; Language Development; Language Difficulties; Language Stimulation; Questions.*

Language Stimulation
You can stimulate your child's language development no matter what your child's age is. Talking to your baby is essential because it

- *will encourage your child's interest in language.* Even though he can't understand what you say, your child will begin to imitate some of the sounds you make.

- *promotes communication.* Slow-motion replays of filmed mother-baby interactions reveal that a baby appears to fit his vocalizations into the gaps between his mother's sentences, almost as though he's listening to what is being said and then replying. Talking to a baby involves him in this prespeech "conversation."
- *ensures your close attention.* This shows your child that language has positive dimensions.

Many mothers use "motherese" when they talk to their baby, that is, they speak slowly, in exaggerated tones, using short sentences with clear gaps between the words. Research has proved that a baby will pay closer attention to an adult who speaks to him in motherese than to one who speaks to him in a normal style. Adopting some of these speech qualities is worthwhile when you talk to your baby. This doesn't mean you should use baby talk. Your child has as much chance to understand the meaning of the word "dog" as she has to understand the word "bow-wow." Baby talk has no advantage over normal words, and in fact can impede your child's skills. Do the following to encourage your baby's language development:

- *Name everyday objects involved in your baby's regular routine.* When you dress him, for example, tell him what you are doing ("This is your sleeper," "Here is your hat.").
- *When your child makes sounds, give a response.* For instance, if your child makes a cooing, gurgling noise, you might say, "Good, you seem to be happy today." Use lots of facial expressions when you talk to your child.
- *Play action rhymes that are basic and that physically involve your child.* Elementary rhymes such as "Round and round the garden" or "This little piggy" will make your child chuckle with delight.

One of your main aims at the toddler stage should be to improve your child's listening skills. This can be achieved in two ways. First, listen to your child when he talks to you—if you don't, he will have no incentive to use speech. Second, encourage your child to listen to you; when you give him instructions (such as "Please come over here."), make sure that he acts on them, even if he appears to ignore you.

Broaden your child's use of words, grammar, and sentence structure using the following strategies:

- *Don't constantly correct your child's speech mistakes.* While there is no harm in doing so occasionally, nagging about errors will reduce your child's self-confidence and may make him hesitant to speak.

- *Model appropriate language.* For instance, your child might say, "More juice," to which you could reply, "I can see you would like to have some more juice." This provides a model for your child to imitate and is quite different from correcting him.

- *Use the same word in different contexts.* For instance, your child will learn the significance of "on" faster if you say, "I'm sitting on a chair," "Your cookie is on the plate," "Your toy is on the floor," rather than using it in one context only.

Try these activities:

- *Ask your child to tell you about something that has just happened.* This forces your child to concentrate, to recall details of a previous experience, and to find the words to describe it to you.

- *Play lots of word games with your child.* He will enjoy hearing action rhymes and songs, singing with you, and reciting simple nursery rhymes. Listen to songs and music together; your child will probably want to join in when he hears familiar tunes.

- *Explore picture books and read storybooks.* This is a marvelous way to increas your child's vocabulary and, at the same time, develop his early reading skills. Children of this age love to hear the same story read over and over.

Between three and five years, your child's language becomes even more sophisticated. Now, he chatters away endlessly and asks you lots of questions, which you should answer at a level appropriate to his understanding. Remember that every child should be given plenty of opportunities to talk. Family life is hectic, and you may have more than one child eager to have a turn. Each child needs a chance to express his thoughts, not just the talkative ones. Ensure the quiet child also tells you his news, no matter how many others want to speak. These activities will encourage your preschool child's language:

- *Teach your child useful concepts, such as color, shape, and size.* Pick one concept at a time (for example, color) and work on this for a few weeks. Begin with matching activities: "Which one of these blocks is the same color as the sweater you're wearing?"; then sorting activities: "Put blocks of the same color in the same pile"; then identifying activities: "Find me all the green blocks"; and last, naming activities: "What color is this?"

- *Play memory games with your child.* For instance, bring out a tray with perhaps a dozen common objects on it (ball, scissors, pencil, doll, spoon, etc.). Tell your child you will take the tray away, and that he should try to remember as many as he can. After two minutes, cover the tray with a cloth; then ask your child to tell you the objects he can remember.

- *Watch a children's television program together and then talk about it.* Programs such as *Sesame Street* can help broaden a child's world because they can give him access to events he may not have experienced himself, such as a visit to a factory. Your child will derive more enjoyment if you spend a few minutes discussing the program with him.

See also Hearing Assessment; Hearing Loss; Language Development; Language Difficulties; Language Learning; Questions.

Laziness Everybody needs motivation before they are prompted to activity—this is human nature. If you aren't motivated by hunger, you won't eat; if a student isn't motivated by the desire to learn, she won't attend class. And if your child isn't motivated by the wish to please you, she might not do as you ask.

Motivation is the driving force underlying all human behavior.

Yet your child may be one of those who appears to lack all motivation, and as a result, you may describe her as "lazy" because she has no drive or enthusiasm, makes no effort at anything, and is content to watch television all day without moving from the chair. However, the word "lazy" suggests that the low level of activity is an inherent personality characteristic, something inside your child that makes her unwilling to put in any effort. As such, it may be misleading, and it can lead to conflict as your efforts to blast your child into action are matched by her efforts to remain inert.

A more positive way to approach the situation is in terms of motivation. Instead of criticizing your child for her apparent laziness, ask yourself what can be changed in your child's immediate environment so that she'll become more enthusiastic. One common source of controversy in a family is a child's reluctance to tidy her room, which usually ends up with her parents accusing her of laziness. There may be other reasons why the child doesn't tidy her room; for instance, the task is so overwhelming for her that she doesn't know where to begin (in which case you can help by encouraging her to tidy a little at a time, following a plan), or it could be because she knows you will eventually do it for her (in which case you can help by making it clear that tidying the room is her responsibility, not yours).

Likewise, a young child's failure, say, to regularly practice playing a musical instrument often has absolutely nothing to do with laziness and everything to with the fact that the child doesn't enjoy the activity—she'll only practice regularly when she likes the instrument. And a child who doesn't seem to try hard to achieve in school may lack motivation because she has a poor self-image and expects herself to fail. Calling that child, or indeed any child, lazy will serve no purpose at all.

So if you do think that your child is lazy, consider the specific situations in which that unmotivated behavior is seen, and try to determine what feature demotivates your child and also what could be added to the situation to fire her enthusiasm. One of the best ways to establish this is to ask the child herself!

You may find that her suggestions are very straightforward—such as doing the activity at a different time, or at a different pace. Lack of motivation sometimes occurs when a child feels she is not involved in the decision-making process: for example, the art class was selected by her parents, not by her. Your child is more likely to have a higher level of motivation to complete a task when she has positively selected the task herself.

See also Criticism; Self-Confidence.

Learning Difficulties (LD) Children experience learning difficulties for many reasons:

- In some instances, a child is of below-average ability and, as a result, is expected to have difficulties with school work. Such a pupil has a general learning difficulty.

- In other instances, a child is of at least average ability, uses language well in discussion, gives an impression of being bright, and yet has unexpected difficulties with reading, writing, and spelling. Such a pupil has a specific learning difficulty.

How can learning difficulties be recognized? Generally, students with learning difficulties have

- uneven academic results;
- difficulty organizing time, work, and materials;
- trouble with social relationships;
- trouble sequencing size, shapes, and distances;
- noticeable gaps in learning;
- trouble with fine motor and/or gross motor development.

Learning difficulties have an emotional component—a child with learning difficulties whose condition has not been properly identified may have a poor self-image because he thinks he is not as bright as his classmates. He may lack confidence with any task that involves schoolwork, and often describes himself as "stupid." The longer the child's learning problem goes undiagnosed, the worse his psychological problem will become. That's another reason why early identification is important.

Children with learning difficulties often have a history of slow speech development in the preschool years, and there is often a family history of speech and learning difficulties, perhaps involving parents, aunts and uncles, or other relatives. These signs, however, are only guidelines, and their presence does not mean your child has learning difficulties. Many children without learning difficulties also show these features in the early stages of learning to read, write, and spell. You should become concerned only if problems persist beyond the first year of grade school.

Often teachers label children as having learning difficulties if they show some of these characteristics:

- immature behavior;
- low self-esteem;
- short attention span;
- impulsiveness;
- argumentativeness;
- inability to cope with the work at the grade level;
- aggressiveness;
- acting out.

A diagnosis of learning difficulties can and should be made only by a psychologist after having fully assessed the child in the following areas:

- *Level of intelligence.* This must be measured using a standardized intelligence test. Weaknesses with specific learning skills can also be identified (such as in auditory or visual short-term memory, pattern recognition, ability to recall sequences, spatial skills).

- *Level of attainments in reading, spelling, writing, and math.* The psychologist will establish the exact level of the child's progress in each of these areas. The first stage will be to find an age level (for example, a nine-year-old child may read at a level normally associated with a five-year-old, and hence has a reading age of five).

- *Pattern of errors.* Aside from quantifying the child's educational attainments, the psychologist will consider the types of mistakes that the child makes in reading, writing, spelling, and math, since this will enable future learning support to be targeted most effectively.

- *Learning attitude.* The attitude that a child has toward learning partly determines his level of success or failure. Children with learning difficulties often appear to make little effort in any task that involves literacy. These children should not be accused of laziness—rather, it's as though they have given up trying altogether because they expect to fail.

- *Developmental background.* A diagnosis of learning difficulty can only be made after the elimination of other, external factors that could depress progress in school. These factors could include stress at home (such as recent divorce, bereavement), lack of stimulation in the preschool years (possibly due to long periods of hospitalization), and hearing or visual difficulties.

Certain strategies can help the child with learning difficulties, both at home and at school:

- *Praise your child whenever he does something well.*
- *Ensure that you have the child's attention before you give him instructions.*
- *Stay close to your child to help him maintain his focus and attention.*
- *Help your child avoid situations where he is bound to fail.*
- *Keep distractions minimal.*
- *Help your child break big jobs into smaller tasks.* Do them one at a time. The tasks should be focused and structured to be relevant in the child's life.
- *Give your child one instruction at a time.*

- *Realize that simple tools can sometimes cause injury.* Your child might not be able to use a stapler, scissors, paper cutter, or pencil sharpener.
- *Give your child lots of structure.*
- *Avoid open-concept classrooms; they often prove to be full of distractions.*
- *Have your child sit at the front of the classroom, if at all possible, under the eye of the teacher.*
- *Remove superfluous materials because they are a source of distraction.*
- *Use taped books to reinforce your child's visual reading.*
- *Ask your child to pronounce his spelling mistakes.*
- *Present learning materials in a variety of ways: verbal, visual, and tactile.* Teachers should present any new material using several different methods.
- *Present new concepts in class.* Your child should never try to learn new material as "homework."
- *Review, review, review, and review.*
- *Be realistic.* Your child will need longer to do tasks. He has to be taught in a way that is cooperative, to ensure his ongoing development of skills. He cannot be competitive or he will fail.

Surprisingly, children with learning disabilities often need more, not less, organized stimulation. Ways to provide this include the arts, music, drama, sports, and dance.

See also Attention Deficit Disorder (ADD); Dyslexia; Hyperactivity.

Learning Skills Your child's learning skills change frequently during the preschool years, each stage allowing your child new ways to learn about her world (the following ages are only approximate):

0 to 1 month   Most of your baby's responses are reflexes—for instance, she turns her head toward anything that gently touches her cheek; she sucks automatically when a nipple is placed in her mouth; her toes fan out when the outside of the sole of her foot is scratched; she grasps any slim object placed in her palm. Your baby soon learns from experience how to modify these reflex responses.

1 to 4 months   Your baby no longer gazes passively, but looks around her more purposefully and makes specific responses to specific objects—for example, she smiles at a familiar face. She repeats basic actions that involve parts of her body, such as thumb-sucking or twiddling her fingers.

4 to 9 months   Your child's explorations continue, but now they are directed toward objects other than herself. You may find that she becomes determined to whack her mobile or that she tries to hit the activity center attached to the side of her crib. Reaching out and grasping is more frequent at this stage.

9 to 12 months   Now your infant can combine two or more strategies in order to make more discoveries. She is able to knock away a cushion that conceals her favorite toy; and when she has done that once, she is able to apply this same strategy to any similar situation that confront her.

12 to 18 months   Experimentation is the order of the day, as your child tries out new ways to play with objects. She may slowly push her spoon off the high chair, then hit it away quickly, then drop it gently off the side, each time finding new ways to make the spoon hit the ground. She's just naturally inquisitive. Her ability to walk means she can venture farther than before.

18 to 24 months   Your toddler begins to develop the ability to use symbolism, which means she can now use one object to represent another. This is a completely new skill that opens up a vast array of play opportunities. A building block can become a dog, and a doll can become mom or dad.

In the remaining preschool years, these learning skills expand and develop further. Until the age of five or six, a child's thought processes continue to be significantly different from those of an older child in two main ways:

- *A preschool child tends to be egocentric* (she can only see things from her own perspective), and she may not realize that she can view situations in other ways. Try sitting your child at one end of a table, so that she faces her favorite teddy, which is positioned in a chair at the opposite end. Put a ball and a building block side by side—exactly in the middle of the table—with the ball nearest to your child and the block nearest to the teddy. Then ask your child, "What toy does teddy see first? The ball or the block?" If your child is still egocentric, she will tell you that her teddy sees the ball first—because this is what she herself sees.

  This limitation of a young child's learning skills means that you have a better chance to get your child to understand something when you explain it to her in personal terms. Psychologists have found that young children understand sentences that contain their own name more easily than equally complex sentences that do not contain their names. Remember to include your child's name when you explain something to her.

- *Your child tends to focus on one part of a problem only.* Try to show your child two drinking glasses, one short and fat, the other tall and thin, but each capable of holding the same amount of liquid. Fill one glass with water. Let your child see you pour the water from this glass into the other, and then ask, "Which glass holds the most water?" Your child will probably focus on the height of the glass and tell you that the tall glass holds more water than the fat glass. Only when your child is five or six will she realize that although one glass is taller, it is also thinner, and both glasses hold the same amount.

Your child's learning skills expand and develop naturally, but you can nonetheless encourage the process along in the following ways:

- *Make sure your child has plenty of opportunities to practice her developing skills.* Your child can explore and discover without your help, but her curiosity will be increased by interesting surroundings, such as an attractive mobile above her crib, a colorful array of teething rings and rattles, and a varied range of toys, games, and books. Ensure you read together frequently.

- *Get involved!* Your child will have much more fun if you are involved and look as though you're enjoying yourself. This doesn't mean you should take over—in fact, you should definitely not do that. But your child will be more interested if you are with her, giving her your attention and encouragement.

- *Give your child lots of repetition.* Just because your child has completed a puzzle once doesn't mean that you have to give her a new one. She'll discover something new every time she solves the same puzzle. Encourage her to play with toys more than once.

- *Show by example.* Of course, your child wants to discover things by herself, but sometimes she needs a helping hand. So if she's struggling to fit a shape into the shape sorter, don't be afraid to show her how to do it, occasionally.

- *Don't push too hard.* When choosing a toy, pick one that is at a higher level of complexity than the ones your child has, but that isn't frustrating. She will make progress gradually, step by step.

- *Set limits when you have to.* Much as your child would like to explore wherever she wants, to touch whatever attracts her attention, and to discover the qualities of the most fragile objects, you have to set down some clear rules about what she can and can't do. Explain that certain objects, or areas of the house, are out of bounds, and redirect her interest elsewhere. Distraction works wonders.

See also Concentration; Knowledge; Learning through Play; Play.

Learning through Play Play and learning are
connected in three ways:

- *Learning can occur directly through play.* In exploratory play a child deliberately manipulates a toy in order to discover its qualities. This type of play allows your child to discover aspects of his immediate world. In play with such things as jigsaws, shape sorters, and matching activities, your child learns problem-solving skills.

- *Learning occurs indirectly through play.* A typical six-month-old child will want to play with any toy given to him. While he discovers how to play with it, he will probably put it in his mouth, bite it, lick it, smell it, and bounce it off the wall. Although the infant's main attention is to play with the toy, these other actions teach him about texture, shape, weight, and size. This incidental component of learning has a major influence on a child's intellectual abilities, particularly in the first few years of life.

- *Learning occurs instrumentally when children are suddenly faced with a particular problem that they have to solve before their play can continue* (for instance, learning how to climb a tree in order to search for dinosaurs).

The following guidelines will help you choose suitable toys to stimulate your child's learning ability through play:

6 months   Your child will enjoy playing with rattles, activity centers, and small toys that he can pick up in his hands—but they must not be too small, because at this age an infant still tends to put toys in his mouth. He will try hard to get hold of an object that is put just outside his reach.

12 months   A child of this age can imitate adult actions (such as banging two small wooden blocks together to make a loud noise). He will be fascinated by any object that rattles. Put a couple of wooden beads inside a small box, and shake it—your child is likely to open the box in order to find out what's inside. This type of play stimulates a child's interest in puzzles.

18 months   Your child will begin to show an interest in elementary shape sorters. Most good toy shops sell shape sorters with just one or two shapes in them. If an adult demonstrates how the shapes fit into the board, the child will try to imitate the action.

2 years   Your child enjoys stacking building blocks, one on top of the other; he may be able to build a tower of up to six or seven blocks before it falls over. He enjoys playing with a set of plastic nesting toys, the type that fit inside one another in a fixed sequence.

3 years   Your child's interest in puzzles and shape sorters with up to seven or eight pieces in them continues. Games in which he has to sort objects, such as blocks, according to color, size, or shape may attract his attention—and build his learning skills at the same time.

4 years   Puzzles with up to twenty pieces often fascinate a child of this age. He will also enjoy crayons and paper. His drawings of mom or dad will probably include details such as eyes, hair, hands, and mouth.

See also Gender Play; Knowledge; Learning Skills; Play.

Left-Handedness We live in a right-handed world.

Since most people use their right hand for manual tasks (such as opening doors, cutting with a knife, using a pair of scissors, lifting a cup), we tend to forget that this doesn't apply to everyone. About one boy in ten, and one girl in twelve, is left-handed.

Hand preference is not present at birth. When your baby starts to explore the world with her hands, she will show no preference for one over the other and will be able to use them both with equal competence. Only toward the end of the second year do toddlers begin to develop hand preference. You may find that even at this age your child will use one hand for months at a time, then switch comfortably to the other. Hand dominance is usually firmly established by the age of three or four, although some children remain ambidextrous throughout their life.

Psychologists are unable to say whether left-handedness is innate or whether it is learned. Both points of view have supporting evidence. Parents who are concerned about their child's possible left-handedness can gently encourage her—up to the age of twelve or fifteen months—to use her right hand. This does not mean pressuring your child to use her right hand all the time. Rather, it means providing opportunities for your child to use her right hand—for example, by handing things to her right side. If your child appears agitated or uneasy about it, allow her to use whichever hand she feels more comfortable using. After the age of twelve to fifteen months, the choice of hand should definitely rest with the toddler.

The significance of left-handedness must be kept in proper perspective. Being left-handed can make life a little difficult for a young child, especially when she is trying to learn new manual skills such as cutting and sewing, or when she is learning new sports such as racquet games. Left-handedness is not a handicap; it is not something that parents should lose sleep over. In fact, some studies show left-handed people are right-brained, and so are highly intuitive and creative. A child learns to adapt to her world, whether she is left-handed, right-handed, or ambidextrous.

Never force your child to use her right hand when her left one is dominant. This could cause difficulties in other areas of development, since hand preference is controlled by the same part of the brain that is responsible for speech, writing, and reading. Forcing a left-handed child to use her right hand may result in problems when she starts learning to read, and can be linked to stuttering and possibly dyslexia. Undue emphasis on making a child use her right hand will only lead to confrontation and will reduce the child's self-confidence.

A left-handed child will have difficulty learning to cut with a pair of scissors, since standard scissors are made to fit on the right hand, not the left. Fortunately, left-handed scissors can be purchased from most educational suppliers, and every nursery school should have at least a couple of pairs readily available. Aside from making life easier for the child, this strategy will help her achieve success. There is no greater boost to self-esteem than that.

The idea that left-handed children are likely to do less well at reading is a complete myth. Reading surveys have confirmed that reading scores are not different between children who are left-handed and children who are right-handed. The only instance where left-handedness and reading problems can be linked is where a left-handed child has been forced to use her right hand from an early age.

Learning to write is the biggest hurdle for left-handed pupils to overcome. English writing patterns, going from left to right, favor a right-handed pupil because they involve movements that are natural for that hand preference. When a left-handed pupil learns to write, she faces a number of difficulties:

- *Smudging*. A child's hand holding the pencil moves across the words after she writes them, which (if it's a soft pencil) can smudge the writing; fountain pens and felt-tip pens are, therefore, not suitable for a left-handed child.

- *Blocking.* While writing, a left-handed child can't see everything that she has already written because the hand with which she continues to write conceals part of the page.
- *Awkward direction.* Whereas a right-handed child sweeps the pencil across the page from left to right, a left-handed child has to push it across; this is not an easy task—rather like pushing a rake across a lawn instead of pulling it.
- *Cramped position.* A left-handed writer has to hold her arm closer to her body when writing than a right-handed person. This is an unnatural pose for a left-handed child and she may feel restricted. The child would be much happier writing from right to left—that's why left-handed children have a head start when writing languages in which the words go in the opposite direction like Hebrew or Arabic.

When teaching writing to a left-handed child, observe these basic principles:

- *Suggest that the child holds the pencil a little farther away from the tip.* This will give her a clearer view of her completed written work.
- *Make sure the child does not imitate her right-handed classmates by pointing the pencil in the same direction as they do.* She may want to do this because she does not want to be different. Her pencil should follow the line of direction of the arm with which she is writing.
- *Encourage your child to find a comfortable seating position for writing.* She should be allowed to swivel her body slightly to the right if she feels more comfortable in that position.
- *Don't give your child a very sharp pencil.* When she pushes it across the page, the point is liable to catch in the paper and snap off.
- *Discourage your child from using a fountain pen or a felt-tip pen.* Apart from the fact that her writing will be instantly smudged, she will be smeared with ink.

Left-handedness need not be a source of difficulty for a developing child; the child will manage as long as the adults around her show some understanding. A sense of humor also helps. As one child replied when asked which hand she ate her cornflakes with, "None. I use a spoon!"

See also *School Readiness; Self-Confidence.*

Life after Baby You may not believe it at the time of the your new arrival, but there is life after baby! You and your partner will eventually adjust to being a threesome, though the adjustment may take several weeks or even longer. Having a new baby in your family is a wonderful time, as you and your child mesh together and get to know each other. Watching your child develop becomes one of your greatest pleasures, and you delight in all that he does. Undoubtedly, your baby adds whole new dimensions to your life. You also learn a lot about yourself as a parent, perhaps even discovering strengths and talents you didn't know you had. These are the positives.

On the other hand, the relationship between you and your partner will inevitably change during this phase of your lives. Following are the main challenges facing new parents:

- *Lack of sleep.* A new baby is lovable, but he doesn't live his life by the clock. He cries when he wants to cry, plays when he wants to play, and fills his diaper whenever he feels like it. Your baby's schedule almost certainly clashes with your own at first.

- *Loss of privacy.* Your new baby is only one of several intrusions into your life. Other intrusions include planned and unplanned visits from friends and relatives, and phone calls inquiring after the welfare of parents and baby.

- *Reduced disposable income.* Alongside the addition of an extra mouth to feed, more clothes to buy, and extra furniture, there is the fact that women usually stop earning for at least a couple of months when the baby is born. This means less money to go around.

- *Reduced social life.* Your new baby takes up a lot of your time, and by necessity, you'll spend less time going out with your friends than you did before. And when you do go out, you may not have the same level of energy as your did before the baby.

- *Responsibility of parenthood.* Parenting has lots of pluses, but it also brings responsibility. Knowing that you are the one who has to care for this helpless, dependent little baby can make you feel pressured.

- *Lower sex drive.* Few things are more likely to drive passion from the bedroom than the sound of a crying baby. Add in a higher level of tiredness, and it is a small wonder that new parents often struggle to reestablish their sex life.

Fortunately, with careful planning, all of these challenges can be overcome so that you and your partner can rediscover yourselves as individual adults, not just as your baby's parents. Perhaps the most important step to take in this new phase of your life is to have honest and candid communication with each other. You will do no harm by admitting to your partner that you are exhausted, that you are afraid you are less than perfect as a parent, that you lack confidence in your ability to cope. Concealing negative feelings will not make them go away. Make time for these discussions—you'll be so busy that you will have no free moments unless you specifically plan them.

Be prepared to accept help and support from friends and relatives—you don't have to make yourself a martyr. If someone reliable offers to care for your baby for a short time in order to give you a break, grab the chance when you can. Use this time for a rest, or for relaxation. You deserve it.

Parents with a new baby often find a plentiful supply of advice showered upon them from well-meaning experienced adults who have clear ideas on matters of child care. Listen to this advice, but then make up your own mind. Remember that what works for somebody else's child may not work for yours. Your are the parent now, so it's up to you to make decisions independently.

Within a few weeks after the baby is born, you and your partner will begin to reestablish a social life, though it won't be the same as before. Make time to go out together, if only for an hour or so. Don't expect these times to be wonderful—chances are that you both may be tense and unable to relax—but make an effort to get out anyway. And within a few months you will have also resumed your sex life. If you still feel stressed and down long after your baby is born, professional counseling might be useful.

Rebuilding your life after the baby arrives is hard work. Yet it's worth the effort. As long as you avoid the temptation to become a slave to routine, to become an individual who responds only to the baby's needs and not to your own, then you'll quickly see light at the end of the tunnel. Family life with three is so much more satisfying than family life with two, especially once the initial adjustment process has passed.

See also *Parents; Postnatal Depression.*

Lying When you catch your two-year-old child red-handed, in the middle of an act of destruction, chances are that she'll deny doing it. Most toddlers will deny misbehaving in these circumstances, either because they genuinely wish they hadn't committed the offense or because they know they are in deep trouble and just want to get out of it any way they can. At this age, children have difficulty distinguishing fantasy from reality.

This isn't lying, in the true sense of the word. A child should only be accused of lying when she is old enough and able to tell right from wrong, and when she deliberately tries to conceal or distort the truth. These two features are not usually present in very young children. Of course, this doesn't mean that mischief and misbehavior should be ignored by parents, but they should be kept in perspective. By the age of three or four, however, a child begins to develop moral awareness and has the ability to tell lies.

Studies of child development have established two important principles:

- *Every child is capable of lying, depending on the circumstances.* Most children will try to hide their wrongdoings if they think the consequences of discovery will be very unpleasant. Be reassured, however, that no evidence suggests that a child who tells lies will grow up to be a criminal,

- *A child who is too frightened to confess will make even more of an effort to justify her initial lie.* If you punish your child every time you think she has told a lie, she will soon learn to become a better liar in order to avoid the inevitable consequences. Strike a balance between being too punitive and too lenient. Spanking your child for telling lies only encourages her to lie even more, because her fear of discovery becomes greater.

Not all childhood lies involve concealment. A child might, for instance, tell greatly exaggerated stories about how well she's doing at school, or how much the other children want to play with her. This type of bragging isn't lying, though—it is more likely to be a sign of lack of confidence. Never ridicule your child for telling this sort of boastful tale; in this situation, your child benefits more from your support and attempts to boost her confidence.

There is also the make-believe lie—often a normal part of imaginative play—in which a child embellishes her everyday experiences with fantasy. Don't be alarmed when your four-year-old insists she was chased by a monster; she's just trying to make her life more interesting. She'll grow out of it.

Your child models much of her own behavior on yours—that's why if you tell lies in front of her, chances are she'll do the same. Although you probably don't tell lies as a matter of course, you may occasionally be guilty of "white lies," those little untruths designed to protect other people's feelings (such as when you told your mother-in-law you liked that horrible vase she gave you, or when you completely forgot an appointment and later gave the excuse that you were unwell). Don't be surprised when your child imitates this—only she won't be able to tell the difference between serious lies and white lies.

Dealing with a child who persists in telling lies can be extremely frustrating. You will find these guidelines helpful:

- *Stay calm.* Instead of instantly reacting, spend time considering why your child is lying. Bear in mind that some lies stem from a child's lack of self-confidence.

- *Explain to your child why she shouldn't lie.* Give her reasons she can understand. For instance, "If you tell lies, people won't trust you." Children who are taught the difference between right and wrong, rather than simply being punished for lying, are less likely to tell lies in the future.

- *Make punishments reasonable.* It is far better to deprive your child of candy, or to put her to bed ten minutes early, than to tell her she's not allowed out to play for two months. Punishments that are too extreme rarely have much positive impact on a child's behavior.

- *Reassure your child that you still love her.* A child who is afraid of losing her parents' love for being naughty will lie fiercely to cover up whatever she's done wrong.

See also *Boasting; Discipline; Guilt; Scapegoat; Self-Confidence; Stealing; Swearing.*

Manners A young child usually takes great delight in the sort of habits that adults regard as bad manners: first, because they usually ease feelings of discomfort, and second, because of the response that greets them.

Belching and farting are guaranteed to raise a laugh, spitting out half-chewed food causes onlookers to squirm, and nose-picking (and flicking) makes others feel sick. Elicits a response, doesn't it? Other examples of bad manners, such as interrupting a conversation or barging to the front of the line also ensure that the child gets what he wants.

Consistently displaying bad manners will, in the long run, have two psychological effects:

- *The child will become unpopular.* Of course, the child will get a laugh from others at first. We've all seen a group of young children burst into squeals of delight when one of them breaks wind. Eventually, the joke wears off, and others won't want to sit beside him because they think he is disgusting. And a child who constantly pushes others out of the way is unlikely to be liked.

- *The child himself will feel uncomfortable.* He'll be following one set of social rules while everybody else is following another. Suppose you tried to play soccer when everyone else was using the ball for volleyball. You'd feel strange because you'd be aware that what you were doing wasn't in harmony with those around you. This is the sort of feeling a bad-mannered child will experience.

Children don't start out in life fascinated by habits that adults regard as "bad manners." A baby does these things with complete indifference: he passes gas without embarrassment, he explores his body cavities quite naturally, and he shouts out when he wants something. These habits are normal, from the child's point of view. His parents encourage most of them because they know he feels more comfortable afterwards.

Adult perceptions change as a child matures, however. What was considered acceptable from a baby is no longer endearing when the child reaches toddler or preschool stage. Adults expect an older child to have greater understanding of the world around him and to be more aware of social conventions. A child's perception also changes. Somewhere between birth and the next five years, the child begins to realize that adults consider some behavior to be "good manners," although he doesn't know precisely how this distinction is made.

Later on, the child will discover that many of these rules are only a matter of social convention, and that they are not universal. He'll also learn that some aspects of good manners are very subtle. Some people, for instance, think that it is good manners to leave a small amount of food on their dinner plate, because that lets their hosts know that they've had enough to eat; other people think it is bad manners to leave food on the plate because it suggests to their hosts that the meal was not tasty enough to finish. You have to learn to read each situation.

In the meantime your child becomes aware that adults start to frown when he makes a "rude" noise during mealtimes. Or he is reprimanded for picking his nose while watching television. That's the exact point when he becomes fascinated by these habits. Tell your child not to do something—particularly if you don't give him a good reason why not—and you can be sure he'll do it again. The more you giggle when your child passes wind, the more he will continue to do so. Children do find these habits intrinsically enjoyable, just as adults do, because in most cases they do relieve a feeling of physical discomfort. But it is certainly not the habits per se that fascinate the children; it's the adults' reaction to them that give children such joy.

If you want to discourage your child from persisting with actions that you regard as bad manners, do the following:

- *Set a good example yourself.* You can hardly expect your child to stop picking wax out of his ear, if he sees you mindlessly drilling deep into the side of your own head. Make sure you do not ask your child to follow a set of rules that he knows you ignore.

- *Don't laugh at your child's behavior.* Once your child thinks you regard his behavior as funny, you will have a hard time convincing him otherwise. Better to discourage it right from the start.

- *Keep things in perspective.* Chances are, some of your child's bad manners will make you feel genuinely disgusted. By all means use a firm voice and a scowl to indicate your displeasure; but try not to be extreme. A balanced reaction works better.

- *Use meaningful explanations.* Tell your child why you think good manners are important, and be very explicit about the benefits of being well mannered. Always use explanations that your child can understand (for example, "You won't get invited to parties if you pick the icing off the cake.").

- *Reinforce good manners.* Praising your child for behaving well will encourage him to repeat the behavior. So let your child know that you are pleased with him for showing good manners. Make your comments quite specific and clear. "I was so proud when you waited quietly for your turn."

See also *Eating; Eating Out; Modeling; Politeness.*

Masturbation
Interest in the genitals is normal in childhood, even in the preschool years. Preschool boys can have erections, although they don't ejaculate. Nearly all boys and girls explore their genitals at some stage, just as they explore their noses, ears, and other body parts. You may be embarrassed when you see your child masturbate, but the habit is not harmful.

Manipulation of the genitals to bring pleasure and relaxation is a phenomenon found throughout every society. Research has revealed that almost half of all children under the age of five engage in genital handling. This is probably an underestimate, since many children masturbate in secret. Some parents might find the habit embarrassing because they associate it with sexual pleasure. Preschool masturbation (unlike adult masturbation, which ends in orgasm) gives comfort, not sexual stimulation. Like other comfort habits (such as thumb-sucking, hair-twiddling), masturbation soothes a child and provides a feeling of relaxation and security. Never use old wives' tales to discourage a young child from masturbating. Threats of blindness or warts will only frighten your child, who will then learn to associate genitals with fear. The stronger the reaction that you show to your child's masturbation, the more likely it is that the habit will intensify.

Take a low-key approach, by gently informing your child that you don't want her to masturbate in front of you. Use terms she can understand, such as, "Do that in private, please." Do this calmly. Try to divert your child's attention away from herself to another activity, such as playing with a toy or listening to a story. Frequent masturbation may be a sign of stress, and you'll only stop the habit by discovering, then eliminating, the source of the stress.

See also Pacifiers; Security Objects; Sexual Curiosity.

Memory Memory is how we store information and then recall it later. Learning cannot take place without memory, because an individual who cannot recall previous events has no basis on which to build further understanding of the world around him. Children who have difficulties with memory may have problems learning.

Psychologists are unable to specify what actually happens in the human brain when memory is used, but they have proved that memory skills are present before birth. In one investigation, mothers who were six months pregnant read a children's story out loud, three times a day for several weeks. Soon after their babies were born, they read this same story along with two others. The researchers found that the babies made a greater response to the story they had "heard" while in the womb! Memory capacity constantly increases as your baby grows through his first year:

1 week	A baby can recognize his mother's voice, and shows preference for the smell of his mother's breast milk.
1 month	Memory improves to the point where a baby can remember specific speech sounds if he has heard them often enough.
2 months	In an experiment involving two-month-old babies, a mobile hung above each baby's crib was attached to his foot with a ribbon. Eventually, the child learned to move the mobile by kicking. The mobile was then taken away, but replaced after a few days or a few weeks. Would a baby of this age remember how to make the mobile move? Observations confirmed that the child's

memory of the previous exposure to the mobile lasted up to four weeks.

3 months   An infant will respond positively when familiar feeding objects are brought to him. He will recognize them immediately and possibly thrust out his hands in the general direction of the food source; he will also show anticipation of familiar situations, such as bath time.

7 months   A baby remembers people he hasn't seen every day—such as a family friend, a baby sitter.

9 months   A child of this age is able to use his memory more purposefully. When sitting in his high chair, if he accidentally drops a toy from his tray, he will look for it in the right direction. If he sees you put an object under a cup in front of him, he will instantly lift the cup because he remembers that the object is there.

From nine months, an infant demonstrates his memory in play. He begins to show pleasure at hearing familiar songs and rhymes, and may want them to be repeated over and over again. He can remember where his toys are kept, which means he can find them on his own. This ability allows him a much wider variety of play and learning experiences, all of which provide him with endless opportunities to improve his capacity to remember even more.

The memory of an adult is greater than the memory of a young child. This difference is not so much in the size of memory as in the techniques used to store and recall information. Adults tend to have more efficient strategies for remembering than children. After a child reaches age five, you can help him improve his memory by encouraging him to use the following techniques:

- *Rehearsal.* A young child can increase his recall through the use of rehearsal—repetition of information over and over. He is more likely to remember a group of objects if he has spoken their names out loud several times while trying to memorize them. Try this: place a tray of twenty common objects in front of your child and let him look at them for a minute; then remove the tray and ask him "How many can you remember?" Repeat this activity with another set of objects, but this time encourage your child to say the name of each object several times while the tray is in front of him. He will probably remember more from the second tray than from the first.

- *Organization.* Information is easier to recall when it has been stored in memory in an organized way. Try this with a child who can read: compile a list of twenty objects (for example, five foods, five articles of clothing, five modes of transportation, and five pieces of furniture), putting them in a random order. Give your child this list and let him look at it for one minute; then remove it and ask him to tell you how many he can remember. Then repeat the activity with a similar list. This time, put the objects into their categories, so that your child sees four groups of items. Chances are, he will remember more of the second list because he stored them in his memory in a more organized way.

- *Retrieval.* A child's ability to recall from a previously learned list can improve when categories are suggested to him, even though he may not have been aware of the categories at the time he learned the list. To demonstrate this, give your child the first jumbled list of objects (as above) without mentioning any of the categories, then note how many he can remember. Do the same with a second jumbled list of the same objects, but this time, at the point when you ask him to recall the list, suggest to him that the objects can be grouped into "furniture," "transportation," "food," and "clothes" and that he should try to remember them in these categories. Your child's efforts with the second list should be more successful.

Practice these strategies for a few minutes each week to enhance your child's memory. Such activities are suitable for a child as young as four or five, as are memory games such as "lotto," and "When I went on holiday I took with me a..." Have fun together as you practice your child's recall with him, for a few minutes at a time.

See also Concentration; Intelligence; Knowledge; Learning Skills.

Milestones Detailed study of child development by doctors, psychologists, and child-care professionals has shown that there are a number of "milestones," that is, significant points of development. Most children pass through these milestones at about the same age. For instance, most children are able to sit independently at the age of six months, most start to put two words together at about the age of eighteen months, and most are toilet-trained by the time they are five. Such milestones are important because they provide guidelines for a child's expected rate of development. Every child develops at her own pace. Milestones are only approximate points, nothing more, and often vary widely among children. One baby might show her first smile at six weeks, while another may not do so until she is twelve weeks old; one may be up on her feet at twelve months, while another may not walk independently until sixteen months. These variations are normal and are not a cause for concern.

Here are some key milestones in the development of walking and talking of which you may want to make a special note:

Walking   at 3 months, your child's back becomes firmer and straighter when sitting on your knee;

at 6 months, your child sits on the floor without any support from you;

at 9 months, your child may be able to stand using a low table as support;

at 12 months, your child may take her first few unsteady steps;

at 15 months, most children are on their feet, often unconfidently;

at 18 months, your child can walk comfortably around the room;

at 21 months, with your help, your child can walk up and down stairs;

at 24 months, your toddler can run and kick a ball, without falling over.

Talking

at 3 months, your baby can make a couple of distinct sounds;

at 6 months, your child babbles more consistently;

at 9 months, your child starts to use two-syllable babbling and possibly her first word;

at 12 months, your infant may be able to say up to three clear words;

at 15 months, your child recognizes her name when it is spoken to her;

at 18 months, your child has at least a dozen words and probably more;

at 21 months, your toddler starts to combine two words into a short phrase;

at 24 months, your child's spoken vocabulary runs into hundreds of words.

Sometimes the gap in levels of progress between one child and others of her age does indicate a deeper problem. A severe difficulty is rarely indicated if only one aspect of development is slow. In most instances, a combination of several delayed milestones must be present before more substantial investigation by a qualified professional is needed.

Determining the significance of developmental difficulties is not clear-cut and requires detailed consideration of a child's strengths and weaknesses. If you are worried about your child's progress, speak to your pediatrician. Chances are, you'll be reassured to hear that your child is progressing well. If a problem does exist, then the earlier it is detected the better for the sake of your child.

See also *Coordination; Language Development; Learning Skills; Normality.*

Modeling When you look closely at parents and children, you will nearly always see similarities in attitudes, behavior, and mannerisms. This could mean that these personality dimensions are inherited—but psychologists offer the "modeling theory" as a more plausible explanation.

The theory proposes that, as a child becomes closely attached to his parents, he adopts some of their personal characteristics. The child starts to use phrases that the parents speak, facial expressions that they use, and may even walk with their gait. This immitation makes the child feel more secure, closer to his parents, and increases his self-confidence. As modeling, also known as "identification," intensifies, a child gradually absorbs the attitudes and beliefs of his parents, selecting the characteristics that he finds most desirable.

A child does not only model himself on his parents. He partly models himself on other significant adults in his life as well. A young child who spends a great deal of time with a baby sitter or a nanny will begin to model some of that person's behavior. A child who attends day care regularly will model himself on some of the nursery staff to whom he feels attached. It is very important that you are aware of the images presented by all the adults in your child's life, including you. Your child is just as likely to model an adult's unpleasant features as he is to model their more attractive ones.

See also *Manners; Politeness.*

Mothers A woman's tightly structured role within the family has changed greatly in recent years. The "traditional" family is no longer a routine expectation. Just because a woman becomes a mother doesn't mean that her self-identity comes from ironing shirts, washing diapers, or keeping a tidy house. It no longer means a woman is expected to give up a career, either. Now the term "mother" has more to do with enhancing the social and educational needs of a child than it does with being a "housewife."

The evolving roles of women in contemporary society have destroyed many historical stereotypes of the woman's role as a mother and created more new challenges than ever before:

- *More than one-quarter of today's first-time mothers are single women, unattached to a male partner at the time they give birth.* Many of these are young girls, who in turn live with their mothers, who bring up the grandchild.

- *More and more new mothers are in the work force.* Some women choose to maintain fast-paced careers. Others are forced into low-paying jobs just to try to keep the wolf away from the door.

- *Some new mothers seek job retraining or further educational goals.* Some are trapped in the poverty and welfare downward spiral.

- *A stay-at-home mother is likely to participate in outside activities, such as a playgroup, or to volunteer for nursery school.*

- *A mother must be in touch with her child's needs as never before, and may have to become her child's advocate within the school system.*

- *Some new mothers are caught in the "sandwich" generation, where they have not only the prime responsibility for the care of young children, but also the care and concern for aging parents.*

These changing roles and opportunities for women create new pressures on the downside. This all means a mother's role is more challenging than ever before.

Somebody still has to clean the toilet and vacuum the floor.

While current studies show that when both parents work and males assume some household responsibilities, 88 percent of the household chores are still done by the woman. Of the 12 percent done by the male, the chores are mostly garden work, grocery shopping, or household repairs. These tasks are perceived as having lasting results. Generally, the more educated and the higher the income level, the more the male performs household tasks. Few males will do the daily tasks that become undone immediately, such as dishwashing, cooking, cleaning, scrubbing the toilet, or making the beds. These tasks are usually done by the woman, or they don't get done.

The division of chores can cause role strain and puts stress on all family members. It is important to remember that love, care, nurturing, and mutual support add to life's joy and purpose. It is also important to remember that a mother can't be all things to all people, or she may find herself more vulnerable to chronic stress, illness, and depression.

See also Bonding; Fathers; Older Parents; Parents; Quality Time; Single-Parent Family; Working Mothers; Young Parents.

Moving Psychological surveys have proved that moving to a new house is a very traumatic life event for adults, ranking third in terms of stress, after the death of a spouse and divorce. Moving is also a very stressful life event for young children.

By the age of two, a child is comfortable being in familiar surroundings and has organized his life around the predictability of his home environment. He knows where his toys are, what ornaments he mustn't touch, and where the juice is kept. A break from this familiarity due to a move can be very unsettling. For a child aged four or five, a move can have a more complex emotional effect, because it may also involve a change of school, and probably a change of friends. No wonder that the child may be troubled by the prospect of moving.

Another reason why moving is stressful for a young child is that he doesn't play an active role in it. Choosing a new house is something that adults do, not children. Decisions about area, type of house, size of back yard, placement of furniture, and who uses which room are made by adults. A child has to rely entirely on his parents' judgement, and hope for the best. Not all moves are for positive reasons, such as to gain more space or live in a more desirable area; some moves are a result of divorce, bereavement, or unemployment.

When moving a child aged five or under, consider the following:

- *Be positive about the move.* No matter the real reasons for the move, talk to your child about it in a positive way. Explain to him that it will give you all a chance to enjoy a new home, with new surroundings and new friends. He'll be happy about the move if he thinks you are happy about it.

- *Don't take your child house hunting with you.* A young child soon becomes weary when trailed through one house after another while his parents discuss lots of boring details. This doesn't make your task any easier.

- *Once you've purchased your new house, take your child to see it.* Emphasize the advantages to him: now he has his own room, the yard is bigger, a playground is nearby. Talk about how you'll decorate and furnish his room. This will help your child see the move and the new house in a positive light.

- *If the move causes a change of school, take your child to visit the new one before he starts.* Naturally, your child will be apprehensive about meeting new children and teachers, so the sooner he meets them, the better. Do this before you move in.

- *If at all possible, let your child keep in touch with old friends.* His biggest fear may be that he will lose touch with his pals. If your move is local, reassure him that won't happen, and let him make plans to play with his friends after the move takes place. If your move is farther afield, help your child send letters or take him for an occasional visit. This will generate a feeling of continuity.

Moving day and packing will be much more successful if your child is settled. Allow him to help pack some of his own clothes and toys. Let him keep out his favorite cuddly toy if he wants. As soon as the move is over, organize your child's bedroom. A few of his toys and some familiar bedding will make the new place seem like home.

See also Routine.

N

Nail-Biting Many children develop behavioral habits during the preschool years, and nail-biting is one of the most common. While this particular habit can be a sign of anxiety and nervousness in an older child, teenager, or adult, it doesn't have the same psychological significance in a child aged six years and under—a young child usually bites her nails just because she enjoys the nibbling sensation, likes having a finger in his mouth, and derives a sense of achievement from shaping her nails.

Even though nail-biting is a comfort habit, you may want to discourage your child from doing so for a number of reasons:

- *The danger of infection.* Your child may bite her nail so hard that the skin surrounding the nail becomes broken, which allows infection to set in easily.

- *The fingers look unsightly.* A well-chewed fingernail, surrounded by inflamed skin, looks awful—it's even worse if every finger has this appearance.

- *The child looks immature.* Fingers in the mouth is something associated with a younger child, and a four-year-old child may look babyish and immature.

A positive approach—in which you reinforce the times when your child doesn't bite her nails—will be more effective than a negative approach that involves punishment or disapproval when the child does bite them. Strategies such as painting your child's nails with a bitter-tasting fluid, wrapping tape around her fingers so that she can't access her nails, or even making fun of her, won't help. If anything, these strategies are more likely to strengthen your child's determination to continue the nail-biting habit.

Explain to your child what you intend to do (help her stop biting her nails), why you want to do this (for example, because other children won't want to play with her), and how you intend to help her (for example, by showing how pleased you are with her when she doesn't bite her nails). Then gradually do exactly all of these things. When your child does cope with an activity without biting her nails, make a fuss over her, so that your approval is obvious.

See also Masturbation; Pacifiers.

Nightmares Bad dreams occur most frequently in young
children between the ages of four and six years, although research indicates that at least 25 percent of children between six and twelve years still have nightmares. Don't be concerned if your child has an occasional disturbed night, even though he may become upset by it.

Bad dreams can be due to many different factors, some of which can be avoided:

- *Specific foods eaten late at night.* Some children are more prone to nightmares after they have had a late-night snack of cheese or chocolate, or a soft drink with a high level of coloring, sugar, and additives. Serve a healthful snack instead.

- *Television program.* Most children have vivid imaginations, and an action-packed television program or video just before bedtime can cause nightmares.

- *Ill-health.* When your child is incubating an illness, before the symptoms have fully emerged, his sleep at night may become unsettled. A sudden run of restless nights, coupled with nightmares, can be a warning that your child is about to develop an illness. Watch for this.

- *Worry.* What may seem trivial to you (such as not being able to sit beside a friend during juice time at playgroup) can seem momentous to a young child. Anxiety over small incidents can cause nightmares.

If your child wakes up distressed in the middle of the night, comfort him and stay until he has settled down again. Your child needs your reassurance that it was only a dream, that it didn't really happen, and that he is perfectly safe now. In a calm, unhurried voice, tell your child that the dream is over, that he'll soon get back to sleep, and that he won't have another bad dream like that one. He may calm down more quickly if you take him to the toilet, or downstairs for a drink of juice. Remember that your child will be all right in a few moments, and don't let your anxiety show.

Repeated nightmares can be a sign that something is wrong. Once you have eliminated all the factors mentioned above, you should consider the possibility that your child has a deep-rooted fear. Maybe he's not getting along well with friends, or perhaps his self-confidence is low because he is not as good at games as he wants to be. A child may have nightmares if he thinks his mom and dad are not getting along well. If your child regularly has bad dreams, talk to him about what's happening in his life. Try to find out what's troubling him. You may want to seek professional advice if the problem persists.

A night terror (pavor nocturnis) is an extreme form of nightmare, in which a child screams in his sleep and may even jump out of bed. Or the child may sit up, with his eyes wide open, and yet still be convinced that he can see something frightening. Twenty minutes may pass before he accepts that he is awake and that the night terror is over.

Always stay with your child during a night terror, all the time reassuring him that he's safe. Do this until your child calms down. He will probably forget all about it by the following morning. Night terrors are rare, but frightening, both for a child and for his parents, who see their child so distressed. As with nightmares, there is no cause for concern unless the night terrors become regular, in which case something is worrying your child.

See also *Crying Baby; Dreams; Fears; Self-Confidence; Sleep.*

Normality While professionals know the physical, intellectual, social, and linguistic skills expected of each child at each age, no clear line divides normality and abnormality in childhood, although some aspects are easier to define than others. When it comes to identifying normal behavior, the position is less clear, because a child's behavior by itself does not necessarily indicate abnormality. Bed-wetting, for instance, is a common early-warning sign that a child is under emotional stress, but many children wet the bed simply because they have not been toilet-trained, or because they are ill.

Before a child is judged to be normal or disturbed, her actions should be examined in the broader context of what is happening in all areas of her life. Most types of behavior found in children who are disturbed—including jealousy, aggressiveness, shyness, attention-seeking, withdrawal, excitability, tearfulness, and boisterousness—are found in normal children at some time in their lives or, to a minor extent, indefinitely.

Calculating the incidence of psychological disturbance in childhood is difficult. Studies that have used acceptable criteria for making such judgements confirm that most preschoolers have emotional or behavioral problems at some stage in their development. These difficulties are usually only temporary, and can be alleviated by timely intervention from the child's parents. Surveys estimate that at most only 15 percent of children experience psychological problems that are severe enough to interfere with their development. Of these, only a few require professional psychological help.

See also *Aggression; Bed-Wetting; Jealousy; Manners; Milestones; Modeling; Security Objects; Shyness; Unhappiness.*

Older Parents Many people postpone having children
until they have their careers or education in place. Some career
women decide to become a single mother when their "biological clock" starts to tick loudly. Many people marry and decide
to start a family later rather than sooner.

Society puts less pressure on couples to have children in the
years immediately following marriage. Many couples are now in
their second marriage. It is no longer rare to be a first-time parent at age forty or over.

Older parents should take into account certain health considerations when planning to have a first child. Medical research
reveals that women who conceive after the age of thirty-five are
more likely to have a child with a developmental problem. For
instance, a pregnancy between the ages of twenty and thirty-five
runs a six hundred to one risk of having a baby with Down's syndrome, whereas the risk increases to about one hundred to one for
mothers between the ages of forty and forty-five. Advanced medical techniques allow for the early detection of such conditions.

First-time pregnancy over the age of thirty-five carries a higher risk of stillbirth, and the possibility of having a longer and
more-difficult labor is greater. The incidence of these problems is
reduced when the mother is in good physical health.

The next hurdle that older first-time parents have to face is
the massive disruption that accompanies the arrival of a baby.
Few events are more likely to involve change than the birth of a
baby. All new first-time parents discover they can no longer go
out when they want, eat when they want, sleep when they want,
go on vacation when they want, or spend what they want. A
couple who has postponed pregnancy may be more accustomed
to their freedom, and consequently may miss it more.

Giving up the role of career woman for that of mother is
sometimes more difficult for an older mother than it is for

someone fifteen or twenty years younger, because an older woman will probably be on a higher rung of the corporate ladder. Despite advances in employment legislation, few women are able to return to their premotherhood employment status, unless they are back at work within a certain period of time after the birth. An older first-time mother who plans to stay at home for a while could pay a high price in terms of her future employment prospects.

This change of role may mean that an older first-time mother finds the contrast between her former lifestyle and her current one much greater than she had expected. The danger is that anxieties over loss of status may turn into resentment toward her new baby, or into a megadose of postnatal depression.

Age can also have advantages when it comes to parenthood. One benefit of maturity and life experience is increased self-confidence. Older first-time parents are more likely to be at ease with themselves, more able to handle the pressures of life that often overwhelm younger parents. Older parents have already enjoyed many years of living only for themselves, and don't have such a strong need to prove themselves personally or financially. A couple's pleasure in caring for a child can easily offset any of the disadvantages of being older parents.

Young babies have a tremendous capacity to tax their parents' stamina. Parenthood, with the physical demands of sleepless nights and hectic days of washing, changing, and caring for the baby, can be exhausting. No wonder some people argue that parenting—like inline skating and all-night parties—is a younger person's pursuit.

The so-called "generation gap" (the difference in outlook between successive generations of parents and children) can occur with parents of any age—some couples behave as though they are old when they are in their twenties. And some older couples often have a very young outlook. However, while it depends on the individuals concerned, a generation gap is more likely to occur as the age gap between parent and child widens.

There is another type of generation gap. Most people socialize with others who have similar interests. Likewise, most tend to have friends with children around the same age as their own. This gives them the opportunity to share ideas and to discuss common problems with each other. Older parents may not have this type of peer-group support; instead, all their friends may have grown-up children, and they may find that these friends have forgotten the everyday worries of first-time parents. This lack of common ground with others can sometimes increase an older couple's sense of isolation.

See also Parents; Postnatal Depression; Working Mothers; Young Parents.

Only Child An ever-increasing number of families has only one child. The main difference between only children and first-borns is that only children rarely have to compete with anyone else for their parents' attention. Unlike an oldest child who is forced out of her central position in the family, an only child enjoys the limelight throughout her childhood. The child never has to wait her turn and she doesn't often have to share her toys.

Being an only child has obvious advantages—the child has a strong feeling of security, a sense of ease in the company of adults, and a higher level of material comfort than do children in larger families. It can also have disadvantages, such as a tendency to be selfish, difficulty when it comes to sharing, and lack of confidence when mixing with other children, especially when the child first starts to attend nursery school. Life can be lonely for an only child, if she doesn't have an opportunity to mix with others. Only children tend to be more self-interested than other children of their own age, and they frequently seek the approval of authority figures. This extends into adulthood—many only-child employees rely heavily on the approval of their managers. Only children usually relate better to older people. Being raised in the company of adults makes them feel comfortable with more mature individuals. Only children also make good leaders, which can be a tremendous asset in situations where initiative is needed.

An only child will not automatically turn out to be selfish

and overindulged, but if yours develops these characteristics, concentrate on the following strategies:

- *Encourage your child to share her toys with friends and classmates.* Since an only child has little opportunity to share at home, at first she will probably have difficulty doing this when she is with others. Your encouragement will be helpful.
- *Try to involve your child in outside activities.* Where possible, make sure your child joins in activities that involve sharing and turn-taking with other children.
- *Let your child play with other children of her own age.* The best way to do this is to send your child to playgroup or nursery school and to invite other children to the house to play with her. When your child has visitors, encourage the children to play independently of the adults.
- *Give your child responsibility.* Some children expect everything to be done for them. As parents, you have to encourage your child to take more responsibility for the everyday events in her life, such as washing, dressing, feeding herself, and tidying up.
- *Don't always make your child the center of attention.* Learning to share adults' time with others is not easy. It is your responsibility to help your child solve any problems she may have in this respect—for example, by playing games in which she and her friends take turns, or by having small group activities where every child is given a chance to participate equally.
- *Share your attention with other adults.* Your child must learn to share the attention. Adults want their time in uninterrupted adult conversation, too.

See also Birth Order; First-Born Jealousy.

Overfeeding
Food serves a physical and a psychological purpose. Physically, food provides essential nutrients that enables the body to grow; psychologically, it provides comfort and reassurance. The very act of preparing and serving a meal is an act of

love and a sign of care and concern. For both children and adults, food and love are intertwined.

Difficulties can arise, however, when food becomes a substitute for parental love and parental interest. This process works in two ways. First, there is the child's perspective. For instance, a three-year-old child who is unhappy because his parent has little spare time for him may compensate by eating more than necessary. In the child's mind, the food becomes a substitute for love—and what his parent won't give him in terms of quality time, the child will take in terms of extra food. Adults sometimes eat out of sadness and low self-esteem, and children do this as well. Second, there is the parental perspective to overfeeding. The parent may believe that giving a baby additional food is a sign of love. Or the parent may overfeed an infant because the parent feels unable to relate to the child in any other way. Not all instances of obesity are a result of food being used as a substitute for love, but some do stem from this connection.

Overfeeding can be used as a way to win a child's love. Most children form an instant liking for sweets, especially if they are introduced into their daily diet early on, and look very favorably on any person who provides an ample supply. So the temptation to give your child too many sweets can be very strong. Similarly, you may be tempted to use sweets as a reward for your child's good behavior, but this too encourages overfeeding.

If you are concerned that your child is overfed, do not rush him into a diet plan. Instead, think about your child's emotional development very closely, to establish whether this pattern of overfeeding has a psychological basis. Should this be a realistic possibility, try to identify the source of the problem (for example, your child wants you to spend more time with him; he is insecure about his achievements in school; he is worried about his popularity; you are afraid he doesn't love you enough). Once the emotional difficulty has been resolved, the psychological need for overfeeding will dissipate.

See also Eating; Eating Out; Fussy Eaters; Healthy Eating; Snacks; Weaning.

Overorganized You probably recognize the importance of your child using her leisure hours purposefully.
Watching a young child fritter away hour after hour in front of
the television—staring at a video she has viewed dozens of
times already—is extremely frustrating for parents, especially
with the plethora of extracurricular opportunities available for
children nowadays (such as music, skating, swimming, ballet,
drama, gymnastics, soccer, ballet). This type of leisure activity
can play an important part in your child's life.

Learning to move to music in music class or play simple
percussion instruments at four years of age, for example, can
stimulate a lifelong interest in music. Activities have other benefits too. Being a member of groups that involve interaction
with other children can help develop your child's social skills;
learning to swim could save her life; appearing on stage for the
end-of-year drama show is a great boost to self-confidence. The
list of potential advantages is endless.

You probably encourage your child to be occupied when
she's at home, perhaps by making sure she regularly has a friend
over to play after school, so that she is never bored. Most children enjoy this sort of arrangement.

However, you should place a limit on the amount of free
time your child has organized for her—she also needs time to
herself. A child with an overorganized day may

- *lose her independence.* Every child wants to become independent, to be able to do things for herself. Part of the process
  of establishing this independence is making decisions about
  how free time is spent. An overorganized child is denied
  such decision-making opportunities, and her independence
  will suffer as a result.

- *have low self-esteem.* Psychological research confirms that a
  child's self-respect takes a tumble when she is not involved
  in making decisions about basic aspects of her life, such as
  what she eats, what clothes she wears, and with whom she
  plays. A child who has all her leisure time organized for her
  by her parents may experience similar feelings.

- *be unable to make decisions.* An overorganized child will be so used to having her parents make all the choices for her that she won't know what to do when she has any free time. Quite simply, when left to her own devices, she may not be able to decide how to entertain herself.
- *be a "jack of all trades and master of none."* Logic dictates that your child has only so many hours in the day to devote to leisure pursuits. Involvement in too many means that she doesn't have time to become skilled in any of them.
- *appear more tired than usual.* A child who spends most of her time actively engaged in leisure pursuits may not have sufficient opportunity to rest; she may become overtired.
- *lose interest in her toys.* An overorganized child may not have the chance to play with her toys at home because she is so busy. She may even start to feel that there is nothing of interest at home, and that she can only enjoy herself when she is somewhere else or with another child.

These disadvantages outweigh any benefits a child may derive from having an exceptionally busy life. So think about your child's leisure time and the way it is spent.

To help you judge whether your child's day is purposefully organized or overorganized, ask yourself these questions:

- *Is my child having fun with this activity?* If your child has been in a gymnastics class for three years and complains because it's too difficult to do the moves, perhaps you should consider whether she is deriving any benefit from this activity.
- *Does my child look forward to going?* Most teachers will tell you that nothing is worse than an unenthusiastic pupil who gets pushed along every week because mom and dad want her to be there. Your child should anticipate the activity with at least some spark of enthusiasm.
- *Is my child being kept busy in order to suit my schedule?* Perhaps you have organized your child's day in order to give yourself free time to pursue your own interests. Nothing is wrong with that occasionally, but don't let it become routine.

- *Does my child bicker a lot with her friends?* Having friends over to the house to play with after school can be great fun, but it may mean that your child doesn't have enough time on her own. Your child's dissatisfaction may show itself in irritability with the children who come to visit her.
- *Is my child able to structure her free time?* One test of whether you are overorganizing your child is to observe her when she has no planned activities and the TV isn't on. Can your child entertain herself?
- *Do I spend enough time with my child?* Add up the amount of time your child spends in the company of other people (excluding nursery school), and then add up the amount of time she spends just with you. If the total time spent on out-of-home activities is substantially more than the time she spends with you, then your child may be overorganized.

As with every part of child rearing, scheduling your child's activities is a question of balance. A child who is never allowed to participate in extracurricular classes, or to have friends over, is just as disadvantaged, though in different ways, as an overorganized child. One of your tasks as a parent is to ensure that your child's full potential is maximized. Structuring your child's day can be one way to achieve this, but overstructuring it is not.

See also *Friendships; Independence; Self-Confidence; Supervision.*

Overprotectiveness Just as animals have an instinct
to protect their newborns, humans instinctively protect their children from any danger or threat to their health. This natural tendency, found in all parents, ensures that a child will remain in good health until he is mature enough to look after himself. However, some parents become overprotective; for instance, they continue to do things for their offspring long after he is capable of being independent, or they fuss over their child when he is playing, or they worry constantly about his diet and sleeping habits.

You have to tread a fine line to allow your child the independence he needs as he needs it. Yet you have to protect your child's best interests when he can't take care of his own needs. Parents sometimes become overprotective when their child has had a serious illness in the early years. The stress and worry brought about by ill health make them extremely cautious about letting their child face routine challenges. Or they may become overprotective as a result of family bereavement, the death giving them a feeling of insecurity, which they redirect to the child. Whatever the cause, overprotectiveness restricts a child, and the effect can be to impair his development and self-confidence.

However, insufficient concern for your child's welfare is more harmful than too much. You have to find a balance in your parenting style, so that your child is allowed a degree of autonomy and, yet, is not allowed to put himself in danger. Only then will your child learn to tackle everyday challenges confidently.

See also *Illness; Independence; Spoiling; Supervision.*

Overweight Despite intensive medical research over many years, nobody knows whether a child's tendency toward fatness is inherited or whether it is due to food consumption.

Probably a bit of both is involved. However, the following is known:

- About 40 percent of children who are overweight during their primary-school years will continue to be overweight in adulthood.

- Although a high proportion of parents worry that their child is fat, only between 2 and 25 percent of North American children are obese. The figure is higher in the United States than Canada, which is attributed to the difference in the amount of exercise and the amount of TV watching between the two countries.

- Very few plump babies grow into plump children.

- If you and your partner aren't fat, there is a one in ten chance your child will be fat; but if you are both fat, there is a four in ten chance.

Table 1 Average Growth Rates

age (years)	average height (inches)		average weight (pounds)	
	Girls	Boys	Girls	Boys
1	29.3	30.0	21.0	22.5
1.5	31.9	32.4	23.8	25.3
2	33.3	33.7	26.0	27.1
2.5	35.2	35.6	28.6	29.7
3	37.0	37.4	31.1	32.2
3.5	38.5	39.0	33.3	34.6
4	40.0	40.5	35.2	36.8

Height and weight are directly linked. A child who gains weight faster than height will become fat. But remember that assessment of your child's correct body weight for your child's height can only be made using standard growth charts, which are available from your pediatrician.

Table 1 provides a rough guide to average growth rates, but it doesn't take into account acceptable individual variations.

Never put an overweight child on a rigorous diet to reduce the *amount* of food the child eats, unless you are medically advised to do so. Instead, exercise more control over the *type* of food your child eats. Following are common problems causing fatness during the toddler and preschool years:

- *Too many desserts, candy, and potato chips.* You may not be able to cut out sweets altogether, but try to reduce them. Your child might not even notice that you gave her an orange instead of a cookie.

- *Too many sweet drinks.* Encourage your child to drink fresh fruit juice, water, or milk instead of soft drinks. Milk consumption should follow the daily food guide for the age of your child.

- *Too many fats.* Spread butter and margarine more thinly (or give your child toast without any at all), serve boiled potatoes instead of French fries, and reduce the amount of fried food you serve.

- *Too many snacks.* Nothing is wrong with snacks as long as they are nutritious and infrequent. Don't give your child a high-sugar or high-fat snack every time she asks for something to eat. Give her fresh fruit or raw vegetables instead.

- *Too little exercise.* We are becoming a chair-bound society. A toddler can push her stroller along the street; a four-year-old can run, jump, and climb—this activity decreases the opportunity for fat to build up. Turn off the television and go for a walk together.

See also *Additives; Eating; Eating Out; Healthy Eating; Snacks; Overfeeding.*

P

Pacifiers Sucking a pacifier is a comfort habit that some parents encourage. A pacifier is specially shaped to fit the contours of a young mouth, and is designed so that it cannot be swallowed. Most pacifiers are made of plastic, are nontoxic, and can be washed and sterilized.

Parents usually allow their child to use a pacifier for three reasons:

- *To silence the child.* Placing a pacifier in your child's mouth is a sure way to quiet him. This may be preferable to having your child wail while you are trying to talk. The use of a pacifier can be a quick and effective way to achieve the desired goal.

- *To help the child fall asleep.* A pacifier may bring about a state of relaxation in a tired infant—something you may be desperate to achieve. If you take the pacifier out of your child's mouth just before he falls asleep, he is unlikely to become dependent on it for falling asleep.

- *To soothe the child.* A child who is accustomed to having a pacifier will be calmed by it when he is distressed or afraid. Sucking it will have the effect of reducing his tension.

If you do let your child use a pacifier, ensure it is clean and germ-free. Many children take enormous pleasure in throwing their pacifiers onto the ground. This increases the risk of germs ending up in your child's mouth. Sterilize the pacifier regularly; otherwise your child will pick up an infection. That is hardly likely to bring him peace and tranquillity. Never dip the pacifier into anything sweet. That could cause your child's teeth to rot even before they emerge through his gums. For the same reason, avoid giving your child a bottle at bedtime.

One of the prices to be paid for using a pacifier is that your child's early explorations may be restricted. Young babies learn about the world around them by gumming objects, such as toys and rattles. This is a natural phase of development. A pacifier in your baby's mouth will prevent him from exploring his toys.

One potential problem with encouraging your child to use a pacifier is that it can create dependency on an object. You may find that your child doesn't want to give up the pacifier. He may want it at times when he isn't tired or unhappy. This habit can be extremely difficult to eliminate once it has started. You must be prepared to eliminate your child's pacifier when he is older.

See also Learning through Play; Masturbation; Security Objects; Teeth.

Parents Most couples experience mixed feelings at the prospect of becoming parents, especially with their first child. First comes excitement at the thought of having a baby in the family, someone extra to love and care for. Then comes apprehension: won't a baby cause an enormous disruption to their existing lifestyle? It's also the time when many of us realize that the ability to be a good parent beyond the basic instinct to protect is not innate.

Animals seem to be better equipped than humans when it comes to being natural parents; they are very capable of protecting their babies. Nobody tells animals to behave in this way, and they don't attend prenatal classes. Neither do they have obstetricians, nurses, or psychologists advising them. They instinctively do a good job.

Animals, though, are not concerned with the higher issues of parenting, such as giving their offspring creative and beautiful toys or ensuring that their child fulfills her full intellectual potential. Animals are not concerned with many of the issues that we regard as central to our parental role. The main goal of animal parents is to make sure their babies survive until they have learned enough skills to hunt for themselves and to avoid danger. Our own concerns are far more complex. While you, too, have a natural desire to protect your child from danger, you want much more than that for her, including a good education, a happy home life, a suitable career, and probably, a satisfactory marriage. These higher-order goals are not instinctive.

Some inborn tendencies pull parents and child together. For instance, when a baby comes into the world she is preprogrammed to interact with her parents. The baby's hearing is tuned to human voices. Her vision is set to focus best on her parents' faces when they feed her. She can use her voice to let them know when she is unhappy.

Other biological forces act on parents and encourage them to look after their child, such as the mother's natural production of breast milk following birth. In addition, the minimum delay before the mother can have another child—at least nine months—means that their baby doesn't have to share their attention with other babies in the family, although the arrival of twins, triplets, or more throws this particular natural plan into disarray!

Aside from these basic tendencies, most aspects of parenthood have to be learned. Your starting point for deciding how to act as a parent probably stems from your own experiences (both negative and positive) in childhood. Some people have such a miserable time as children that they are determined to raise their own child in a totally different way, while others find their childhood so satisfying that they replicate their parents' style of parenting with their own children.

Think about your own childhood. What do you think were your parents' main priorities when they raised you? Make a list of them—it might contain answers such as "keeping me clean and tidy," "encouraging me to be well behaved," "taking me to music classes so I could learn to play the piano," "teaching me to read before I started primary school," or "helping me to be friendly to other children." Now make a list of the priorities you have established for your own children. Are there similarities, or are the lists completely different? How much do you consider that the priorities for your child have been influenced by those of your parents? Chances are, you will see a connection between your parents' skills as mother and father and your own views on how you would like to be as a parent.

Previous generations of parents had one substantial advantage over today's. They were often part of a large, close-knit family network. Many helpful—and experienced—relatives and friends were always close at hand to give practical advice on matters of parenthood. Those earlier generations had less need to ask for advice and help on day-to-day matters, since they already had a bank of folk wisdom immediately available. This made parenthood easier to manage.

The current generation of parents does not usually have that luxury. The basic concept of the extended family has broken down, and new parents no longer have the family support as they once did. One of the many effects of divorce or separation is that one entire side of a child's family may no longer be accessible. Many divorced parents cite this feeling of isolation as the main distress factor when bringing up their children.

Even when a family is intact, a child's grandparents may not be on hand. In previous decades, grandparents would probably have lived close to their married children, ready to help out whenever needed. Today, the grandparents probably live in a different city or, even if they live nearby, they may have outside employment for at least part of the day, or have their own active lives.

Many moms and dads who want to be good parents, but

who also know that parenting doesn't come altogether naturally, deeply feel this loss of access to caring family support. Never
feel guilty or insecure when you find you don't have all the
answers to questions about child rearing. You're no different
from anyone else. Ask your friends and family. Read books and
talk to child-care professionals.

See also Bonding; Fathers; Grandparents; Mothers; Older Parents;
Separation and Divorce; Single-Parent Family; Working Mothers;
Young Parents.

Personality Psychologists define personality as the sum
of the emotional and behavioral attributes that combine to
form a unique individual. Every child has his own unique personality, whether he is quiet or talkative, confident or insecure,
sociable or solitary. From birth, a baby shows that he has a personality of his own and responds to his parents in a unique way.

Little evidence suggests that personality is genetically transmitted from parents to child. Studies of identical twins (who
have the same inherited characteristics) have found that each
child develops a distinctive and individual personality. There are
few signs that identical twins ever have identical personalities.
However, personality probably has a small inherited component.

Numerous psychological theories explain personality development in terms of upbringing. For instance, Sigmund Freud
proposed that personality is formed in early childhood as a
result of parents' attempts to control their child's natural self-
centered instincts. B. F. Skinner's theory of behaviorism claimed
that personality is formed as a result of conditioning: for example, a child who is rewarded for behaving in a certain way will
repeat that behavior until it becomes part of his personality; and
a child who is punished for behaving in a certain way will learn
not to repeat it.

On balance, your child's personality probably develops from
an interaction between inherited characteristics from you and
your partner and environmental factors, including the way he is
brought up. So your child is not the way he is simply because
"he was born that way," or because "you made him like that";

both sets of influences combine to determine your child's eventual personality.

See also Genes.

Phobias Phobias are similar to normal fears, but more pervasive. For instance, a child who fears cats may cross to the other side of the street to avoid one. But a child who has a phobia about cats will have a much more serious problem. It is not just that the child avoids coming close to cats: the child cries when she sees a cat on television, when she sees a picture of a cat in a book, or even when another child casually mentions a cat.

To judge whether your child's fear is a harmless phase that she is likely to outgrow, or whether it is a phobia, consider the following points:

- *Fear at the mere thought.* A child who has a fear will show anxiety only when she actually experiences the dreaded event. A child with a phobia will become terribly upset even at the thought of the event.

- *Intensity of fear.* In most cases, a child's fear will pass within a few minutes, and she will then settle down. A child with a phobia will remain terrified for much longer, perhaps for several hours.

- *Impact.* Fears usually have very little impact on a child's life, except for the few minutes when the child has a face-to-face encounter with the object of her fear. Phobias are more sweeping and may take over the child's life, to the point where she is too afraid to cross the threshold of her home.

- *Resistance.* Most children can be helped to overcome their fears quite quickly, and welcome their parents' support in this. Phobias are much more resistant to change, tending to persevere despite all efforts to remove them.

If you think your child's anxiety is a normal childhood fear, then (if you are right) it will almost certainly pass as your child grows older and more confident. If you think her anxiety is a phobia, then (if you are right) it may have greater psychological significance, and merits closer consideration. Such fearful behavior may be a symptom of a deep-rooted insecurity. You should look closely at your child's life to establish the underlying cause of her behavior. Genuine phobias are rare in childhood. Sometimes psychological advice may be necessary to help the child overcome the difficulty; this can be arranged through your pediatrician.

See also Fears; Unhappiness.

Physical Disability Any physical problem affecting
a child's mobility can also have a significant effect on his psychological development. Following are some reasons for this:

- *A child's self-confidence is affected by his physical appearance.* Disabled and nondisabled children share the same beliefs about personal attractiveness; both groups have the same ideas about their ideal body shape. Therefore, the self-confidence of a child with a physical disability can be particularly low.

- *A child may be forced into adopting roles not normally associated with childhood.* He may have to miss class because he has to attend physiotherapy or sit out during gym class.

- *A disabled child may be denied normal childhood experiences.* Most children take for granted their ability to run around on the playground or move around the school without help. A child who has physical difficulties can't do this, and this can make him unhappy.

Most children with physical disabilities are integrated into ordinary primary and secondary schools, unless the difficulty is so severe that the child has no independent mobility whatsoever or has other contributing medical complications. Practical arrangements, such as ensuring the availability of wheelchair toilets, can usually be made by the local school board before the child's school placement begins. Some schools designate a teacher with specific responsibility for supervising the welfare of pupils with physical disabilities.

See also Cerebral Palsy; Clumsiness; Coordination; Integration, Educational; Self-Confidence; Special Needs; Spina Bifida.

Play Every style of play stimulates the development of a different aspect of your child's life. The particular form of play in which your child engages at any one time will depend on her level of maturity, her individual interests, and her toys. The following categories of play are not mutually exclusive. Any one sequence can have several purposes:

- *Exploratory/discovery play.* This kind of play is most commonly seen in babies up to the age of eighteen months to two years. Through exploratory play a growing baby discovers the world around her. By reaching out and exploring, a baby begins to make sense of her surroundings. That's why crib and bath activity centers are so popular. Your baby is fascinated by the various noises and sights these toys make. The more discoveries your baby makes, the more she wants to explore. Exploratory play may involve only touching, or gumming, or listening to sounds, or watching, or batting at her mobile. It doesn't involve her whole body.

- *Physical/energetic play.* Once your child is able to move around independently, she plays more adventurously. She moves her entire body. Physical play, whether crawling, running, jumping, balancing, climbing, or kicking, encourages your child's independence and boosts her self-confidence.

- *Creative play and imaginative play.* Creative play involves a child making an item from materials, such as a model, a block tower, a picture, a puppet. Imaginative play involves a child playing a role, such as pretending to cook a meal, or dressing up. Two points are common to these activities: First, they involve symbolism; your child pretends that one object represents another. Second, they allow your child to express inner feelings, feelings that she may not realize she has.

- *Social play.* Social play occurs when two or more children play together. Solitary play is the earliest stage, lasting up until about age two, when a child is content to play on her own. Parallel play usually emerges between the ages of two and three; two children play in the presence of each other, although they do not actually play together. Cooperative play, the last stage in the development of social play, usually emerges around ages three and four. This takes place when two or more children learn how to play together. Through genuine cooperative play, children learn how to get along, how to take turns, how to follow simple rules, and how to be fair.

- *Manipulative/cognitive/problem-solving play.* Play of this sort includes activities in which a child learns by solving problems. Puzzles, shape-sorters, building blocks, lotto, matching games, and memory games all involve this type of play. Problem-solving play encourages a child to think about her actions and their consequences, to plan strategies for tackling new problems, and to learn through trial and error.

To understand these different types of play, and the varied benefits they bring your child, remember any single action can serve several purposes. Throwing a ball to another child is social play because it involves cooperation; it is physical play because your child's whole body is involved; and it may be imaginative play if the ball turns into a space vehicle in your child's mind.

Although you may be reluctant to interfere or upset the spontaneous nature of your child's play, do join in and play with your child. Research into the effects of mother's involvement in the play of their children (aged eighteen months to two years) at home has revealed the following patterns:

- A child is likely to play longer when her mother participates.
- Although most pretend-play sequences are initiated by toddlers, few of them are actually completed when a child plays independently; but when mothers play, the toddler completes the pretend-play sequences.

Adult participation can increase the imaginative quality of children's play. A group of five-year-olds took part in a number of twenty-minute demonstration sessions in which an adult introduced a theme based on the children's interests and then used pipe-cleaner figures to act out a story about the theme. The children were encouraged to make up their own role-play situations, using a range of materials, such as Play-Doh, pipe cleaners, and fabrics. The researchers found that these children (compared with a matched group of children who hadn't received tutoring), showed more imagination and creativity in their play, as well as more concentration. These improvements were still present more than two months after the demonstration sessions had ended. Sensitive adult participation can enhance a child's play.

Parents can develop their child's play experiences in three principal ways or styles:

- *Prestructuring.* With this style, a child's play is to a great extent prescribed. Usually this happens when the child has a toy that can only be used in a specific way; for instance, a jigsaw puzzle by its nature determines what a child can do with it, whereas building blocks can be used in many different ways. Parents also prestructure their child's play by telling her how to play with a particular toy, rather than letting her investigate for herself. While a prestructuring style can inhibit imagination and creativity, it can encourage a sense of direction in a disorganized child.

- *Redirecting.* The young child initiates the play activity, but then the parent redirects the play in a specific way. This often happens in nursery school when the teacher subtly changes a child's original play activity into one that apparently has greater educational value. For instance, a child may be happily playing with water, thoroughly enjoying the fun of filling up empty containers and then emptying them back into the sink. The teacher then suggests that the child should count the number of small containers she can fill from the contents of the large container. The redirecting style can make a dull play sequence more interesting.

- *Extending.* The extending style stimulates the expressive and imaginative dimensions of play. Evaluate the play activity from your child's point of view. When your child forms shapes from Play-Doh, you can offer suggestions, or when she builds a block tower, you can help make more-complex structures. This style of play is very helpful for a child who lacks self-confidence.

When you join your child's play, consider which style of involvement you want to adopt. Think about the reasons you choose that particular style of play and anticipate the possible effects it might have. Your child's play has room for all three types of parental involvement. Always try to ensure that your child has a wide range of play experiences.

See also *Coordination; Gender Play; Imaginary Friend; Imagination; Knowledge; Learning through Play; Sociable Play.*

Playgroup/Nursery School Starting playgroup

or nursery school involves a separation that is a two-way process: it's as hard for you as it is for your child. While all parents want their child to stand on his own two feet, feelings of regret that your child is growing up are natural. Both parents and child need time to adjust to this new phase. Playgroup or nursery school may be the first time your child goes out into the world on his own. Although playgroup provides a child-centered environment, it can be daunting. Some children cling tearfully to their parents at the playgroup door, not wanting to let go; and the parents may be just as upset, though trying not to let it show. Yet other children arrive full of anticipation, happy to wave good-bye to their parents without so much as a backward glance.

You can take positive steps to help your child through this stage.

- *Prepare your child for the event by talking about it beforehand.* Visit the playgroup to familiarize him with the staff and the building.

- *Be calm and relaxed when taking your child to the center.* If your child appears anxious, reassure him that there is nothing to worry about.

- *Don't linger.* Make the separation brief, even if your child appears upset.
- *Talk about the day's activities with your child when you pick him up at the end of the session.*

All these measures reduce your child's anxieties.

One advantage that a playgroup can have over day care is that parents may take turns participating in the group. This can have a settling effect on a child, especially if he is apprehensive. But it can work the other way as well—a manipulative child can use his parent's presence to draw attention to himself. Some children behave perfectly with everyone, except their parents.

Should your child seem apprehensive at the thought of being away from you, do not panic. Your child needs you to be calm. Some parents feel embarrassed when they realize that other children are settling down while their child is not. You shouldn't be embarrassed; your child will settle down in time. You'll find that after a couple of weeks he no longer needs you to be with him. With his new-found independence, your child will be a stronger, more-mature individual. When, at a later stage, your child attends school, the experience of succeeding with playgroup will have given your child extra confidence.

Preparation for leaving you can be made in other areas of your child's life. Attendance at leisure activities where parents are not constantly present (such as dancing classes, gymnastics, swimming lessons), provides your child with an opportunity to develop on his own.

See also Independence; School Readiness.

Playing with Bowel Movements Young children are usually fascinated by bowel movements; a sense of dislike, perhaps disgust, at bodily waste products doesn't develop until later. In the meantime, don't be surprised if your toddler shows great enthusiasm and interest in her bowel movements. You may even find that she reaches into the potty to play with them; to you, that's a revolting action, to her, it's a healthy expression of her inquiring mind.

Before you start toilet training your toddler, decide how you feel about bowel movements. This may seem a silly thing to do, but the attitude that you have toward toilet training will directly influence your toddler's attitude. For instance, if you react with loathing every time your child has a bowel movement, she'll eventually react the same way, too. On the other hand, if you react with ecstasy every time, then your toddler will be so happy that she'll want to play with her creations. A balanced approach is best, in which you show pleasure at your child's achievement in using the potty effectively (and not simply pleasure at the product), while at the same time explaining to her that the contents of the potty now have to be flushed away. This way, your toddler will recognize that depositing her bowel movements in the potty, followed by their removal, is the desired goal.

There will probably be times when you leave your child sitting on the potty while you engage in another activity, only to return to find her staring avidly into the potty or perhaps even bringing her bowel movement to show you proudly. In these instances, remind your child how pleased you are with her for using the potty, and tell her in a matter-of-fact voice that she shouldn't touch them. Your own calm response—combined with specific suggestions for her behavior in the future—lets your toddler know what is expected of her. Her initial curiosity about bowel movements will soon fade.

See also Masturbation; Toilet Training.

Politeness

The way a child behaves toward others has a direct effect on the way others behave toward him. Politeness is part of this. Politeness, however, assumes less significance than it did in previous decades. What is accepted by many contemporary parents would have been frowned upon by previous generations.

But this doesn't mean that all forms of manners in children should become a thing of the past. Politeness brings a child a number of benefits. For instance, politeness is likely to make your child popular with others. A child who says "please" when he wants to borrow a toy from a friend will be more liked than one who simply snatches it out of the friend's hand without asking. Politeness has practical benefits, too: for example, a child who says "thank you" when given a present is more likely to receive another present than a child who takes it without comment or as his due. Your child's politeness can help put others at ease, because they will probably assume that the child will also be well behaved, even though this isn't always the case.

Your child's attitude toward politeness stems directly from you and your behavior. If your family values include being polite and respectful to others, then your child's behavior will show this. Hearing you say "please" and "thank you" provides your child with a model to imitate in his own friendships. Do show politeness toward your child as well, not just to other adults—there's every reason to treat children politely. Encourage your child, from the age of three or four, to say "please" and "thank you."

Don't get angry with your child when he isn't polite, especially before age five. Chances are, your child has simply forgotten what you told him, or he didn't really grasp the idea in the first place. Your child may not pick up social conventions easily, and so you may have to specify the expectations: for instance, that he should say "please" when he wants something, that he shouldn't barge in front of others in a line, that he should apologize when he realizes he has made a mistake. Your child will understand and follow your rules eventually.

See also Manners; Modeling.

Postnatal Depression

All new mothers experience mixed emotions immediately after the birth of their baby. Almost 80 percent of women have mild feelings of depression and anxiety in the first few weeks following their baby's birth. Known as the "baby blues," these emotions are so common as to be regarded as normal, and are an almost-predictable first reaction to the onerous responsibility of caring for a baby. Like most stresses caused by fear of new situations, the baby blues soon pass, as the mother gains self-confidence and the bonding process proceeds.

Some women are very excited to have a healthy baby to care

for, while others are more apprehensive. Thoughts such as "Will I manage all the changing, feeding, and washing?" or "Will I learn to love my baby in the way that all my friends love their children?" run through the minds of all new mothers.

In addition to these typical worries, new mothers, who are now often routinely discharged just hours after giving birth, are still recovering from the exhaustion and physical strain of the birth process itself. This takes its toll on her stamina. Increased tiredness resulting from the baby's regular feeding schedule is a further pressure, and there may be additional stresses, including lack of privacy with her partner, because of visits from friends and relatives, and unhelpful comments and well-meaning advice from other people ("I don't know how you manage with a baby screaming all the time like that.").

Many women with the baby blues are too embarrassed to admit their feelings to their partner or friends. The image of motherhood promoted in the media is one in which the new mother sits holding a silent, contented baby in her arms, while she chats proudly to her admiring husband. It takes courage for a woman to accept that the reality of motherhood is different from that rosy picture, and to admit to herself and to others that not everything is going according to plan. As a result, a new mother may hide her true feelings and not admit her exhaustion. Pretending that negative emotions do not exist isn't the answer. Denial of the baby blues won't make them go away. So if you experience anxiety and depression—however mild—in the postnatal period

- *speak candidly to your partner.* Tell him exactly how you feel, no matter how irrational your worries may seem.

- *talk to other new mothers.* You may be surprised and reassured to find that your experience is not unique. Sharing worries with another new mother can be supportive.

- *don't feel guilty.* Harsh comments, such as, "You should be ashamed of yourself, feeling this way when you've got a lovely new baby," are totally unhelpful, only produce pangs of guilt, and should be ignored. This pull-yourself-together approach falls short of the sensitivity required to help some-one manage anxieties.

Postnatal depression is a more-severe and long-term condi-tion, occurring in approximately 25 percent of new mothers in the United States. Symptoms can include inability to sleep, appetite loss, episodes of tearfulness, loss of sex drive, and anx-iety attacks. The significance of postnatal depression has only relatively recently been acknowledged by professionals as a gen-uine psychological disorder.

Women who suffer from postnatal depression often say that they don't know what it is that their baby wants from them and that they are unable to care for their baby adequately because they don't understand what she needs. This inability to inter-pret nonverbal communication causes distress for both mother and baby. Of course, it's not possible to say whether it's the mother's depression that reduces her ability to communicate nonverbally with her baby, or her reduced ability to communi-cate nonverbally that increases her depression. Either way, this breakdown in communication causes psychological problems.

Bonding between mothers and babies with visual difficul-ties can be badly affected because of their relatively poor non-verbal communication. Compared with a baby with normal sight, a baby who is blind tends to smile less frequently and less intensely, makes no eye contact, has a narrower range of facial expressions, and appears more somber and morose. This restricted level of body language means that mother and baby can have difficulty forming an emotional attachment.

The cause of postnatal depression is disputed. Most medical practitioners emphasize the role that hormones—natural chemi-cals that control bodily reactions—play in the condition. The marked chemical changes that occur throughout the prenatal and postnatal periods, claim medical scientists, are directly linked to the appearance of postnatal depression. Drug therapy aimed at resolving the hormonal difficulty is an increasingly popular form of treatment, with new advances being made all the time.

Other professionals reject this explanation of postnatal depression. Many psychologists maintain that the baby blues and postnatal depression are linked to a woman's personality and the pressures in her life. Evidence for this comes from studies that have found that many women experiencing this form of depression had a depressive nature before their pregnancy, or were subject to prepregnancy stresses (such as money worries, marital difficulties).

The true explanation probably lies somewhere in between. Effective management of postnatal depression combines both the psychological and the medical approaches, and could include the following:

- *Drug treatment,* prescribed by a general practitioner after detailed medical examination;
- *Psychotherapy,* from a qualified therapist who is able to help the mother gain insight into her anxieties and concerns;
- *Contact with self-help groups,* organized by other mothers who have experienced similar problems. Local health clinics have the relevant contact numbers;
- *Sleep,* especially uninterrupted sleep.

Hospitalization is necessary only in the very extreme form of postnatal depression (puerperal psychosis), which affects approximately one in five hundred new mothers. This psychological disorder causes a new mother to lose contact with reality; she may become confused, thought-disordered, and almost certainly unable to care adequately for her baby. Treatment for puerperal psychosis is lengthy, and a full recovery may take more than two years.

See also *Bonding; Fathers; Mothers; Parents; Working Mothers.*

Praise Life as a parent is so hectic that parents have a tendency to ignore things that go right (such as when your child behaves well) and to give attention to things that go wrong (such as when your child misbehaves). But this only encourages your child to misbehave in order to get your attention. To avoid this, make praise an important part of your relationship with your child.

Praise for a specific positive action gives a very clear message to your child that you value what he has done, that you value him, and that you love him. (Of course, love and praise shouldn't be entirely conditional on your child's good behavior, because he has a need—and a right—to be loved by you no matter what he does. Therefore, your child deserves general praise just for being himself, just for being the unique and special child that he is.) Aside from raising your child's self-esteem, praise is a very effective way to encourage appropriate behavior and should be a constant component of your family discipline.

General praise is great, as far as your child is concerned, but he may not know exactly what it was he did that made you happy. When giving out specific praise, make it clear to your child what pleased you. For instance, your approval when your child tidied up his toys can be for a number of reasons: for example, he did what you asked, he saved his toys from breaking, he helped you. You may have to spell these reasons out to him so that he knows what to do the next time.

Like all forms of reward and reinforcement, praise is effective when it occurs immediately after the behavior. If the time gap is too long, your child may have forgotten what he did that earned the praise—this is especially true with a young child. Praise your child immediately following the positive behavior; this enables him to understand the connection between the two events.

Your praise should be construed as desirable by your child, not only by you. A four-year-old child may not thank you, for instance, for a big hug and kiss in front of his friends—in fact, that particular gesture of praise may ensure that he never repeats the behavior again! Much depends on your individual child, his likes, his personality, and his age. An older child tends to prefer more subtle gestures of praise, such as a loving touch on the shoulder, a gentle stroke on the cheek, or a positive comment, whereas a toddler may prefer a more obvious reaction, such as a big cuddle, a round of applause, or a favorite story read to him. You know your child's likes and dislikes better than anyone, and will quickly learn the type of praise to which he responds best.

See also *Attention-Seeking Behavior; Crying Baby; Discipline; Ignoring; Punishment; Spanking; Tantrums.*

Prenatal Development Life inside the womb is fascinating! The process of development from the moment of conception to the moment of delivery is divided into three phases:

- *The ovum.* This phase lasts about ten to fourteen days; it is the period from the moment when the nucleus of the sperm fuses with the nucleus of the ovum until the fertilized ovum becomes firmly implanted in the wall of the uterus. From then on, the ovum is dependent on the mother, and the next phase of prenatal life begins.

- *The embryo.* Progress is rapid in subsequent weeks. The embryo becomes surrounded by membranes, which form a sac filled with a watery liquid. The embryo floats in this liquid, but is attached to the sac by the umbilical cord, which itself is attached to the placenta. The placenta acts as a filter for the embryo (and fetus). During this period, which lasts until about eight weeks after conception, an embryo starts to develop many major organs, including eyes, ears, the mouth (which can open and close), limbs, and the all-important spinal cord.

- *The fetus.* This third period of growth lasts from about two months until the birth itself, and sees further development of body systems already laid down during the embryonic period. By twelve weeks, muscles are well developed, eyelids and lips are present, toes and fingers are observable, and the sex can be identified. Around the end of the sixteenth week, a mother may report that she feels her fetus moving. The fetus is now more than four inches long, and the ears are formed. By twenty-four weeks, eyes are completely formed (but closed), and taste buds appear on the tongue. A fetus is capable of surviving if born at this point.

Knowledge of fetal capabilities from the twenty-fourth to the fortieth week has been compiled from two sources. First, studies of premature babies born from the twenty-fourth week onwards have been able to plot changes in the senses of the fetus. By week twenty-four, a baby's nervous, respiratory, and other bodily systems have advanced to such an extent that it can survive outside the womb, with special help. As a result, we now know, for instance, that a fetus born at

- twenty-eight to thirty-three weeks will make mild attempts to avoid bright lights and loud noises, may have a weak cry, and will have some movements;
- thirty-three to thirty-six weeks has stronger movements, a stronger response to bright lights and loud noises, and will give a good cry when hungry;
- thirty-six to forty weeks will begin to track movements of objects with its eyes, will be active, and will have a very solid cry when distressed.

The sensory abilities of premature babies under forty weeks are not developed to the same extent as those of full-term babies. For instance, premature babies' sense of touch is not so highly attuned, and they are not very sensitive to pain. Yet they do respond to other types of sensory stimulation. Research has confirmed that babies born from twenty-eight weeks onwards can differentiate basic tastes such as sweet, sour, salt, and bitter, and basic odors.

A second source of knowledge about the sensory skills of an unborn fetus comes from the widespread use of ultrasonography. Examinations carried out with this technique demonstrate that a fetus spends a great deal of time moving around the womb. And since these movements tend to be coordinated, this probably means the baby has a good sense of balance. Ultrasound techniques have shown that an unborn child will give a startle response to a loud noise. Eye movements have also been detected.

With this level of sensitivity, it is hardly surprising that a fetus can be affected by stimulation outside the womb. The fact that an unborn fetus at twenty-eight weeks responds to noise does not mean that it hears these noises in the same way as an already-born baby of similar maturity. Remember that an unborn fetus is surrounded by fluid, which is not a very good transmitter of sound. Think for a moment about swimming in your local pool. The pool area may be very noisy, with lots of people shouting to each other and splashing around. The sound echoes loudly from one wall to another. However, as soon as you put your head under water, sounds become muffled. Submerged in water, you have great difficulty picking out individual sounds and specific voices. Scientists believe that's what it is like for a baby surrounded by liquid in the womb.

In addition, the outer ears of a fetus are covered by a creamy material known as vernix, which acts as a further barrier to clear hearing inside the womb. Studies have also shown that although an unborn baby may be startled at first by a loud noise (indicated by an increase in fetal heartbeat), the effect soon fades.

There is no direct connection between the mother's nervous system and that of her fetus. Yet, as early as the 1940s, scientists proved that a mother's emotional condition is indirectly connected to her fetus's physiology. This happens because emotional arousal—such as anger or fear—causes a physical reaction that releases chemicals into the bloodstream. Hormones are also secreted. These biochemical changes are transferred through the placenta, causing the fetus to become agitated. Fetal movements in the womb increase many times over when the mother experiences emotional stress. If the period of excitation lasts for weeks, the fetus may persist with this higher rate of movement for the remainder of the pregnancy.

See also Memory; Ultrasound.

Punishment
One of the problems with punishment is that it teaches your child what he shouldn't do, but it doesn't teach him what he should do. Punishment is also negative because it occurs at a low point in a relationship, because it is something your child dislikes, and because it is something that you probably dislike, too. Yet there can be a limited place for punishment within your overall family discipline. Try not to use punishment in isolation; always try to counterbalance with more positive dimensions of discipline, such as attention for good behavior, praise, reward, and encouragement.

For punishment to be effective, it should be all of the following:

- *Infrequent.* The more you punish your child, the less effective the punishment becomes because, like most things, its impact quickly attenuates. Parents who punish frequently have difficulty changing this model of discipline.

- *Appropriate.* Although matching the punishment with the misdeed is not always possible, make sure that the punishment is not too extreme. If your child recognizes that the punishment is unfairly harsh, then he won't be sorry for his actions.

- *Effective.* A punishment that is effective for one child might not work for another. For instance, your friend's child might dislike being confined to his room, whereas your child might thoroughly enjoy that experience

- *Overt.* Your child should know beforehand what the punishment will be when he misbehaves in a particular way. Tell him in advance so that he knows the consequence of his actions.

- *Consistent* Threatening your child with punishment and not carrying it out is pointless; your child will quickly learn that your threats are empty, and that you don't really mean what you say. Punishments should be applied consistently

- *Immediate.* As with rewards and praise, punishments should be carried out as soon as possible after the misbehavior. Leaving too long a gap might mean that your child completely forgets why he is being punished.

- *Nonphysical.* Plenty of research evidence confirms that hitting your child is not an effective punishment. Spanking is likely to turn your child's guilt at his misbehavior into anger at you.

- *Varied.* Use a range of punishments with your child (such as having time out from you for a few minutes, going to bed a few minutes earlier that night, not allowing him to play with his friends that afternoon, and so on).

See also *Attention-Seeking Behavior; Crying Baby; Discipline; Ignoring; Praise; Spanking; Tantrums.*

Q

Quality Time Family life is hectic, no matter what the age of your children. When your children are babies, their physical care takes up so much time, with the constant washing, changing, and feeding. When they are toddlers, they demand a lot of attention because they want to be amused so much of the time. When they're preschoolers there's the carpooling to playgroups and activities, and the endless rounds of parties. When they reach school age, they become involved in a whole new range of educational and social activities that occupy much of the day. You have your own busy lives to lead, too.

No wonder that family communication can falter in the hubbub of everyday life. That's why it is so important to make "quality time"—a time when outside pressures are laid aside, when every member of the family sits down and shares his or her feelings and ideas, while the others listen. Quality time is the opportunity for parents and children to keep in touch with each other about what's happening in their lives.

Quality time can be individual—for instance, between you and just one of your children. It can be achieved by setting aside a specific time each day to be with your child, talking to her about her experiences that day, or perhaps playing a game with her. Some children are pleased just to have the chance to talk about their daily activities with their parents. Even if you can manage this for only a few minutes each day, your child will benefit.

Quality time can also be a whole-family event. Mealtime is often the best time, since this is perhaps the only moment of the day when all the members of your family sit down together. Turn off the television and make a point to encourage a family meal. Make sure that everyone around the table has a chance to share their experiences. A small amount of quality time gives a large amount of psychological satisfaction to everyone.

See also *Bonding; Emotional Deprivation; Working Mothers.*

Quarrels No parents can deal with all the stresses and strains of everyday life without occasional disagreements, but no child likes to witness mom and dad arguing.

Tension between you and your partner can show itself in many ways. Raised voices are not the only means to convey the fact that ill-feelings are present in the household. Many parents hold the mistaken view that if they do not actually scream at each other in front of the children, the children will have no idea there is any problem. Unfortunately, the statement "We may not get along well with each other, but at least the children don't see that" is rarely borne out in reality.

The nonverbal communication that goes on between couples—the gestures, the unsaid comments, the looks on faces, the expressions in the eyes—is just as meaningful to a young child as the spoken word. Children are as sensitive to body language as they are to what is actually said.

Research has shown that young children are sensitive to specific marital tensions: tension over dissatisfaction in the sexual relationship, tension over one parent feeling that the other is not as considerate as he or she should be, tension arising from emotions not being expressed openly, tension about matters not being discussed openly, and tension over one spouse feeling dominated by the other. If you and your partner do have conflicts over these or any other issues, treat them as high priorities and make an effort to resolve them as quickly as possible.

Regular quarrels between parents can have a bad effect on their child for a number of reasons:

- *A child needs a stable family in which to thrive.* If your child feels this stability is threatened—by repeated disagreements between mom and dad—he'll become unsettled. Loss of family security disturbs a young child.

- *Parents who fight frequently with each other are more likely to disagree about how their child should be disciplined.* This confuses a child.

- *A child imitates his parents.* If they quarrel a lot, then the child is likely to quarrel with others.
- *A child is affected by parental arguments because he wants to remain loyal to both of them, irrespective of the reasons underlying the arguments.* Witnessing mom and dad fighting tears a child's loyalties apart.

Disagreements are a normal part of family life. Every child has to learn to manage this. Negative emotions, such as anger, dislike, and jealousy, are experienced by everybody at one time or another. This is perfectly normal. But some parents feel that they, and their children, should always repress these negative feelings, in the hope that they will go away. Repression tends to have the opposite effect. Repression of such feelings injects even more tension into a relationship. A child brought up to think that only pleasant feelings are allowed free expression will eventually feel guilty every time he has an unpleasant thought. The child has to learn that there are appropriate ways to express anger and ill-feeling and that the release of negative emotions need not be destructive.

Discuss rather than conceal your feelings. Of course, this doesn't mean that you should never have arguments in front of the children. A child who sees that his parents argue, yet still love each other, will eventually understand that arguments and love are not mutually exclusive. He will learn that it is possible to be angry with a person and to love that person at the same time. An occasional parental disagreement in front of the children need not be harmful. When a child sees that arguments can have a beginning and an end, that they do not have to drag on for days and days, and that two people arguing can settle their differences, then you have achieved something positive. You can teach your child, by example, that disagreements can be resolved without any long-term damage to a relationship. This will help your child handle conflicts in his own relationships.

There are certain limits to this. Physical aggression, or even the threat of physical aggression, between you and your partner should never be witnessed by your child, under any circumstances. A child will always become terrified and insecure if he sees one parent hit the other. He may become afraid to leave the house in case something dreadful happens when he is out, or he may become afraid that one day he himself will be hit.

See also *Aggression; Body Language; Fighting; Modeling;*
Separation and Divorce; Unhappiness.

Questions Once your child starts talking, she will soon realize that asking questions is one way to find out more about her world. The wonderful thing about asking questions is that it involves social contact with you; it's a very pleasant way for her to learn. A young child's questions generally fall into one of these categories:

- *Facts.* "Why is grass green?" "Who makes dogs have a tail?" "When is my favorite TV program on?" "Why is rain wet?" These kinds of questions enable your child to acquire information about specific aspects of her life that interest her. Some of these questions can be very complex, even though they appear straightforward.

- *Permission.* "Can I have another candy?" "Will you take me to the park?" "Is it all right if we play outside?" "Can I draw now?" These questions let a child test the limits of acceptable behavior and help her establish the boundaries within her immediate environment.

- *Ideas/feelings.* "Why are you crying?" "What will happen if I don't go to school today?" "What do ice cream and fries taste like together?" These questions allow your child to express her ideas and feelings, and to assess how other people react to them.

You may find that your child asks you the same question even though you gave her a satisfactory reply a few minutes ago. She does this for a number of reasons. First, your child may not understand the answer you gave, even though she seemed satisfied at the time. Asking the question again gives her another opportunity to think about the issue and to confirm what you originally told her. It is highly unlikely that she repeats questions just to annoy you! Second, asking questions is a good way to get your attention, because most parents are pleased when their child shows interest in something; your child will soon realize that this strategy is very effective. In some instances, two-year-olds and three-year-olds repeat questions solely to attract more attention.

Always answer your child's questions in a way she can understand. Explaining theories of nutrition to a four-year-old who asks why hamburgers are so tasty is absolutely pointless. Don't be tempted to give the sort of in-depth reply you would give to an adult who asked you the same question. Look closely at the expression on your child's face when you answer her—if she seems bored and disinterested, then you have almost certainly gone over her head.

You may find your child is adept at asking questions that you can't always answer. For instance, do you know why the sky is blue? Probably not—and there's no harm admitting that to your child when she asks. Tell her you don't know, and look up the information in a reference book together.

Your child may ask a question you find embarrassing but which she, in her innocence, does not (for example, "Why do you always fight with each other?" or "Where do babies come from?"). A young child is much less inhibited and is quite happy to ask about these issues. Such questions might make you feel uncomfortable, perhaps because the question is about sex, or because your child asks it very loudly in a crowded supermarket. You may say, "Let's talk about this when we get home," and then do it. Whatever your own feelings, if your child cares enough to ask a question about something personal then she deserves a reply—one that is honest, yet worded so that she understands what you say. Never tell your child that she shouldn't ask such questions, since she may become afraid to express herself openly.

See also *Knowledge; Learning Skills.*

R

Reading Your child will learn to read when he starts school, but you can do a lot before that to stimulate his interest in this vital educational skill. Start the process early by having lots of books in your child's room at home, by singing him songs, by telling him nursery rhymes, by playing word games with him, and by reading him stories. This will trigger your child's interest in reading during the first few years of life.

Later on, when your child is about the age of three or four years, he'll want to get more involved in reading itself. Instead of passively listening to the story, your child will sit beside you, looking closely at the book, even though he can't read a word of it. Your child may point to the words and ask you what they are. At this stage, he doesn't even know that the letters represent sounds. Encourage your child's enthusiasm by discussing the story with him and answering any questions he raises. Let your child see that the book starts at the first page and finishes at the last, that it should be held upright, and that you read the words from left to right. Always choose books that are suitable for the age of your child.

These prereading activities are most effective when they are fun. Spend a few minutes every day running through them with your child, building up his confidence slowly and steadily. He should find such activities enjoyable, fun, and relaxing—so don't get anxious, tense, or angry with your child. He'll develop reading-related skills at his own rate. By the time your child starts school, he will probably be able to recognize his own name and also be able to identify some street signs.

See also *Language Development; Language Stimulation; School Readiness.*

Reflexes Healthy new babies have a number of automatic, or reflex, actions, some of which are used by pediatricians to assess your child immediately after birth. You may have noticed that as soon as your baby was born, she was briefly examined by medical and nursing staff, who gave her an Apgar assessment. Devised in the 1950s by an American doctor, the Apgar system gives a rating of two, one, or zero to the following physical characteristics: heart rate, breathing, muscle tone, reflexes, and color. The higher the score, the better. A healthy baby will probably score at least seven; a score of less than this indicates the baby may be at risk, and a score of four or under indicates the baby may be in a critical condition. The assessment is repeated five minutes later. Reflexes are a crucial part of early development.

A newborn baby's reflexes include the following:

- *Swallowing.* Your baby knows how to swallow and breathe at the same time, without choking.

- *Sucking.* When a finger or nipple is placed in your baby's mouth, she automatically starts to suck.

- *Rooting.* Your baby will turn her head toward a finger or nipple that gently strokes her cheek.

- *Grasping.* When an object or finger presses down on the palm of your baby's hand, she will grasp it firmly.

- *Walking.* When held upright with her feet barely touching the floor, your baby will take a few small steps.

- *The Moro, or startle, reflex.* If your baby hears a loud noise, or is moved suddenly so that her head drops back, she will fling out her arms and legs, open her hands, arch her back, and then bring her arms together as though trying to catch something.

Some of these reflexes persist throughout a baby's life and are necessary for basic survival (for example, sucking, swallowing), while others fade during the first year (for example, the Moro reflex, rooting). Some scientists believe that many of the reflexes that disappear soon after birth were useful at an earlier period in human evolution, but are no longer required. For instance, a grasping reflex would have been helpful when humans' ancestors lived in trees.

Although reflexes are inborn and are essential for healthy development, a baby also begins to learn actively about the world around her from birth.

See also Knowledge; Learning through Play.

Religion
Many families are deeply religious. A home life with religious commitment provides a structure that can be a source of comfort and security for young children.

The mind of a child is particularly receptive to a belief in God. Your child might not have the same concept of God as adults, but he will happily accept the existence of a deity. He won't challenge the view that God makes the world the way it is, because this notion makes sense to him. If you respect religious values, then your child will almost certainly follow your example in the preschool years. When your child grows older—especially when he reaches adolescence—he may begin to look at alternative systems of belief.

Children usually take great delight in religious ritual. Attending a place of worship can prove a fascinating experience for an eager young mind. The rituals and prayers can be a source of wonder. When a child develops an interest in religion early in life, it is often maintained, perhaps even into adulthood. A strong religious tradition within a family can give a growing child a sense of respect for himself and others.

See also Religious Differences.

Religious Differences
Parents don't always share the same religious beliefs. In many marriages partners have different religious backgrounds. In such instances, a child may find religion confusing rather than comforting, especially if her parents have not reconciled their differences.

The time for a couple to sort out their religious differences is before children are born. The best time is before the marriage itself—this way, the couple has plenty of time to consider all the angles. Religion usually engenders strong feelings. Giving up one religion for another—even when this conversion is in the best interests of the family—can be a very painful process. Discussions about the religious upbringing of children should never be left to the last minute.

Some couples in a mixed marriage take the view that their child should be brought up to experience both religions in the home, and that when she is old enough she should choose for herself. Although this may seem a common-sense solution to the predicament, giving a child an opportunity to choose her religion places too great a responsibility onto young shoulders. Religious systems are complex; many adults cannot explain the ins and outs of their own religion. It is unreasonable to expect a young child to make such a decision. Parents must make the choice for their child. In later years, the child may elect to challenge her parents' religious views. That is part of growing up. But parents should provide firm guidance at the start.

Even where partners in a mixed marriage agree on one religion, problems can arise through pressure from friends and family. Wars start through differences in religious belief, so it is hardly surprising that family skirmishes can erupt for the same reason. A child who experiences religious tolerance within his own family is likely to adopt a similar attitude herself outside the home.

Both partners need to have their own views clear before they can hope to provide an adequate example for their child to follow. If religious differences between husband and wife are not resolved, and if they continue into married life, their children will come to regard religion as a source of conflict, not as a source of security.

See also Religion.

Responsibility
Part of growing up involves learning about responsibility for others, about caring for others, and about considering the feelings of others. Although your child doesn't start of with a sense of responsibility, this will develop gradually during the preschool years, with your help. You can do a lot to encourage responsibility in these formative years.

Consider the following three main strategies: First, set an example. Young children learn best by imitating their parents and, to a lesser extent, by imitating siblings. This is particularly true for a toddler around the age of two years. Demonstrating basic acts of responsibility at home (such as pouring your child a drink of juice, helping him tidy his toys) show your child how to behave responsibly. And the effect of these demonstrations is increased by telling your child what you are doing ("I'm tidying your toys for you because that helps you keep your room nice."). The more you and your children behave in a caring way toward each other, the more responsible they will become.

Second, explain why responsibility matters. If possible, try to tell your child the significance of responsible behavior. Use words that he can understand, and point out that acting responsibly benefits everyone. For instance, remind your child that if he helps his siblings, they are likely to help him when he needs their support. Persist with these explanations, even though your child may seem disinterested or unconvinced. He'll eventually grasp the reciprocal nature of these sorts of actions.

And third, give your child tasks that involve responsibility. A toddler can carry out a simple household chore (such as putting a piece of paper in the wastebasket), and an older child can carry out a more-complex chore (such as setting the table for the evening meal). The act of behaving responsibly is a very powerful form of learning how to be responsible. You may want to establish a small list of minor chores for your children to follow on a reasonably regular basis.

Keeping a pet is another way to teach the concept of caring. Small pets, such as a hamster or gerbil, can be looked after by a young child (under supervision), and this helps your child develop the concept of social and personal responsibility.

See also Kindness; Modeling; Sociable Play.

Road Safety
You are responsible for teaching road safety to your child. You can't wait until your child is at school. By then, it might be too late. Set a good example yourself. If you jaywalk and take risks, so will your child.

Pedestrian accidents are the major cause of death among children: figures from the World Health Organization show that pedestrian accidents constitute between 35 and 50 percent of all accidental deaths of children under the age of fourteen years. Children are a vulnerable group of pedestrians, but the children between five and nine years of age are most at risk. About twice as many boys as girls are hit by cars.

You must explain to your child the dangers of traffic (and, depending on her age, you might even have to explain what "traffic" is)—about the effect that a car has when it hits a pedestrian and about the need to stop, look, and listen for cars when crossing the road. This explanation is a very important part of road safety, but it won't be sufficient on its own.

Give your child a basic explanation. Then go out to the street with her, in order to demonstrate that some parts of the road are better for crossing than others. Specify why (because you can see, and the traffic is less heavy) and emphasize that she should always use a pedestrian crosswalk or traffic light when getting from one side of the road to the other. Give your child first-hand experience crossing at a traffic light and at a pedestrian crossing.

While showing your child how to cross the street, ask her lots of questions. What might happen if she runs across the road without first looking for cars? When should she start to cross? What should she do if the "don't walk" signal starts to flash when she's half-way across? How should she cross the road if she can't find a suitable crossing point? Encourage your child to think about road safety, and to see the purpose of it. This way, your child is more likely to be safe. Encourage her to notice traffic when she is outside with you. Your child should be able to differentiate busy roads from quiet roads, and trucks from cars. She should also know that she can be seen more easily when she wears light-colored clothing. She should realize that crossing at a place with no parked cars is safer than crossing between parked cars. Your child's awareness will help ensure her road safety.

See also *Hazards; Streetproofing.*

Routine Every child needs consistency and structure in his life. Knowing that some events in everyday life are predictable gives your child a sense of security, a sense of well-being. A regular routine, especially in early childhood, also gives parents a sense of well-being. Ask any mom and dad who are woken up regularly through the night by a baby who wants to be fed or to play—they'll soon tell you how much they want to establish a nighttime routine with their infant!

Routines help an older child as well. Most three- and four-year-olds like to know that they go to playgroup on Mondays and Wednesdays, that they go swimming on Fridays, and that weekends are for family outings. This sort of structure enables a child to plan ahead. Later in life, he'll be much more able to organize himself if he's had the experience of doing it in childhood.

However, too much structure and routine can be counterproductive. Some parents preplan their child's day to such an extent that he is propelled from one activity to another, without having any time to reflect on his enjoyment of them. Your child's days and weeks should always be flexible enough to allow for a change of plan; and your child should always have some free time in which to plan his own activities.

Try to involve your child in planning his own routines, even at a very early age. Naturally, your child's idea of a suitable time for bed will be different from yours, but he is more likely to feel comfortable with a routine that takes his own views into account than with one that he feels has been imposed upon him.

See also Bedtime; Discipline; Hospital; Illness; Overorganized.

Rules Every child needs structure and consistency in her life. True, a toddler seems to spend more time challenging rules than following them, but without them she would be totally confused. Insecurity and anxiety would soon set in. Rules serve a number of psychological purposes for your child during the preschool years:

- *Comfort.* We all need to know that our lives have some degree of structure, and that knowledge makes us feel safe, secure, and comfortable. Rules reduce ambiguity and replace uncertainly with a clear plan of action, which makes us feel better.

- *Predictability.* Of course, novelty is exciting for children and adults. Yet, we are generally happier when we are able to anticipate what comes next. Rules allow your child to predict how you and others will behave toward her.
- *Reassurance.* The reciprocal nature of rules is reassuring for your child because she knows that the rule "No hitting" applies to her siblings as well as to her; in other words, it protects her as much as anyone else. This makes your child feel safer.

Another benefit of rules is that they safeguard your child's physical safety. Most rules for young children are concerned with protecting them from accident and injury. Although your child may not appreciate this at the time, she will gradually understand that following rules normally saves her from danger.

Try to be flexible with rules at home. While having rules but not keeping them consistently is pointless, there is always a place for flexibility. Sometimes you don't apply a particular rule, perhaps because your child is unwell that day, or because it is a special occasion and you are prepared to give your child a little extra freedom. That's fine, as long as such exceptions don't become too regular. Flexibility reinforces the value of rules, while showing that they are always open to interpretation.

See also Discipline; Routine.

S

Scapegoat Some children get blamed even when they haven't done anything. Psychologists use the term "scapegoating" when one particular child always gets blamed for mishaps, whether he is actually responsible for what has happened or not.

This type of scapegoating occurs when parents deal with stress by inadvertently redirecting their anxieties onto their child. Scapegoating happens to some extent in every family; few parents are able to resist the temptation to shout at their child from time to time when they themselves are upset. Such incidents, if isolated, will not cause long-term psychological problems for your child, though he won't like it, and you may feel thoroughly guilty yourself after your temper has cooled.

When parents or teachers regularly scapegoat a child, more serious emotional effects could result. The child may become locked into a vicious circle of ever-lowering self-esteem. Scapegoating makes a child lose his self-respect, which adversely affects his relationships with others, which in turn decreases his self-respect.... And so it goes in a never-ending cycle.

To determine whether scapegoating is happening in your family, ask yourself these questions:

- *Is my child willing to take the blame for things that go wrong at home, even when he is almost certainly not responsible?* A child who is scape-goated becomes conditioned to admit to any mishap, and automatically stands first in line to receive punishment even though he is totally innocent.

- *Do I nag at my child constantly over trivial matters?* Of course, your child may be going through a genuinely difficult phase, and your nonstop complaints may be justified. However, it could be that your child has become a convenient punching bag on which to release your own frustrations.

- *Does my child accept every reprimand without challenge, even when he initially appears surprised at the accusations?* Most children become upset when they think they are unfairly blamed. A child accustomed to being scape-goated soon stops defending himself because he knows it's not worthwhile.

Do you feel under a lot of stress, and do you also feel that your child never gives you any time to be on your own? Emotional pressure diminishes our patience to deal with the minor hassles of everyday life. In this situation, your child's normal demands can seem intolerable, and you may reprimand him when he's really not misbehaving at all.

The following suggestions may help you reduce—or avoid altogether—scapegoating in your family:

- *Talk openly with your partner about your worries.* Honest communication is the best way to alleviate the sorts of personal stress that can lead to your children being scape-goated.

- *Be prepared to accept that you are not perfect, that you can make mistakes just like anyone else.* Parents who have trouble accepting their fallibility will always try to put the blame on someone else—probably their child.

- *Explain to your child why he's being punished.* Instead of merely blaming your child for his actions, give him reasons for your action. Your child is less likely to feel scape-goated if he is given an explanation for each reprimand. You may even discover, when you hear your own explanation, that it isn't a very valid reason for punishing him.

- *Be willing to say "I'm sorry" to your child if you have wrongly accused him of something he didn't do.* You are not weak to apologize. Your child deserves honesty from you, and your willingness to show regret sets a good example.

A child may make himself the family scapegoat—even though he isn't consciously aware he's doing so—as a means of getting attention. If you think this describes your child, then it is you who has to change your behavior, not him. Instead of attending to your child only when he misbehaves, give him attention when he behaves. Tell him how pleased you are that he's not breaking any rules, and find a few minutes each day when you and your child can spend time together. This will reduce your child's need to attract blame in order to get your attention. Try to ignore some of your child's disruptive misbehavior. The more your child realizes that making himself a scapegoat doesn't get extra attention, the less likely he is to behave this way.

See also *Attention-Seeking Behavior; Bullying; Guilt; Lying; Stealing; Swearing; Victim.*

School, Choice of In some school boards, parents can't choose the school their child will attend. In others, you have a choice. Most parents select their local primary school because most of their child's friends will attend that school. Starting school is a new stage in your child's life, and the experience will be easier for her if her friends start school with her. Another reason to choose your local school is that your older children may already attend it; having children at two or three different schools can cause practical problems.

Whether your child goes to her local school or someplace else, you should be satisfied that the school you choose is the one most able to meet your child's needs, the one you definitely want your child to attend. The only way you can find this out is by visiting the school yourself or, when choosing between a number of schools, by visiting each one. This may be time-consuming, but this time is well spent—after all, your child will spend six or eight or ten years there!

Phone each school well in advance—in the term before your child's starting date—in order to make an appointment with the principal. The response you receive to your telephone call will give you an initial idea of the way the school reacts to visitors. Don't bring your child with you when you go on your initial visit.

During this visit, you must know what to look for—for instance, the general atmosphere, the reading program used at the primary levels, musical activities. The following list gives suggestions for the issues you should probably consider, but you may be particularly concerned with some others. Make a list of questions and take it with you.

- *Classroom teacher.* If possible, meet the teacher who will be responsible for your child's class. Talk to the teacher about the work he or she does, the equipment he or she uses, and the range of activities he or she provides for pupils. During your discussion—and don't be afraid to ask lots of questions—assess the teacher's attitude toward children, and decide whether you are comfortable with the ideas the teacher presents. Would you like to have this teacher if you were starting school?

- *Staffing.* Aside from your child's teacher, you will want to know the number of other teachers and the total number of pupils. The school may have specialist teachers who have responsibility for such areas as pupils with learning difficulties, music, drama, or science. You can also inquire whether additional help is available from an assistant teacher.

- *Building.* A clean, solid school building does not necessarily mean that teaching standards are satisfactory. But children do learn better in a fresh, appealing classroom with adequate heating, than they do in a cold, shabby building, with paint peeling off the walls and water coming in through the roof. Have a good look around your child's prospective classroom—it should have a stimulating appearance, with plenty of wall displays, separate work and play areas, and a good range of books and equipment.

- *Educational standards.* The early stage of schooling focuses more on settling in, learning to handle a routine, belonging to a group, and following class rules, than it does on learning in the academic sense. But your child will make great educational strides in these first few years, so ask about the school's approach to the teaching of reading, writing, spelling, and math: the approach should be systematic and well planned.

- *Breadth of curriculum.* The school curriculum consists of more than the three Rs. Many subjects traditionally associated with secondary schooling are now also taught in primary schools, such as science, environmental studies, history, geography, and modern languages. The principal will tell you which of these are covered, and how frequently they appear in the curriculum. You may also want to inquire about other subjects, such as drama, art, music, library programs, and physical education.

- *Computer technology.* Although you may not be familiar with computers, your child will be by the time she leaves school. Most primary schools have computers available for their pupils, but not all of them use them in an effective, structured way. Ask the teachers about how they use computer technology as part of the curriculum, and the amount of time available for individual children to have hands-on experience.

- *Parental liaison.* Parents have a right to be made welcome in their child's school, and to be kept up-to-date with her progress. This can be achieved through home-school diaries, parent afternoons, parent helpers in the classroom, and parents' nights. Many schools operate an "open-door" policy for parents.

After talking about these points during your visit, you'll be ready to make an informed choice. If you are still uncertain, think about the issues that trouble you, and perhaps make a second visit before reaching a decision. This advice also applies to private schools; don't assume that all private schools are of a high standard simply because parents pay for their children to attend.

See also School Readiness.

School Readiness Most children are psychologically and physically ready for school when the first day of kindergarten finally arrives. But some are not, and they may find school a daunting experience because they will be unable to meet some of the demands placed upon them. You can help your child reach a state of readiness for school by ensuring that, by the time your child is of school age, he is competent in the following key areas of development:

- *Social (independence).* Your child should be able to
    - go to the toilet on his own, and tidy himself afterwards;
    - wash his hands and face;
    - take his coat off and hang it on a hook;
    - share and take turns;
    - listen to an adult and follow basic instructions;
    - tidy up toys and books when requested to do so;

- play happily with a small group of children his own age;
- deal with difficulties without having a tantrum;
- manage eating, without help;
- separate from you without becoming unduly upset.

• *Educational.* Your child should be able to
- listen attentively to a short story;
- identify colors and give their names;
- correctly name one or two basic shapes;
- know his name, address, and phone number;
- talk clearly in sentences;
- recite a few favorite nursery rhymes;
- concentrate on an activity for at least five minutes.

• *Physical.* Your child should be able to
- put on his shoes and jacket;
- catch a large ball thrown gently to him;
- walk steadily along a straight line;
- run quickly without falling over;
- jump off the ground, with both feet in the air at the same time;
- take off his shoes and then put them on again.

Having these skills doesn't mean your child will manage everything in school without difficulty, but it will help him settle in more easily. If your child isn't able to do all these things, it doesn't mean that school will be too demanding for him, but do practice them with him at home, in order to boost your child's competence and self-confidence.

See also *Concentration; Coordination; Hand-Eye Coordination; Independence; Knowledge; Learning Skills; School, Choice of; Social Development.*

Security Objects Most children have a comforter, a security object when they are tired or unhappy, at some stage in the preschool years. The object could be a teddy bear or a tattered crib blanket. You may be amazed at the importance your child places on such a scruffy object, but it's the familiarity of its smell, appearance, and texture that matters to your child.

Psychologists claim that the use of comforters originates in the early months of life, when a baby begins to associate particular items with pleasant, loving sensations. A teddy bear becomes associated with love because your baby hugs it close in her crib as she falls asleep; the crib blanket becomes associated with warmth and security because you wrap your child in it while you cuddle her. Although your child learns how to obtain emotional satisfaction in other ways as she grows up, this does not eradicate the pleasant memory of babyhood. Your child's comforter becomes a way to relive these earlier happy life experiences, because she still associates warmth and kindness with the object. Even though this association is formed early in your child's life, it remains strong in later years.

A child can have a comfort habit, such as thumb-sucking, rather than a comfort object. Adults often become annoyed with preschool children who thumb-suck. Dentists are aware that continuation of the habit beyond the age of five may push the child's second set of teeth out of line. When this happens, orthodontic treatment to correct the defect is necessary.

If you do want your child to stop thumb-sucking (or any irritating habit), do the following:

- *Decrease the habit gradually.* An adult who wants to give up smoking often finds it easier to do it gradually; so does a child who needs to stop thumb-sucking. Set a time scale of, say, eight weeks, during which time you hope to eliminate the habit.

- *Explain to your child why she should stop the habit.* Use language your child can understand; for instance, tell her that the habit looks awful, or that her teeth will be damaged. A child aged three or more will understand this sort of explanation.

- *Select one short occasion, during which your child usually sucks her thumb, and use this as your starting point.* It may be when your child watches television, or perhaps when you read to her. Give your child advance warning that you don't want her to suck her thumb on that specific occasion on that specific day.

- *Slowly increase the number of occasions your child has to manage without thumb-sucking.* Build up gradually from once every two days, to once every day, to twice every day. Decide on a clear plan of action, and stick to it.

- *Give your child lots of praise when you see progress.* Each day that you see the thumb-sucking decrease, let your child know you are pleased. Make a big fuss over her achievements.

- *Don't use techniques based on avoidance principles.* Strategies such as painting your child's finger with pepper sauce or covering the offending thumb with a bandage, rarely work. This usually makes a child more determined to persist. You may get lucky and have instant success, but if you take an aversive approach you run the risk of confrontation.

Constant use of a security object can be a sign of insecurity. If your child reaches the stage where she cannot go anywhere without it, then her dependence on the object has become too great. This may be the first sign that your child is deeply unhappy. Young children become anxious for many reasons. Failing to get something right at school, having a poor relationship with parents, being reprimanded by mom and dad, not being invited to a birthday party, catching a cold, noticing that a pet is unwell, experiencing a family bereavement—all these can undermine a young child's sense of well-being.

Rather than getting annoyed at your child, take a closer look at her life to establish why she may feel insecure. Sensitive consideration is necessary. Once the reason for your child's unhappiness is identified and resolved, then her reliance on the comforter will ease.

Security objects can be used positively to help a child through difficult experiences. In some situations, the calculated use of a security object can boost your child's self-confidence enough to help her cope with stress. For instance, when a child ends up in the hospital as a result of an accident or ill health, taking a favorite toy with her will make your child feel more at ease. She may be emotionally vulnerable without it, and you will do no harm by letting your child have the object in these circumstances. The same applies to vacations. Strange rooms with unfamiliar noises can make your child distressed when she tries to sleep at night. Having her favorite blanket can ease your child's anxious feelings, and make everyone's holiday more enjoyable.

See also *Masturbation; Pacifiers; Teeth; Unhappiness.*

Self-Confidence
Children with low self-confidence are more likely to experience emotional and educational difficulties, have little faith in their ability to deal with everyday problems, be afraid to express their own ideas for fear of ridicule, and prefer to play a passive role in social relationships.

The foundations for self-confidence are laid at home—the way you interact with your child plays a major part. The more positive the interest you take in your child's life, the more likely he is to realize you value him, and the more likely he is to value himself. Spend a few minutes listening to your child's stories—no matter how boring and trivial they may seem; your attention will have a positive effect on your child's self-confidence.

Consider how often you make derogatory comments to your child about his behavior. If your child is going through a particularly difficult phase, in which he whines and demands lots of attention, try to avoid falling into the habit of constantly reprimanding him. Repeated negative remarks from parent to child will reduce the child's confidence. It is better to ignore the small incidents, or to take action without actually saying anything: for instance, by simply removing the pen he is using to draw on the back of his hand.

Psychologists have shown that self-confidence is also related to the way discipline is exercised at home; children with lots of self-confidence tend to have parents who have clear expectations about behavior and who are prepared to follow them consistently. A child thrives best in a family environment that has predictable and consistent standards. Sometimes you knowingly let your child break the rules, perhaps because you are too tired to bother. This is perfectly normal, but if it becomes a regular pattern, and if discipline fluctuates from day to day, then your child's self-confidence will drop.

The use of praise is important. Parents of children with high self-confidence tend to use praise to encourage their child's good behavior rather than punishments to discourage bad behavior. While discipline undoubtedly has its place, repeated punishment has the effect of focusing attention on a child's wrongdoings. Punishment emphasizes the child's negative characteristics and weakens his self-confidence. A more effective strategy is to praise your child when he behaves well, when he does what you expect of him. This technique makes a child more aware of his positive characteristics.

You can increase your child's self-confidence by letting him make basic decisions about his day-to-day care. Family life is hectic, and it is often a lot easier for you to make all the decisions, yet your child needs to have some control over his world. Allow your child the opportunity to make some choices, whether he wants Cheerios or granola for breakfast or whether his new shoes will be brown or black. A child who makes such decisions will tend to have higher self-confidence.

Succeeding in a challenging task is the greatest boost to self-confidence. You know what it's like when you try to learn a new skill. At first you think you'll never do it. Then (after extensive practice) comes that sweet moment of success, that moment when you feel everything connect. A great feeling, isn't it? A child feels the same way when he achieves success.

Whatever skill your child tries to master, a useful approach is to break the task into very small steps, each one a slight progression ahead of the previous one. For instance, the first stage in learning to ride a bicycle could be for your child to sit on the bike, hands on the handlebars, while you hold the bicycle steady. The next step could be for your child to sit on the bike while you push it along the road. Continue this progression until you reach the last step, when he can pedal the bicycle himself. Each stage should be just a little bit harder than the previous one, yet not so difficult that your child feels it is beyond his reach. At every stage that your child is successful, shower him with praise.

See also Attractiveness; Discipline; Emotional Deprivation; Learning Skills; Routine.

Separation and Divorce Every married couple
argues from time to time; that's part of normal married life. With some couples, the endless arguments are a symptom of much deeper relationship difficulties. For these partners, the outcome may be separation or divorce. Many children will spend some time living in the home of a single parent.

This increasingly common breakdown of family life happens for a number of reasons:

- *Female independence.* Women as a social group are at their highest-ever level of independence. Many women are able to take on the role of provider, following separation or divorce, because they have a career.

- *Female identity.* Many women realize that they have skills and talents of their own, that they are not simply adjuncts to their husbands. This increase in self-confidence and self-awareness means that a woman will not necessarily be prepared to sacrifice herself to years of unhappy marriage.

- *Male ego.* Some men feel threatened by the change in a woman's position within the family and within society, and are unable to accept what they regard as an imbalance in their relationship; this eventually leads to the collapse of their marriage.

- *Social tolerance.* Being a single parent has less social stigma attached to it than, say, twenty years ago.

Members of older generations often yearn for the days when "marriages were for life." This philosophy fails to acknowledge that many marriages that were superficially happy in the "good

old days" were actually miserable. Staying together in such circumstances may have looked good to outsiders, but those inside
the marriage—including the children—suffered emotionally.

There is no psychological justification for the advice that a
couple should continue with their unhappy marriage solely for
the sake of their children. Some parents claim that, although
they have no love for each other, their children are unaware of
the true feelings existing between them. They believe that since
they have not openly flaunted their disagreements at home,
their animosity is concealed. But long silences at mealtimes, an
absence of loving response between them, and a subdued family atmosphere all tell a child that something is wrong.

Parents who desperately love their children, and who don't
want to separate because of this, may find this gives them enough
motivation to change their marital relationship so that their partnership can continue in a revitalized way. This is totally different
from staying together in a stagnant relationship for the sake of the
children because it involves positive change. It is a forward step.

Social attitudes toward divorce fluctuate from decade to
decade. Children will always be at risk psychologically when
their parents separate:

- *A child needs stable family relationships.* Failure to form at
  least one firm emotional connection with an adult by the
  age of three or four can have long-term detrimental effects
  on personality development. Parents have difficulty giving
  their children essential love and attention when they struggle to manage life.

- *A child models her behavior on her parents.* In a family beset
  with hostilities between the mother and father, a child is
  presented with a disturbed model of behavior that she is
  likely to imitate.

- *Parents who fight constantly are likely to use their children as a
  way to retaliate against their partner.* One parent may deliberately exercise different levels of control to aggravate the other
  parent. Using a child in this way will only upset the child
  even further.

- *Every child wants to have both parents and will do her best to remain loyal to both.* The end of a marriage does not mean the end of a child's love for either of her parents. The child does not want to have to choose one over the other, or to form a negative opinion about either parent.

Evidence from psychological research reinforces the positive value of a child maintaining contact with both parents following separation or divorce. One study of divorced families found that five years after the divorce about a third of the children managed well and had no emotional difficulties, about a third managed reasonably well, and the remainder showed signs of emotional difficulties. The main difference between the copers and the other two groups was that the copers saw both parents regularly. The children with emotional difficulties tended to be those who seldom, if ever, saw one of their parents.

The high incidence of divorce in recent years has allowed psychologists to look closely at its long-term psychological effects. Encouragingly, research confirms that children from disrupted families are no more likely to be delinquents than other children, nor are they more likely to have educational problems or social difficulties.

Most of the bad psychological effects of divorce seem to lessen once the family rebuilds itself and adjusts to the new circumstances. The responsibility for carrying the family through the crisis rests with the adults, not with the children. Any emotional damage that results from parental separation will not be permanent if the adults act in a sensitive and reasonable way.

See also Fathers; Modeling; Mothers; Quarrels; Single-Parent Family; Stepparents; Working Mothers.

Sex Education Even if you don't tackle the subject of sex education directly, your child will learn about sex based on what he hears others say in the schoolyard, on what he sees on television, and on your reaction when he asks you questions. A child who isn't given sex education by his parents may evolve his own ridiculous or possibly frightening theories. Sexual understanding now will better prepare your child for personal relationships in adulthood.

To be ready for your child's questions, you must clarify your own ideas and feelings. If you feel embarrassed talking about sex, your child will sense it. Practice out loud using sex-related words until you feel comfortable saying them. This will help reduce your own tension. Every family has its own ideas on nudity, but very often, in families where the parents sleep naked, or where the young children are allowed into the bathroom when mom or dad takes a bath, the children are able to talk about body parts in a casual way, without feeling embarrassed or guilty.

"Where did I come from?" is usually the first question that an inquiring four- or five-year-old asks about sex. A satisfactory answer is to say that he came out of mom's tummy. Most children of this age will accept such an answer and will ask no further questions, because their thought processes are not as mature as adults'.

Answer at your child's level of understanding. Don't go into unnecessary details unless he asks. Telling a child under the age of five about the ins and outs of the male and female reproductive systems, about eggs and sperm, will only confuse him. Keep your replies simple and direct; treat sexual inquiries as you would treat any other aspect of his curiosity.

Your child may ask the same questions over and over again, and require the same explanation to be repeated many times. Be patient—this repetition is a natural part of your child's learning process. Simply because you tell him once that a baby comes from mom's tummy, doesn't mean that he will remember it, or even that he will believe it! Your child should always feel able to approach you about sex.

Older children want to know how he got into mom's tummy in the first place. At this point, your explanations should start to involve the fact that sex occurs within a caring relationship. Of course, you know that sexual intercourse frequently occurs in a casual nonloving relationship, but leave that aside until your child is older. Sex discussions should always be set in the context of a loving partnership. Explain that dad and mom loved each other so much that they wanted to have a baby, so dad put his seed into mom. Give just enough information to answer every question. Your child may quickly become bored with anything more complex; you may even find that half-way through your detailed explanation, your child's eyes glaze over.

Books written specially for children can provide a useful starting point for sex education. Most of them provide very basic information on conception and birth, within a family setting. The advantage of using this sort of book is that it will give you the chance to prepare your ideas in advance. Your local library will probably have a reasonable selection; make sure the book you choose portrays sex in a way with which you are comfortable. For example, some books show the adults walking around the house naked, and this may not reflect your own family values; some may use terms that you don't use, and this could cause confusion. Read the book carefully from cover to cover before you select it for your child.

Sex education is a lifelong process that continues with, or without, parental guidance. If you use opportunities to discuss sex with your child, as they arise out of everyday life, your child will have a basic understanding of sex by the time he is seven or eight. If you discourage sex discussions in the earlier years, you leave your child vulnerable to the influence of the misguided gossip that circulates in the schoolyard.

See also Masturbation; Questions; Sexual Abuse; Sexual Curiosity.

Sexism
You probably don't regard yourself as sexist, and you are probably confident that you give your children equal opportunities irrespective of their sex. But think about your own attitudes for a moment.

Have you ever bought a pink outfit for a baby boy, or a blue outfit for a baby girl? Chances are, you automatically associate pink with girls and blue with boys. Have you ever described a boy as pretty or a girl as handsome? Probably not; we have certain words that we use to describe boys and others that we use to describe girls.

Virtually all of us are sexist to some extent (we have a stereo-typed view of the behavior and emotions that we expect from boys and girls), even though we may not be consciously aware of having such an outlook. Children are affected by this attitude. The sex-role stereotypes that you hold will influence your children's gender identity (their sense of "boyness" and "girlness").

Psychological studies have revealed that women behave differently toward boys than they do toward girls—without realizing it—especially when the children are under five years old. For instance, mothers tend to keep a baby girl closer to them and spend more time in direct contact with her than they do with a baby boy. They tend to encourage boys to be more adventurous than girls. They also tend to praise and criticize girls more than boys.

Another investigation focused on the emotions that mothers assume their young children have. Detailed interviews with a number of mothers of children aged from two to three years revealed that they are reluctant to admit that girls have negative feelings such as bad temper and aggressiveness. Yet they have no difficulty attributing these emotions to boys. In other words, mothers expect boys to be angry, hostile, and antisocial at times, but not girls.

Your attitude toward gender will be reflected in your child's attitudes. If you have a lifestyle that is traditionally associated with your gender, then your child is likely to regard this as the normal pattern. If you have the attitude that boys are better than girls at sports such as soccer and baseball, then your child will begin to think the same way. Children are more likely to be broad-minded when their parents are less sexist in outlook.

Sexism is often seen in children's literature. While most contemporary writers of children's books present a more balanced perspective, this change is relatively recent.

Children as young as two have very clear ideas about sex roles. At this age both boys and girls tend to think that girls like to play with dolls, help their mother, cook dinner, clean the house, talk a lot, play without hitting, and ask for help frequently; and both boys and girls think that boys like to play with cars, help their father, build things, and tell others "I can hit you." By school age, these ideas have become even more firmly fixed. Most children at this age hold the following beliefs:

- Males have more physical strength than females.
- Boys fight more than girls.
- Girls get hurt more easily than boys.
- Boys and girls wear different clothes.
- Boys are not expected to show feelings as openly as girls.
- Girls are expected to be more helpless when under stress.
- Girls respond to polite requests more than boys do.

If you want to encourage your child to have a less-conventional, less-stereotyped view of sex roles, do the following:

- *Be aware of your own views.* You must have a clear and honest understanding of your own thoughts about sex roles—only then will you be ready to change (if necessary) the way you interact with your child.

- *Provide your child with a wide range of toys.* Make sure you have a range of so-called "boy" and "girl" toys, and at times encourage your child to play with toys traditionally associated with the opposite gender.

- *Be discriminating in your choice of children's books.* Read all books before you give them to your child. This way you can avoid any material that is stereotyped in the way sex roles are presented.

- *Offer examples of unconventional sex roles.* Make your child aware that many people occupy jobs that are usually associated with the opposite sex. Top chefs, for instance, are often men, and more women are engineers and pilots than ever before.

See also *Gender Play.*

Sexual Abuse Physical contact between parent and child is a normal, healthy part of healthy family relationships. Sexual abuse, however, is a criminal offense, and does not necessarily involve physical contact. Sexual abuse is any interaction between a child and an older person where the child is used for a sexual purpose. Following are several types of sexual abuse:

- sexual interference;
- invitation to sexual touching;
- sexual exploitation of a child;
- parent or guardian procuring sexual activity from a child;
- exposing genitals to a child;
- incest;
- indecent acts;
- sexual assault.

Following are some questions that parents frequently ask about sexual abuse involving children:

Q. *Does child sexual abuse occur spontaneously, and is it due to the abuser's sudden and uncontrollable sexual urges?*
A. Although some acts of child sexual abuse are spontaneous, most abusers are quite calculating in their actions. They often manipulate their child victims into obedience and silence by threatening further abuse ("If you tell, I'll kill you."), or by introducing the notion of shame ("Your mother will be so ashamed of you if she finds out what you've been doing."), or even loyalty ("You shouldn't tell on me because we're related."). The idea that child sexual abusers have no control over their actions implies that they have no responsibility for what they do.

Q. *Does sexual abuse occur only in families who live in poverty and environmental deprivation?*
A. Sexual abuse is not confined to one particular social or economic class, or ethnic group. It exists at all levels of society in many different countries.

Q. *Is child sexual abuse really such a big problem, or is it simply a case of the media blowing up a few isolated incidents out of proportion?*
A. Precise figures are difficult to determine because many victims are afraid or embarrassed to disclose sexual abuse. It is estimated that

- one in four girls is sexually abused before the age of eighteen;
- one in eight boys is sexually abused before the age of eighteen.

Q. *Who are child sexual abusers?*
A. The majority of child sexual abusers are males in their teens to early thirties. Be wary of any adult who wants to be on his own with a child, or to be in situations where the child undresses, bathes, or goes to bed. Most offenders are not strangers; they may be relatives, baby sitters, coaches, and camp counselors. Sexual abuse often takes place in the perpetrator's own home.

Q. *Don't some children encourage adults to touch them?*
A. Blaming the victim turns attention away from the perpetrator of the abuse and toward the child. This is wrong. Children are open and trusting; love and affection are essential parts of the childhood years and so a child often willingly seeks physical contact with an adult. Sexual abusers take advantage of this innocent child behavior to meet their own pernicious needs.

Q. *Is it true that girls most at risk for sexual abuse are those who have reached puberty, and who therefore have developed secondary sexual characteristics?*
A. Studies have revealed that prepubertal girls are most at risk of sexual abuse, especially during the primary-school years. (Girls also tend to be sexually abused at a younger age than boys.)

If a child of any age tells you that he has been sexually abused

- *Believe in the child, no matter how difficult it may be for you to accept.* Children rarely make up stories about this type of abuse.
- *Listen calmly, and allow your child to explain the situation in his own words.* Find a quiet, private place where you will not be disturbed.

- *Reassure your child that he did the right thing by telling you, and that what has happened is not his fault.*

- *Report the incident as soon as possible to the police or your local child protection agency.*

See also *Sexual Curiosity; Violence.*

Sexual Curiosity

Children are fascinated by breasts, bottoms, penises, and vaginas. Most giggle uncontrollably at the very mention of these body parts—or even at the suggestion that they might be mentioned. It's not surprising that children react this way, because these are the organs about which adults get so anxious and make considerable effort to conceal. With this almost-taboo atmosphere surrounding nudity and sexuality, no wonder young children can't wait to find out more.

If children were left to their own devices, without parental interference and restriction, they would probably demonstrate a significant amount of sexual interest anyway. As early as 1927, a researcher investigated the behavior of a primitive tribe that neither encouraged nor discouraged their children from sexual explorations, and found that a large part of the children's spontaneous play was sexually orientated.

Some parents attempt to control their child's sexual behavior—whether it is active inquisitiveness involving another child or simply passing curiosity. Punishing your child with a stern warning about the consequences of a future repetition, or rebuking her with old wives' tales that misinform about the dangers of sex, sidesteps the central issue of the child's sexual curiosity and runs a risk of encouraging the child to associate her genitals with guilt. Your child may think anything to do with sex is naughty, and if this feeling persists in subsequent years, her adult sexuality may be adversely affected.

If you do want to manage your child's sexual curiosity satisfactorily, then do the following:

- *Avoid showing embarrassment about sex.* You can't expect your child to develop a mature sexual attitude if you start to giggle and blush every time the subject is raised. Your child will sense your discomfort.

- *Fit your explanations to your child's level of understanding.* Your advice should be very specific. "Your friend won't want to play with you if you keep pulling her pants down."

- *Keep calm.* If you overreact, your child will soon realize that such behavior is one way to gain your attention. This realization can make her feel very powerful, and may encourage her to persist. It's far better to stay relaxed and level-headed than to let your child see you become angry.

- *Explain about the importance of privacy.* Everybody—no matter what age—has a right to decide who touches them and who does not. Just as your child has times when she doesn't like being kissed and cuddled, so do other people. Explain that the parts of the body covered by a bathing suit are private. Explain to your child in very basic terms about respecting the personal rights of others. If masturbation worries you, tell your child that other people don't like to see her do that; it's private.

- *Take direct action to stop your child's overtly sexual behavior*— such action is not harmful as long as it isn't punishment, and as long as you explain the underlying reasons to your child. If your child always takes off her clothes when she is alone with a particular friend, don't invite that friend to your home for a while. Tell your child why you are unhappy about her behavior, and let her know that she can play with that friend again once they are able to play differently.

See also *Masturbation; Security Objects; Sex Education; Sexual Abuse; Streetproofing; Unhappiness.*

Shyness Every child is shy sometimes. Even the most vivacious, talkative child can freeze when he suddenly finds himself in a new situation or with strangers.

Shyness depends largely on age. Although every child matures at a different rate, the following guidelines apply to most children:

1 week	A newborn baby does not show any signs of shyness. While some infants will take a feeding only from one person, most babies will happily interact with anyone who shows them kindness and interest.
6 months	By this age, an infant has begun to differentiate familiar faces from unfamiliar faces. He can recognize his parents and his brothers and sisters. He will probably be shy and tearful when he sees a stranger.
1 year	The child now has greater awareness of who is familiar and who is not. He remains shy and clingy in new situations, and may even cover his eyes with his hands or arms when a stranger approaches. At mother-and-tot group, he often sits "glued" to his mother, wanting to join in the fun and games, yet not secure enough to go off on his own into the playroom.
2 years	A child of this age has more self-confidence, yet may still hesitate to talk to people he doesn't know. A stranger is more likely to be greeted with silence than with tears. Because a two-year-old is able to walk, he can now leave any situation he doesn't like. When he feels shy, he simply leaves the room.
3 years	Many children of this age are confident enough to accept attention from people whom they do not know well. A typical three-year-old is more able to handle meeting new children and adults; playgroups or nursery schools are well suited to his social needs.
5 years	By this age, most of the earlier signs of shyness have gone, partly as a result of the increased confidence that comes with growing

up, and partly as a result of the experience
of meeting others. Even so, children over
five may still show shyness in a totally new
situation—for instance, on the first day of
school or when joining an activity.

Although shyness is a passing stage for most children, some
children retain their shyness. Some people remain shy all their
lives. An investigation in the United States studied people who
had been described as shy when they were children and then
interviewed them thirty years later. How had shyness affected
their lives? Shy people (compared to those who weren't shy)
were found to have

- married later;
- become parents later;
- entered a stable career later;
- filled a stereotyped gender role within the family;
- achieved less in their job;
- experienced a higher rate of divorce;
- lived a very conventional lifestyle.

These findings don't mean that a shy person is inadequate
or unhappy. However, if you want your shy child to become
more outgoing, then follow the suggestions below:

- *Build up your child's self-confidence.* Shyness stems from a lack
  of self-confidence in his own abilities, so encourage your
  child to feel competent and capable by emphasizing his
  positive attributes—he's kind, he's a good singer—and tell
  him they will make others like him.

- *Give your child lots of opportunities to play with others.* You
  can't expect a shy child to become outgoing unless he meets
  other children. If your child is not at a nursery school, make
  sure he has the chance to play with children of his own age.

- *Don't let your child avoid people.* A shy child would much rather be on his own—but the more you let him avoid meeting other children, the more his shyness will increase.

- *Encourage your child to think of other people.* When a shy child meets someone, he usually spends the first few moments thinking about himself (about his appearance, about whether the other child likes him, about what he will say next) instead of meeting the other child halfway. Suggest that your child imagines what the other child is thinking and feeling; this will distract your child's attention from himself.

- *Teach your child "opening strategies."* Show him specific approaches to use when he meets new people (such as inviting the other child to play a game, or asking him about his favorite television program). A definite plan of action will help your child cope with those first awkward moments.

See also *Friendships; Playgroup/Nursery School; Self-Confidence; Sociable Play; Social Development; Streetproofing.*

Sibling Rivalry "She always gets more than me," or "Why can she stay up later than me?" and "That's not fair!" are familiar cries in most families. Jealousy between children—"sibling rivalry"—is normal and arises because siblings have to share their parents' attention, time, interests, and financial resources.

Most parents will readily admit that family arguments are frequently caused by jealousy between their children. Sibling rivalry can affect every child. Although the oldest child is most prone to jealousy, the youngest too will have moments when she is convinced everyone else in the family gets more than she does. Don't disregard your child's cries of "That's not fair!" If your child feels strongly enough to voice her opinion of unfair treatment, then she deserves to be heard. Ask your child why she feels this way. Her accusation will probably be completely irrational—but you should give her a reasonable reply.

Sensible explanations (such as "Your brother stays up later at night because he's older and doesn't need as much sleep as you do," or "Your sister doesn't have to wash the dishes after meals because she's too young to handle the dishes.") are far more convincing than an irritable retort (such as "You'll go to bed when I decide, whether your brother's in bed or not!").

Violence between your children should not be allowed, although statistics reveal that siblings hit one another in approximately 75 percent of all families. The peak age for physical fights between children in a family is when one of the siblings is two or three years old. If you do spot your children in a physical fight, separate them and reprimand them, but never spank them as a punishment. Violence breeds violence, and you will simply set a poor example if you raise your hands to your children in temper. Instead, show your disapproval verbally, tell your children why you dislike physical attacks, and encourage them to resolve their disagreement with words, not fists. Let your children know that having aggressive feelings occasionally is normal, but that transforming these feelings into aggressive behavior is not acceptable.

Parents can unwittingly cause sibling rivalry. It is very tempting to encourage one child in the family to behave better or to try harder at school by comparing her with one of her brothers or sisters. This technique is unlikely to have the desired effect, but it is virtually guaranteed to intensify feelings of jealousy between the siblings. Judging a child's achievements against those of an older brother or sister will only make the child feel inadequate. The older child may not like such a comparison, either. A more effective strategy is to use a sibling's superior achievements as an aid. For instance, a younger child who struggles to learn to read will benefit more from her older sister's help with her reading homework than she will from an unfavorable comparison.

Encourage your children to play together and to share their toys. The more they understand and accept each other, the less frequently jealous tantrums will occur. Make sure the oldest child is not always the one who gets new things to wear—let the younger child have a turn too.

Jealousy will emerge when love is distributed unfairly in a

family. If you do have a favorite child, never show it, either by your words or by your actions. A child has to learn to manage her feelings of jealousy toward her brothers and sisters, and she must develop a way to keep these natural, but unpleasant, emotions under control so that her enjoyment of life is not impaired. You can help your child deal with sibling rivalry in the following ways:

- *Don't confuse differential treatment with preferential treatment.* They are not the same. One of your children may need lots of cuddles before going out to school in the morning, while another may prefer just to have a smile and a wave from you. Each child has different emotional needs, and you should try to meet these needs even though this may mean treating the children differently. This is unlikely to lead to sibling rivalry.

- *Give each of your children individual attention.* Simple logistics dictate that the more children you have, the busier you become. Whenever you have time, spend some of it with each child individually, whether reading a story at bedtime, or taking a walk in the park, or spending a special day together.

See also *Age Gap; Birth Order; Equality; First-Born Jealousy; Jealousy.*

Single-Parent Family This term covers several kinds
of families, each with quite different backgrounds. It can apply to a family that has experienced the death of one of the parents, or to a family headed by a mother who was never married, and who has raised her child alone. However, by far the largest number of single-parent families are those that arise from a dissolved marriage.

The period following separation or divorce is usually one of chaos and turmoil. Every child—especially boys under the age of five—is affected by the impact of changing to a single-parent family, and may become anxious when leaving the remaining parent, or may behave badly at home and at school. Fortunately, these short-term effects pass. The long-term psychological effects of becoming a single-parent family are not entirely predictable;

some children continue to yearn for their absent parent, while others do not.

Living in a single-parent family poses particular difficulties:

- *Physical demands.* A single parent usually has to work in order to pay the bills and, as a result, has little energy left to deal with home life at the end of the day. If the parent does not work, the family may experience the strain of new-found poverty. This takes place against a background of preparing meals, shopping, and managing children who are emotionally weakened by the marital split. The single parent also has to deal with the former marriage partner, in-laws, and friends. The sheer volume of these demands dictates that a single parent cannot do justice to them all.

- *Emotional demands.* The head of a single-parent family has no one to support the everyday decisions, and this can undermine the parent's self-confidence. In a two-parent family a woman has her partner to reassure her that what she thinks and says is valid, and, of course, vice versa; a single parent doesn't. A single parent has no feedback about whether decisions are right or wrong, apart from the children—and they'll probably challenge parental authority anyway. This means a single parent is likely to be less effective and less powerful in leading the family.

- *Age gap problem.* Parents in a two-parent family may use the fact that they are adults to encourage their children to be responsible. In other words, they can use the age gap between themselves and the children to establish their authority as parents. A single parent often confides in the children because a partner is not present to share concerns. This means that the parent may have difficulty acting authoritatively toward the children.

- *Dependence.* In a single-parent family, parent and children depend on each other more than they normally do in a two-parent family. This happens simply because now fewer people are in the house. While this can be very positive and can enhance a parent-child bond, it also means the parent has less freedom to release feelings. When a single parent gets angry with a child, no one else is available to take over the situation—and, also, the child doesn't have another parent at home to whom to turn.

- *Lack of money.* Another difficulty that faces a single-parent family, especially when the woman is the parent, is the abrupt economic change, a factor that has indirect psychological effects. Now that an ex-spouse's income has to maintain two homes (and possibly two families), less cash is available to spend on food and clothes. Luxuries become a thing of the past. This too adds stress.

- *Poor housing.* Single-parent families often have accommodation difficulties. If a marital separation is sudden and unplanned, the newly single parent (usually the mother) may be forced to leave the family home very quickly, taking her children with her. Urgently needing somewhere to live, the family may have to turn to welfare for emergency housing—and anything available under this type of allocation is usually basic. Such an environmental change is yet another pressure on a single-parent family.

Although this sounds a bit gloomy, many single parents are quick to point out that life in a two-parent family also has stress points, especially if the parents have relationship difficulties.

Psychologists have found that children in a single-parent family, when compared with children in a two-parent family, tend to be less capable socially and intellectually when starting school, and tend to achieve less educationally. On the positive side, though, these children tend to have a satisfactory sex-role identity, a keen desire to succeed in life, a good parent-child relationship, and a satisfactory psychological development.

A child from a single-parent family, therefore, experiences a combination of positive and negative influences. The happiest single-parent families have the following features:

- *Good parent-child communication.* Such communication is positively related to the family's mental and physical health; the more openly parents and children can express their feelings and ideas, their anxieties, and their happiness, the better for all of them.

- *Stable home routine.* A clear structure in family life helps a child adjust to having a single parent, and gives him a feeling of security.
- *Frequent access to the noncustodial parent.* In most instances, the child benefits by maintaining regular contact with the estranged parent.
- *No arguments between the parents.* No child likes to see his parents quarreling, whether they are separated or together. A child is more likely to adapt to living in a single-parent family if he doesn't see his parents fight in front of him.

See also Fathers; Mothers; Parents; Quarrels; Separation and Divorce; Stepparents; Working Mothers; Young Parents.

Sleep Isn't sleep wonderful?! Your child may be exhausted at the end of the day, with aching muscles and drooping eyelids, but you know she will wake up fully refreshed after she's had a good night's sleep. Sleep is a way to replace lost energy, a way to recharge her batteries. Yet nobody knows exactly why people need sleep.

Scientists *have* proved the following:

- *Physical changes take place during sleep.* For instance, a child's pupils become very small; the rate at which saliva, digestive juices, and urine are secreted drops sharply; the volume of air breathed diminishes; heart rate slows; electrical brain waves change their patterns; and consciousness is lost.
- *Sleep is essential for physical and mental health.* A child who does not get regular sleep at night will become irritable and depressed, difficult to manage, and will not be able to concentrate in school. She may also lose her appetite, start to lose weight, and eventually become ill.
- *Nobody can go without sleep indefinitely.*

A new baby

- sleeps up to 80 percent of the day;
- takes seven or eight naps every twenty-four hours;
- dreams during 50 percent of sleep time;
- sleeps anywhere and at any time;
- drifts imperceptibly in and out of sleep;
- has her own individual sleep patterns. Some babies simply don't need as much sleep as others.

As your child grows older, she will develop a more predictable sleeping routine, although not every child has settled sleep during the night. In fact, night waking—defined as waking up one or more times during the night, at least four nights a week—is the most common problem reported by parents when their baby is between the ages of twelve and eighteen months.

More than 20 percent of one-year-olds wake up four or more nights each week; at eighteen months, 17 percent wake that frequently. Encouragingly, the rate of night waking then begins to decline, although at four years 10 percent of children are still reported by their parents as waking regularly each night. In addition, at each age, about 10 percent of children wake two or three nights a week.

You can help your child have untroubled sleep, by using strategies involving the following:

- *Comfort.* An uncomfortable child will not sleep, even though she's tired. Make sure your child isn't hungry, thirsty, sick, in pain, cold, or too hot.

- *Contentment.* Your child won't fall asleep unless she feels loved and secure. Soothing cuddles before bedtime relax her; reading a short story to her will also have a settling effect.

- *Routine.* Your child is more likely to sleep well when she follows a predictable routine each evening—for example, undressing, followed by bath time, followed by story time, followed by lights out.

- *Security.* Your child may be unable to get to sleep in the dark. A night-light can be useful—once your child falls asleep, you can turn the light off.

  Following are some thing you should try to avoid:

- *Naps.* Cut out unnecessary naps during the day. Most children older than three or four should play quietly when tired in the afternoon, rather than take a daytime nap.

- *Background noises.* Your child may be disturbed by outside noises, such as heavy traffic, barking dogs, noisy neighbors. Eliminate these sounds where possible, and reassure your child they aren't harmful.

- *Unhappiness.* A troubled child won't get to sleep easily. Worries that keep children awake include arguments with friends, fights between parents, and anxiety about starting playgroup or school. Ask your child what worries her.

Bear in mind that each child is an individual, and that some children need less sleep than others. These individual differences are normal, and should not be a cause for concern. Here are some common concerns:

- *My child doesn't get enough sleep.* If your child isn't irritable and tired during the day, then she probably does get enough sleep. What matters is that your child's bedtime and sleep routines should be consistent, and that she should feel refreshed when she wakes up in the morning.

- *My child wakes up too early.* Some children are early risers. The only difficulty with this is when your child makes a lot of noise and wakes up everyone else, too. Make sure your child has plenty of toys, games, and books near her bed so that she can play with them (quietly) until the rest of the household stirs.

- *My child likes to sleep late.* Again, this is a normal pattern in many children. There is nothing to worry about unless your child sleeps late because she has gone to bed too late the night before. As children grow older, they learn to appreciate the benefits of sleeping late, and previous patterns of early rising may disappear.

- *My child likes to sleep with us in our bed.* This is a matter of personal preference—some parents specifically encourage this behavior, and don't expect a young child to sleep in her own bed. If you want to change this habit, do it very gradually, encouraging your child to spend an increasing amount of time in her own bed before coming into yours.

Ensure that you get enough sleep, too, during these critical early years.

See also Bedtime; Crying Baby; Dreams; Nightmares; Routine; Unhappiness.

Snacks No matter how much effort you put into food preparation, no matter how meticulously you plan your child's meals, sometimes your child will be hungry between meals. Nutritious food is good for him, whether he eats three large meals each day or six small ones.

This doesn't mean your child should have eaten more at lunch. A small, nutritious snack between meals can take the sharp edge off a child's hunger, putting him in better spirits until the next meal arrives, and can turn a bad mood into a good mood. Of course, you don't want the day to deteriorate into a never-ending series of small snacks, because that will reduce your child's interest in family meals—and will also have you permanently stuck in the kitchen. A midmorning and midafternoon snack works wonders for everyone.

A child likes snack-type foods because they are

- small and easy to consume;
- less structured than family meals;
- different from usual main courses;
- selected by him.

These positive reasons mean that your child will probably eat whatever snack you serve him. This opportunity can be used to reinforce good eating habits and introduce new nutritious snack foods. Ensure that the snack doesn't make your child so full that he can't eat the next meal.

Healthy snacks include sliced fresh fruit or vegetables (such as apples, pears, oranges, seedless grapes, carrot sticks, green pepper strips), finger-food (such as meat/cheese sandwiches with whole-grain bread, pizza strips, cheese on toast), and dairy products (such as cheese cubes, yogurt, low-fat cheese spread, cottage cheese). Low-fat chips can be given occasionally.

Never give a peanut to a child under the age of five, because he could accidentally inhale it and choke. Never give small children snacks that could be aspirated; check with your pediatrician first. Never give snacks to a visiting child without first checking with a parent about food allergies.

Snacks and treats are different, although your child may not agree! Candy, cakes, cookies, potato chips, and soft drinks should be avoided. Aside from giving your child an excess of carbohydrates that may turn into fat, candy causes tooth decay. Don't be fooled by supposedly healthy cereal and granola bars: read the contents label carefully, since many cereals and snack bars contain a lot of sugar and fat.

Be realistic. Every parent starts off determined not to let their child eat junk food, yet soon realizes this isn't always possible. At times, you are bound to give your child candy or gum. He'll survive that nutritional lapse! Likewise, don't feel bad because your child has binged on candy, soft drinks, and potato chips at a party. That's what makes it a party.

Opinions vary about "junk" foods. In many instances, fast food has nutritional value (for example, take-out hamburgers, submarine sandwiches, tacos, pizza), as long as it is eaten as one small component of a well-balanced diet. The danger is that these foods might become an integral part of a child's weekly food consumption. So don't feel guilty about letting your child have an occasional fast-food hamburger, or a small piece of fried chicken.

See also *Additives; Eating; Eating Out; Fussy Eaters; Healthy Eating; Overweight.*

Sociable Play
Sociable behavior has three main features, all of which can be encouraged through play:

- *Sharing.* Sharing has two forms. First, a child might share in order to benefit personally; for example, she shares her snack with others in the hope that this will make them want to play with her. Second, a child might share even when she gets no obvious personal benefit; for example, she shares her new toy with her friends simply because she likes them. This, perhaps, is a more genuine type of sharing because it involves a child doing something for nothing.

- *Cooperation.* This happens when a child works with a number of others so that every single one of them benefits; for example, when a group of children work together to build a "den" in which to play. This is quite different from competition that happens when each child works alone, trying to get the reward for herself; for example, when children race against each other on field day.

- *Empathy.* The ability to share and experience the emotional state of another person. An empathic child (unlike an antisocial one) is able to understand and appreciate the feelings of others.

Many parents have an intuitive feeling that specific toys can have an adverse influence on their child's behavior; consequently, they may not allow their child to have toy guns, knives, and swords because of the worry that such toys might encourage the child to behave aggressively toward others. Research findings suggest that this concern has some foundation.

In one study, investigators examined the extent to which the characteristics of a toy determine the way a child plays with it. Over sixty boys, aged between three and six years, were involved; they played in pairs, in a series of twelve-minute sessions. During these play periods, the children were given toys, three of which were designed to present aggressive cues (an inflatable doll in the form of a well-known space villain; mechanical boxing robots; small *Star Wars* characters with a spaceship), and three of which were designed to present sociable cues (a basketball with a hoop that had to be held by one player while the other threw the ball into it; a peg-board that lit up when one child pressed a switch while another inserted pegs; a toy ambulance with small paramedic figures). Results confirmed that sociably cued toys encourage children to take turns and cooperate with each other, while aggressively cued toys encourage them to be verbally and physically hostile toward each other.

Investigate all the toys your child plays with, and categorize them as either sociable or aggressive. You may be surprised to discover the range of toys that present antisocial, aggressive cues.

Psychologists have also found that when children play games that require sociable behavior, they become more sociable and caring toward others. Such games can be very simple. For instance, lay a piece of newspaper on the floor, and tell your child and some of her friends that they all have to place at least one foot and one hand on the paper. The smaller the piece of newspaper and the larger the group, the more fun the game becomes. This activity has the two key characteristics that make a game sociable: first, the children have to cooperate with each other in order for everyone in the group to be on the paper, and second, they have to share the space on the paper with each other. It's great fun—children take great delight in twisting and tangling themselves.

See also Aggression; Gender Play; Kindness; Learning through Play; Play; Zero-Sum Games.

Social Development
When you hear your new baby howling day and night because he's hungry, or because he needs his diaper changed, or simply because he's in a bad mood, it's hard to imagine that within a couple of years this same individual will be able to mix with other children of his own age, will probably be able to share his toys without complaint, and may even be popular. He will. Getting along with others is important. A sociable child has many advantages compared with one who does not mix well—he has greater self-confidence and enjoys a more stimulating way of life. Some children, of course, deliberately choose to be solitary, and they appear to be

very contented; but in most instances an isolated child is an unhappy child.

Despite having inherent tendencies toward social contact, your child still must learn social skills, such as the ability to communicate his feelings accurately. A child who learns to say, "It's my turn next" will be more socially acceptable than a child who simply grabs a toy or pushes in line without any explanation. Even a two-year-old can be encouraged to use simple socially acceptable behavior. Another important social skill is knowing what to say in the first few moments when meeting someone for the first time. Teach your child what to say and do in these situations (for example, your child could offer the other child a toy with which to play).

Encourage your child to think about the way he behaves toward other children and about the gestures he uses. Some gestures are aggressive (shouting, scowling, clenching fists, swearing), while others are pacifying (smiling, showing approval, holding out a hand). Children who mix well are usually those who use more pacifying gestures than aggressive ones.

The three most-important social skills that will help your child get along with others of his own age are the abilities to share, to take turns, and to follow rules. A child who does not have these skills will have social difficulties. Explain to your child why these skills are important (because others will like him), and give him plenty of opportunities to practice them at home (for example, sharing candy with his friend, waiting his turn to have a glass of lemonade, playing games with rules).

Cleanliness is also necessary. Life is unfair, and although it is not your child's fault if he has dirty clothes or is unwashed (this is your responsibility), his unkemptness will give your child an uphill struggle when making friends. Encourage your child to take an interest in his appearance, in his clothes, and in his personal cleanliness. Good eating habits also help.

Your child's social development in the early years occurs in stages:

3 months
Your child will have already shown his first smile (usually around six weeks), and he clearly enjoys the company of familiar people. He will probably watch you closely as you move around the room.

6 months
When your child is happy playing with you, he will smile consistently or even laugh. However, the first signs of shyness may appear when he sees people he doesn't know.

9 months
Your child is now ready to take the social initiative when he is with other children and adults (for example, he may approach another child). He can readily distinguish a familiar face from that of a stranger.

12 months
A typical one-year-old loves action rhymes that involve his parents tickling him or moving him about (such as "Pat-a-Cake" and "Round and Round the Garden"). And he will like to sit on your lap, being cuddled by you.

18 months
The first signs of genuine cooperation appear when your child begins to help to dress and undress himself. He may try to pull his undershirt off himself, or perhaps to put on his slippers.

2 years
Unfortunately, social development takes a temporary downward turn at this age. Instead of increasing his social skills further, your child becomes more concerned with himself: tantrums predominate when others don't do what he wants.

2½ years
Your child likes being with other children, although he won't actually play with them yet. He is still cautious about sharing his toys, and isn't ready yet for cooperative play.

3 years   Your child will love playing fantasy games
                           with other children, each absorbed in their
                           own make-believe role. He is more aware
                           now that games can't take place unless
                           everyone plays according to the same rules.

4 years   Your child should be able to mix coopera-
                           tively with other children of his own age.
                           He may not be thrilled about waiting his
                           turn, sharing, or following the rules of
                           someone else's game, but he can manage
                           this if he wants.

5 years   Your child will have developed social com-
                           petence and will be able to join the compa-
                           ny of others of his own age without much
                           problem. Of course, he may be shy and
                           withdrawn, but he can manage without
                           adult supervision.

See also *Fighting; Friendships; Hygiene; Kindness; Manners;*
Politeness; Shyness; Sociable Play.

Solid Foods
Current medical opinion holds that early
introduction of solids to your child can be harmful. You should
not start your baby on solids earlier than is recommended: they
won't make her grow better. In 1980, the American Academy of
Pediatrics stated that no nutritional advantages result from the
introduction of solids before a child is between four and six
months old. In 1981, a British medical report cautioned against
introducing solid foods before an infant is three months old. By
the time your child is six months old, solid foods should be
gradually introduced, because breast milk or formula alone
doesn't provide enough nourishment for the developing body.

Your baby's behavior is the best way to decide when to start
her on solids, assuming, of course, that you don't break the
three-month limit. If you find that your four-month-old is still
hungry after a feeding, even though you have increased the

amount of formula, then it is probably time to try solids. But don't rush into it.

Approach solids gradually, giving your baby one new food at a time, starting with a single-grain cereal. This will enable you to monitor whether your child likes it, and whether she has problems digesting it, or has food allergies. Give her a drink of breast milk or formula first, then mash a small amount of food and give it to her. You may find that she spits it out at first, but don't worry—she'll probably take time to get used to the new taste and texture. Remember that a baby should always get her main source of nourishment from breast milk or formula until she is twelve months old. Gradually introduce vegetables, more-complex cereals, meat, fruit, and juices, one at a time.

Some parents let their infant taste the food by putting some on their freshly washed finger, which they then place in the baby's mouth. Some offer the baby solids from the tip of a small spoon. Other parents sit their baby on her high chair, place a little food on her tray, and then leave her to explore. Every baby is different. Once you have gotten your baby interested in solids, and she is older than six months, gradually make the food less smooth. Your child should be encouraged to get used to foods of different textures. Never force-feed her.

Commercially prepared foods, in boxes or jars, are very convenient and may suit your lifestyle. Ensure that they don't have added sugar (that could damage your baby's developing teeth), salt, or any kind of additives. The fresh food that you eat will be suitable for your baby, but purée it and avoid adding salt to it. Once your infant is well established on solids, make sure she continues to take breast milk or bottle throughout the day.

See also *Additives; Bottlefeeding; Breastfeeding; Eating; Fussy Eaters; Healthy Eating; Teeth.*

Spanking Studies show that violence is more common in the home than on the streets. One problem with spanking is that because it doesn't work, it escalates into unintended violence. Parent support groups, crisis hotlines, parent education, parent/child drop-in centers, and "parents anonymous" groups can all provide support when you don't know what to do next.

Children have a knack of pushing parents to the absolute limit... and beyond. The constant nagging of a demanding toddler can use up the patience of even the most placid of parents. So can the antics of a five-year-old who thinks it's good fun to draw all over the living-room walls with his felt-tip pens, or run into the busy street.

Like most of us, some time or other you've probably been at that low point where you felt overwhelming frustration and fury at your child's behavior. Following are good reasons why you should never, ever break down and spank your child:

- *It doesn't work.* Studies have found that being spanked does not prevent children from being even more troublesome as they get older. The opposite occurs. Children are more likely to cause problems at age sixteen if they were spanked as children. Toddlers who are smacked are the ones least likely to obey the instructions that go along with the spanking. Spanking has no long-term positive effect.

- *It sets a bad example.* From your child's point of view, if hitting and lashing out at someone else are the way you handle your anger, then it's the way for him to handle his anger. Your child will follow your example. Aggression breeds aggression.

- *It's dangerous.* A very fine line separates a carefully aimed smack on the bottom and a smack that can do unintentional physical damage. Most parents don't deliberately set out to seriously hurt their child, but it happens often.

- *Physical assaults are illegal.* Hitting anyone can be a physical assault in the eyes of the law. Aside from a jail sentence for common assault, more-serious charges of child abuse can arise. It may lead the way to family intervention by social workers, psychologists, and child welfare authorities. You may find your children suddenly placed in foster homes.

Spanking is usually done in a temper. That's a time when people don't have full control over their actions. You might hit your child too hard; or he might move at the wrong moment, causing the blow to land across his face or a vulnerable part of his body.

If you have ever spanked your child, chances are you felt terrible afterwards. No parent likes to see their child look at them with fear. We all want our children to value us, not to be afraid of us.

You can exercise discipline effectively without hitting your child. You will find the following list helpful:

- *Tell your child why rules matter.* Use explanations he can understand—for example, that throwing his toys will break them. Your child is more likely to follow your rules if he thinks they are sensible.

- *Emphasize that your child will benefit from rules just as much as anyone else.* For instance, the rule that children shouldn't punch each other means that your child doesn't need to worry about being hit by another child.

- *Keep rules consistent.* This is very important—if you have set limits, make sure your child sticks to them.

- *Take action when your child breaks your rules.* If you've warned him of the consequences, then stick to them. Empty threats only teach your child that you don't mean what you say.

- *Use praise to encourage good behavior.* Praising a child when he behaves well is very effective.

- *Time rewards and punishments properly.* Discipline and praise will be most effective when given immediately. Don't wait to punish your child for obnoxious behavior, or to praise him for behaving well—take action now. Don't wait for dad.

- *Never try to bully your child into good behavior.* You're bigger than he is and you can intimidate him. But the impact lasts only for a few moments—he'll misbehave again as soon as you turn your back.

- *Use realistic punishments.* Only make consequences that you can live with and that you know you can carry out. Short punishments (such as reducing television viewing time by ten minutes or imposing a "time out") are very effective.

- *Be prepared to reach a compromise.* There should always be room for reaching a compromise with your child. Most rules can be bent for sound reasons.

- *Walk away when you feel tempted to spank your child.* This isn't a sign of weakness—it's a realistic acceptance that you have taken as much as you can at this moment. Take five, and come back to talk it out.

See also *Aggression; Attention-Seeking Behavior; Crying Baby; Discipline; Modeling.*

Special Needs All children need to be loved, to be physically cared for, to feel secure, to have self-confidence, to have structure and consistency in life, and to mix with other children. But some children have special needs in addition to those described above, needs that arise because their development is atypical.

Until the 1980s, these children were called "handicapped," "retarded," or "abnormal," but this form of labeling is no longer used. Now, children with developmental problems are described as having special needs. The problems with the terms "handicapped" and "abnormal" are that they focus on a child's weaknesses instead of on her strengths, they are too general, they don't indicate that certain supportive measures may be taken to help the child deal with her difficulty. Such terms also encourage people to consider the condition rather than the child herself. The shift from "handicap" to "special needs" allows a child to be treated as an individual.

Parental reaction to the realization that their child has special needs varies from shock to denial, from grief to acceptance, from fear to despair. Although some parents don't experience all these emotions, feelings of confusion and distress usually follow the diagnosis that a child has a serious developmental problem. Being honest with yourself will help you get through this early stage. It's not pleasant to know you feel guilty or afraid, but these are common reactions that you shouldn't try to hide. No stigma is attached to feeling anxious or embarrassed about having a child with special needs.

Find out as much as you can about your child's problem and the impact it may have on her development. Ask the professionals who are involved with your child, and keep asking questions, until you receive adequate answers. You may find it helpful to contact other parents who have a child with similar difficulties; sharing your worries with someone else is often beneficial. Find the resources available to aid in the best possible care for your child with special needs. This can usually be arranged through organizations specifically formed to help parents.

Right from birth, play is vital to every child's development because it is through play that the child explores the world around her—she learns through play. A child with special needs may require extra encouragement to play because she may not show that active sense of curiosity that most children have. Be prepared to get involved with your child. If she doesn't reach out for toys, take them to her and put them in her hands; if she doesn't squeeze a squeaky doll, then put her fingers around it and gently squeeze the toy yourself. This will provide your child with a suitable model of behavior that she can copy, and that will also stimulate her interest.

Chances are, you have other children as well (the majority of children with special needs have at least one brother or sister), and their development is just as important. Common complaints from siblings include that they are asked to do too much around the house because their parents' time is entirely taken up by the child with special needs, that they feel neglected because the child with special needs is the center of attention, and that they are pressured to be high achievers in school because their parents expect too much of them.

Bear in mind that all your children have their own lives to lead. They all need to develop their full potential. In the same way that you shouldn't cover up your child's special needs, neither should you make them a permanent and all-encompassing focus. Tensions often arise in a family with a child who has special needs when the other children don't fully understand the nature of those difficulties. Give your other children as much information about the problem as you can, and encourage them to ask you questions.

Many parents become overprotective of a child with special needs, and are more lenient with her than they are with their other children. Parents probably do this because they feel that a special-needs child is more vulnerable than other children. Your child with special needs will benefit from a consistent family discipline, so avoid the temptation to spoil her because of the difficulties she experiences.

See also Cerebral Palsy; Down's Syndrome; Integration, Educational; Language Difficulties; Learning through Play; Milestones; Overprotectiveness; Play; Sibling Rivalry; Spina Bifida.

Spina Bifida This condition is caused by a spinal column defect in which one or more of the bones forming the backbone (the vertebrae) fail to join properly, leaving a gap or a split; spina bifida is one of the most common congenital abnormalities in children. More boys than girls are affected.

The condition varies in severity. At one end of the scale, spina bifida occulta is very mild, and usually goes unnoticed. The visible sign may be a dimple in the back, but most people with this are unaware they have an abnormality because they don't experience any symptoms at all. At the other end of the scale, spina bifida cystica is more serious. The visible sign is a cyst (or sac), almost like a large blister, on the back. It is covered with a thin layer of skin.

There are two types of spina bifida cystica:

- *Meningocele.* This type occurs when the cyst contains some of the meninges (membranes that cover the spinal cord) and the spinal fluid that surrounds the brain and spinal cord. In most instances, damage to the nerves is limited, and so a child with meningocele is only mildly affected.

- *Myelomeningocele.* This type occurs when the cyst contains the meninges, the spinal fluid, and also part of the spinal cord, which is therefore damaged. Myelomeningocele is a more-serious form of spina bifida. It always involves some degree of paralysis. Most children with this condition have difficulty with bladder and bowel control, and may never be entirely continent.

In addition, a baby born with spina bifida usually has hydrocephalus (brain fluid cannot drain into his bloodstream). The effects of hydrocephalus vary, but often include visual and learning difficulties, seizures, and coordination problems. The precise cause of spina bifida is not known, although it is thought to be genetic. The nervous system is one of the first parts of the body to develop, and the neural tube—from which the brain and spinal cord develop—is formed within the first twenty-five days of pregnancy. Spina bifida arises when the neural tube grows abnormally.

Evidence does suggest, though, that spina bifida is at least partly inherited. A woman who has already had one child with spina bifida has an increased chance of having another with the same problem. The chance of an adult with spina bifida having a child with spina bifida is one in twenty. Genetic counselling is available, and tests can also be done to determine whether the fetus is affected.

A large-scale survey found that in more than one-third of families with a child who had myelomeningocele, the mother admitted that she had been counselled against having any more children, and about 25 percent stated that having a child with spina bifida had made them very anxious about the possibility of subsequent pregnancies. However, nearly 20 percent of the mothers felt that having a child with spina bifida had not influenced the size of their family; they either intended to have more children, or had decided before the birth of the affected child that they would not have any more. A small number of mothers reported that having a child with spina bifida made them decide to have a larger family than they had originally planned—perhaps to prove to themselves that they could have a nonaffected child.

Most children with spina bifida are able to attend their local school. Segregated special schooling is recommended only when a child's learning difficulties are so severely impaired, or when his physical difficulties are so extreme, that his needs cannot be met within an ordinary classroom.

See also Hydrocephalus; Integration, Educational; Special Needs.

Spoiling Spoiled children are rarely liked by others. Yet it's unfair to reject a spoiled child, because it's certainly not her fault that she behaves this way. No child is born spoiled, nor does she make herself spoiled. Spoiling is caused by parents and often grandparents. They do it for many different reasons:

- *A desire to give a child everything possible.* Parents who had a very deprived upbringing are often determined to make sure their own child doesn't have that experience. Spoiling can be one outcome of this approach.

- *Compensation for a difficult childhood.* Everyone feels sorry for a child who has long periods of ill health, so it's natural for parents to shower their sick child with toys, games, and as much attention as possible. If they take it to extremes, this form of compensation can turn into spoiling.

- *An inability to say "no" to a child.* A demanding toddler wants her own way, and her parents have to be quite determined to not always give in to her demands. Yet life is easier in the short term if the child gets what she wants, because this avoids confrontation. In the long term, however, this lack of firmness will make the child grow into a spoiled child.

- *A history of spoiling in the parents' childhood.* We all react to the way we were brought up, sometimes by mirroring it with our own children, and sometimes by turning against it completely. Parents who were overindulged in childhood will consider it a normal way to raise their own children.

- *A one-child household.* Holding the center position in the family—without ever having to share it with any other children—means a child may become spoiled as her parents smother her with clothes, toys, gifts, love, and attention.

A spoiled child usually becomes unpopular because she thinks only of herself, because she's unable to share and take turns, and because she's insensitive to other people's feelings. If these personality traits continue into adulthood, rejection and unpopularity will also continue. That's why it is best to tackle spoiling right at the outset.

People differ in their attitudes to overindulging babies. Some think that babies can't possibly be spoiled because they don't know what's going on around them. Others think that spoiling can start at birth, and that an overindulged baby will develop into an overindulged child.

It is true that even a young baby can soon learn that crying is an effective way to get attention from mom and dad, but failure to react to a crying baby can have the serious effect of teaching the child that she is not important. Ignoring a child's cry communicates the message that, although she is unhappy, her parents will not do anything to make her feel better. Repeated experiences like this can reduce a baby's feelings of security, and she may even cry more frequently as a result. The best approach is one that achieves a balance between rushing to a crying baby every time she makes a sound and ignoring her completely when she howls between meals.

Spoiling is not just a matter of giving a child too many toys, or too much attention; it's more about the way these things are given to her, why they're given to her, and how she understands the situation. Occasionally, your child should not be given everything she wants. Naturally, she'll react badly when this happens, but it will teach your child how to adapt when things don't go her way. This is not being cruel or letting her down; rather, it's a sensible strategy to stop your child from becoming spoiled.

You can avoid spoiling your child in other ways, including asking your child to explain why she wants something. It's tempting to accede to nagging, simply for the sake of a quiet life. But then the child may not value what she gets—instead, the act of acquisition may become more important to her than the actual enjoyment of the object. Asking your child to explain why she wants something forces her to think about her request. It also shows her that it's better to ask nicely for something than to stomp about angrily. Try to encourage your child to accept a compromise between what she wants and what you want, and once a deal is struck, don't go back on it later when she starts to nag at you all over again.

A young child who is spoiled sees the world around her

only from her own point of view. She thinks only about herself, and her desires; therefore, she must be encouraged to appreciate other people's feelings—for example, you could point out how terrible her friend felt when she snatched her toy away from her. Your child may be completely uninterested at first in what you have to say, but she'll get the message eventually.

See also Crying Baby; Discipline; Grandparents; Only Child.

Stealing A child under the age of three does not usually have a full understanding of the significance of personal possessions. True, a young child can get very agitated when his friend takes one of his favorite toys without asking, but he cannot generalize this concept to other people's possessions. So he doesn't "steal" in the adult sense of the word; no malicious intent underlies his action.

Your child does have to learn the basic meaning of ownership. That's why minor incidents of theft by a child under the age of four should be dealt with firmly, but reasonably. Tell your child that taking other people's things is wrong, that others won't like him if they think he takes things without asking, but don't make a big issue out of it. If your child does tend to take things without permission, give him a fresh reminder before you visit someone else's house.

By the age of four or five, your child will know right from wrong and will know that stealing is not allowed. He may be tempted to try it out at some time or another, even though he knows he shouldn't do it, for the following reasons:

- *Stealing gives your child what he wants, without having to wait.* A child who wants candy but has no money can solve this problem by stealing money from his classmate's desk or from home. A child who wants a computer game, but hasn't got one, can change the situation by stealing one from someone else.

- *Stealing can appear exciting and adventurous.* The thrill associated with stealing (fear of discovery, excitement at disobeying adult rules) can be very attractive to a child—at least, until he is caught, at which point he wishes he had never thought of the idea in the first place.

- *Stealing may maintain your child's status among his friends.* Your child may be tempted into theft because his friends steal and he doesn't want to be left out of the crowd. It's not easy for a child to resist such pressures.

- *Your child has seen you steal.* You would probably be outraged at the suggestion that you might be a thief. But have you ever brought paper or pencils home from the office without paying for them? Have you ever been undercharged in the supermarket, yet not declared it? Double standards of morality confuse children.

If you do discover your child has stolen something, nip it in the bud there and then. Treat the matter seriously (even if the item he has taken is insignificant), explain the consequences of his behavior, ensure that he is involved in compensating the victim, and discipline him reasonably. As long as your child knows that you strongly disapprove of his behavior, he is unlikely to repeat it again. Remember, though, that the fact that your child has pinched a candy from a shop without paying hardly puts him in the same league as a bank robber. A one-time incident does not mean a regular pattern will be established.

Persistent theft by a school-age child is a genuine cause for concern because it may be a sign of a deeper emotional problem. A child who fails to get love and attention from his parents may decide—perhaps unconsciously—that at least he will get something from them, so he steals money from his mother's purse even when he does not want to spend it, or takes cookies from the cupboard even when he is not hungry. Many psychologists claim that this unconscious motivation frequently underlies incidents of repeated theft.

A child who steals for these reasons still has to have moral rules explained to him and still needs to be treated firmly. But stealing is only the symptom of his underlying difficulty—it is not the real problem. The best way to tackle that more-serious issue is for the child's parents to think long and hard about their

child's development. They must examine their child's life closely, and their relationship with him.

See also Emotional Deprivation; Guilt; Lying; Scapegoat; Swearing.

Stepparents Just as marriage has increased in populari-
ty this decade, so too has remarriage. The remarriage rate is now
more than 50 percent higher than it was thirty years ago, which
means that almost three children out of ten are living with one
natural parent and one stepparent. The chances that a second
marriage will succeed are even less than the chances that a first
marriage will succeed. Of those couples who reconcile their differences and remarry the same partner, more than 50 percent
separate within two years. Of those who marry a new partner,
50 percent separate within three years. Couples in a second
marriage experience different problems from those in a first
marriage. Surveys have shown that difficulties in a first marriage usually stem from emotional immaturity, sexual dissatisfaction, and worry over money problems, with children at the
bottom of the list.

Couples in a second marriage report that the greatest area of
conflict is the management of their children.

Parents shouldn't expect their child to welcome a remarriage
with open arms; previous experience has taught the child that
moms and dads don't stay together forever. No wonder the child
is apprehensive about the possibility of living through another
period with lots of arguments and ill-feeling. The child has to
learn to trust the stability of her new family, and this takes time.

A child's adjustment to a remarriage depends on factors
relating to the following:

- *Acceptance of the previous loss.* Your child may unconsciously deny that her parents have separated. This is a natural
  defense; but the remarriage won't work until the child
  accepts that the previous marriage is over.

- *Gap between marriages.* A short gap leaves a child too little
  time to get over the trauma of divorce before facing the
  impact of the new family. A long gap between marriages is

not the best solution either, because the child may become used to having her parent all to herself and may be reluctant to share the parent with a stepparent.

- *Divided loyalties.* When a family break-up arises from divorce, a child really has three parents: her two natural parents and her stepparent. The child may feel her loyalties are stretched. Yet, in many happy remarried families, a child still sees both natural parents.

- *Parental jealousy.* Ex-spouses may be jealous when their former partner remarries, and this may influence a child's perception of her new stepparent. However, every child is capable of having a good relationship with a stepparent and a natural parent at the same time. Each relationship contributes to the child's development in its own way.

- *Child's age.* Younger children are better at adjusting to a new stepparent than are school-aged children. Adolescents frequently have problems adapting to a new family structure.

- *Parental responsibilities.* The stepfather often assumes full responsibilities too soon, before the stepchild is ready to accept him. It is usually best for a stepparent to take parental responsibilities gradually.

Many second marriages involve an amalgamation of two sets of children from two previous marriages, and there may be jealousy between them. This is most marked when the children are of the same age; each child feels threatened by the other, afraid her parent's love for her will diminish. Most parents are able to form good relationships with their stepchildren when they have their natural children living with them as well.

When a second marriage produces a new baby, any existing children in the family may feel insecure. They need reassurance. Some couples in a remarriage decide not to have a baby of their own because of the detrimental effect the baby could have on the other children. This is a personal decision, but it does seem a rather drastic measure to take in order to avoid a potential pitfall. Every child adds a new and unique dimension to a family. In fact, one study has demonstrated that relationships between parents and children in stepfamilies, and between the children themselves, are better when the couple have children of their own. A natural child in a stepfamily seems to act as a binding force.

Although the fairy-tale stereotype of a stepparent is someone who is wicked, uncaring, and selfish, this pessimistic view has little basis in reality. Studies on the effects of remarriage on children (involving thousands of stepfamilies with at least one stepchild) have found the following:

- *Six out of ten families think family relationships are excellent, two out of ten think family relationships are good, and only two out of ten think they are poor.*

- *The age of the stepmother at the time of remarriage is important.* More stepmothers over the age of forty report excellent relationships with their stepchildren than younger stepmothers. The age of the stepfather does not appear to matter as much.

- *Nearly twice as many children under the age of thirteen have excellent relationships with their stepmothers than older children, although the age of the children has no effect on their relationships with their stepfathers.*

- *Stepfathers are more likely to form close connections with their stepchildren than are stepmothers, particularly if the stepchild is a boy;* stepfathers also tend to be more competent than fathers in intact families.

- *The self-image of a child in a remarriage is no different from that of a child in an original family.* Being in a stepfamily does not adversely affect the way a child sees herself, or alter her feelings of personal worth.

See also *Separation and Divorce; Single-Parent Family.*

Streetproofing

While most child abuse occurs in the home, and most abductions are perpetrated by estranged parents, any child can be victimized, both by other children and by adults. As your child grows and his boundaries expand, you must build confidence in your child's ability to handle the world as it is. This is one area where it is absolutely crucial for you, as a parent, to take charge and help your child to learn how to take care of himself. Before he goes to school, your child needs honest, truthful information about what to do, where to go, rudimentary "facts of life," and the difference between good secrets and bad secrets.

Your best resource for streetproofing is your police community relations officer, who is most in tune with the needs of your own community. Do phone and ask for specific advice regarding streetproofing, and ask if this officer would be able to speak to a community group, or even a group of neighbors about child safety. Seek out the pamphlets, videos, and community information programs that the police have available. Find out about your local Block Parent and Neighborhood Watch programs, and participate. Ensure that your child is able to identify Block Parent homes.

When the time comes to streetproof, plan what you want to say to your child about his safety and think through your own beliefs. It's not enough to say, "Some people are bad to children," or, "Never talk to strangers." These only instill fear and don't provide solutions. Your child's best line of physical safety is first to use his head ("Should I be in this situation?"), then his feet and voice (run, and shout "Get away!" "You're not my mother!" "No, I don't know you!" or "Fire!" which is a good choice, because people will come, when they might not for "Help!" or "Rape!"). Make it clear, your child must never stick around to see what's wrong.

Here are some general safety strategies for all families. Many of them are basic life skills, others are simply smart habits.

- *Your child must know where you are and how to reach you.* If you aren't available, your child needs to know, specifically, to call a neighbor, friend, or relative. Ensure that your child has their phone numbers.

- *Your child must memorize his full name, address, and telephone number, including his area code.* Your child must learn how to use both a dial phone and a push-button phone in an emergency. He should know how to phone from a pay phone. Show him how to dial or press 911 and how to get the operator (0) in order to get the police, the fire department, or an ambulance. If your child goes to day care or nursery school, tape a quarter or two into his backpack or lunch box to be used for emergency phone calls only. Check weekly that they haven't gotten lost.

- *Your child must now what an emergency is.* He must know that an emergency is when he is lost, when someone bothers him, when he needs a ride, when he needs your help, when something is on fire, or when someone is seriously sick.

- *Your child must know where to go in an emergency.* Tell your child that if he ever feels funny, or frightened, or threatened he should run into a crowded place and ask for help. Make it clear: "If you are lost, or in trouble, or scared, you go to a person in charge." A person in charge can be a store clerk; a person in uniform; a bus, subway, or streetcar driver; a police or security officer; a Block Parent; or a grownup you know and trust. If all else fails, tell your child to look for a woman with children.

- *When your child is out playing, ensure that he is dressed for play.* Your child should always be dressed so he can run away, fast. He should never be dressed provocatively. His clothes or belongings should never have his name visible. His clothes should never stand out from the rest of the crowd, so he looks "different."

- *Your child should never wear a visible key.* In addition to being a visual signal that this child is on his own, a necklace key can fly up into your child's face as he plays and chip his teeth. If your child must have a key of his own, tuck his key ring inside his waist or pin it into a pocket.

- *Always pair, or "buddy," your child with a friend, or friends—there is safety in numbers.* A child playing alone is an easy target. Shortcuts are seldom safe, and solitary play in a park, playground, apartment stairwell, or any other public place is never safe. Tell your child, "Take a buddy if you need to use a public washroom."

- *Always have your child walk facing traffic.* If a car stops, and the occupant appears threatening, your child should run in the direction opposite the way the car is facing. The car has to turn around before it's able to follow.

- *Make it clear that your child is never, ever to get into a car without your permission, in advance.* If necessary, your child can use one of his emergency coins to phone you.

- *Teach your child to holler, yell, and shout effectively.* "Go away! I don't know you," "Leave me alone!" "You're a stranger!" are all more effective than screaming "Help!" It is worthwhile to teach your child to use a deeper shout than a high-pitched scream to attract attention. Play often elicits screams; hence, childish screams seldom attract adult attention.

- *Clearly define and enforce your child's boundaries.* Know the routes your child travels. Know where he is, who he's with, and where he's going. Do you have the names, addresses, and phone numbers of his friends' parents? His school? Do you know where your child plays, who his friends are, and who his coaches are? Do you trust them and know their values? Do you know the parents and the house rules when your child visits friends?

- *In the extreme case of your child's disappearance, you should be able to provide an accurate description of your child.* What is he wearing right now? The police will need to know his date of birth, sex, height, weight, coloring of skin, hair, eyes, birthmarks, and other identifying physical characteristics. Many organizations, such as Child Find, provide child identification kits in which you can include a fingerprint and recent photo.

- *You might want to establish a family code word, a secret word to be used in case of a family emergency.* Nobody is ever to go with anyone unless the code word is used. Pick words that have family meanings—names of pets, family nicknames, or hated foods—such as "parsnips," "succotash," or "Marmaduke." Once the word is used, change it.

- *Tell your child that there are good and bad secrets.* Any bad secrets, and especially threats, should always be told to a caring grownup. Tell your child that if he doesn't know, or is not sure about any secret, he should tell an adult he trusts. Good secrets are about presents, surprises, or fun times. Nothing else.

• *Ensure that your child knows the anatomical names for the private body parts for both boys and girls.* He must know that his body, and the bodies of other people, are private. Private means the part of the body covered by a bathing suit. There is good touch and bad touch. Good touch is when a doctor examines him, or when you help him get dressed. Bad touch is any touch that makes him feel uncomfortable, or doesn't feel right. Tell your child that it is always okay to say no to any grownup when the touch feels wrong. Tell your child that a bad touch is like a bad secret, and to tell a grownup he trusts about it as soon as possible.

As your child's boundaries increase, play "what if" games together. It's a great topic for the family dinner at home. Introduce a situation that requires thought, and ask, "What would you do if..." For instance, "You missed the school bus and you know if you walked home it would be dark and lonely. What would you do?" Explore your child's different responses thoroughly, and suggest the most appropriate strategies. For instance, answers to missing the bus might include "Getting a ride with a neighbor we know well, after I checked with you," or "Phoning Dad at work to pick me up on his way home," or "Calling you to come and get me," or "Asking the on-duty teacher to help me," or "Going to the principal's office to ask for help." As your child grows up, add more complicated situations. "Mrs. Johnson offered you a ride to Beaver's after school when she saw you in the schoolyard at lunchtime. What would you do?" or "A man you don't know hangs around the park every afternoon watching all the kids play soccer. Nobody knows who he is. What would you do?"

Most adults and older kids are bigger, stronger, and smarter than most small children. Adults and even other children may carry weapons: guns, knives, or sticks. Regard karate, or any other martial arts, as you would baseball, gymnastics, swimming, music class, or any other sport or activity for your child. Karate will not help your child in a street brawl.

See also *Bullying; Quality Time; Sex Education; Sexual Abuse; Victim.*

Stuttering Statistics suggest that stuttering (also known as stammering) occurs in approximately 4 percent of all children, although this figure drops to about 1 percent by the time they reach adulthood. The onset of stuttering is usually between the ages of two and eight years. Encouragingly, most childhood stutters spontaneously disappear without any additional help—approximately 75 percent of stutters have grown out of this speech difficulty by the time they reach the age of five or six years.

A stutter usually develops gradually, building up slowly until the child's parents suddenly realize that this has become part of their child's speech pattern. Stutters also fluctuate in intensity, perhaps being extremely noticeable one week, virtually nonexistent the next, then returning with great severity soon after that. The main forms of stuttering are repetition of the initial sounds of a word, repetition of the first syllable of a word, or repetition of the entire word at the start of a sentence (or even midway through it). Less commonly, a child who stutters might repeat a phrase of two or three words, or may extend the initial sound of a word. Whatever the nature of your child's stutter, your child almost certainly will be embarrassed by it, perhaps to the point where she will avoid speaking to anyone else apart from you.

Here are some suggestions for interacting with a stuttering child:

- *Never make fun of your child.* This form of verbal abuse increases the child's anxiety, thereby indirectly increasing the rate of stuttering. A stuttering child stutters more frequently when anxious. She cannot be cajoled or teased into shedding her stutter.

- *Let your child speak.* Listening to a stuttering child can be very frustrating, because you probably anticipate accurately what she wants to say to you. But give her time, let her say what she wants to say, and don't guess the missing word for her.

- *Don't correct your child.* Once your child has said the word, encouraging her to repeat it properly without stuttering has no benefit. The correction focuses attention on her previous errors, and makes her feel even more self-conscious about them.

- *Slow down your child's speech.* You'll find that when your child speaks more slowly, the rate of stuttering decreases. So calm your child down, encourage her to talk slowly to you, and try to keep her relaxed. This creates a calm atmosphere that helps her.

- *Observe your child.* Make a note of the times when your child stutters most, and try to identify a common link between them. You may discover that she stutters most when, say, she goes to a party. In that case, make a special point of calming your child before she attends.

Chances are, your child's speech difficulty will clear up spontaneously. However, if you are concerned, seek advice from a speech and language therapist, who is professionally trained to help children overcome a stutter.

See also *Language Development; Language Learning.*

Supervision
Children need adult supervision—nobody would argue with that. What is debatable, however, is the type and level of supervision that parents should exercise over their child at different ages. Should you let your three-year-old play in the living room while you lie upstairs in bed having a short nap? Is it acceptable for your four-year-old to play in a fenced yard while you prepare a meal in the kitchen? Is it reasonable to allow your five-year-old to play in a park with friends while you sit some distance away reading a magazine?

These questions have no easy answers. What suits one parent may not suit another. Yet part of growing up is being allowed an increased degree of independence without mom or dad in close attendance. No matter the age of your child, consider the following factors when determining the level of supervision required:

- *Your child's ability.* Don't leave your child unsupervised during an activity that he doesn't have the ability to cope with on his own. For example, a three-year-old will be unlikely to complete a complex jigsaw puzzle without his parent's help, and so requires supervision in that situation.

- *The nature of the activity.* Some activities are unlikely to cause your child harm—for example, playing with building blocks, drawing with crayons. Here, supervision can be minimal. But other activities are potentially dangerous and consequently need closer supervision—for example, playing near a pond, using scissors.

- *Your child's maturity.* Some children take longer to develop a sense of danger and are unaware of everyday hazards. Closer supervision is necessary for immature children, in case they unknowingly place themselves at risk.

- *Past experience.* If you know that your five-year-old becomes wild and irresponsible the moment he is out of your sight, then clearly he is not ready to be left unsupervised. However, if your child has coped with a reduced level of supervision on previous occasions, then you can afford to lessen it even further the next time.

Supervision should be decreased in slow, gradual steps, as your child progresses through childhood. If you do it too quickly, your child won't be able to handle it. Although your child may moan because he wants to be independent as soon as possible, your supervision keeps him safe.

You can't wrap your child in cotton wool. He has to be given regular opportunities to stand on his own two feet, without you watching over him, or he will never attain a satisfactory level of independence. Too much supervision will reduce your child's self-confidence and his ability to look after himself when he is away from you. In situations where your child doesn't have you to tell him what to do, where he has to make a decision on his own, he will struggle.

As a rough guide, a child two and under should never be left unsupervised. From the age of three upwards, start to allow your child times when you and he are not together—playgroup provides ample opportunities for this—and gradually increase these times over the next couple of years. By the time your child reaches school age, he will probably be mature enough to manage many tasks within his daily routine without close parental supervision. At that age, explain to your child why you want to keep an eye on him for some activities, while you are prepared to give him more freedom for others. Your child may not like what you say, but he will understand it.

See also Hazards; Independence; Overprotectiveness; Road Safety.

Swearing

Watching your child develop language is one of the rewards of parenthood, as you witness her progression from mere babbling toward more mature sounds, and then on to actual words and sentences. This joy soon turns to shock when you suddenly hear your child curse and swear like a pirate.

Since young children do not have well-developed moral understanding, the blame for most instances of children under the age of three or four using foul language can be laid at the door of adults or older children. A preschool child who swears when not obtaining her way is almost certainly mimicking adult behavior that she has seen. She is unlikely to have any idea of what the words actually mean—just that it's the sort of thing grownups say when they get angry.

If you hear your young child swear, you will probably react in one of the following ways:

- *With uncontrollable laughter.* The incongruity of your child using very adult language can seem comical, even though you disapprove of the language itself, and you may burst out laughing. Unfortunately, she may interpret this as your approval of swearing.

- *By giving your child a severe scolding.* You may be so annoyed that you reprimand your child strongly, with the aim of ensuring she doesn't use these words again. This strategy may backfire. If you draw undue attention to swearing, your child will immediately realize that a swear-word is a special word with a special effect—and that it is a good way to get your attention. This awareness may make her want to continue swearing.

- *By ignoring her.* This is probably the best way to deal with an incident of swearing at this age. Chances are, your child has only used the word casually and it will quickly pass out of her vocabulary.

A child of school age is often attracted to swear words precisely because she knows adults use them, and she thinks that by adopting grown-up mannerisms she will become more grown-up herself. Your child also knows the distinction between a "good" word and a "bad" word. So explain to your child that swearing is something neither children nor adults should do, and that other children may not want to play with her if she swears. At home you must set a good example.

See also *Discipline; Guilt; Lying; Modeling; Politeness; Scapegoat; Stealing.*

T

Talking Back Few things are more likely to irritate a harassed parent than a young child who insists on "talking back" whenever he is told to do something or when he's given a reprimand for misbehavior. To a parent, talking back is a sign of insolence, disrespect, and downright confrontation. And when your child does talk back to you, these negative words may suitably describe his behavior and, therefore, he thoroughly deserves your disapproval for such behavior. Yet, your child's back talk may have completely different, innocent reasons.

To your child, talking back often appears sensible, justifiable, and reasonable. After all, his point of view is as important as yours, as far as he is concerned, and the only way to express those genuine thoughts and feelings is to say them out loud. Your child doesn't think he is talking back (in the parents' sense of the phrase), rather that he is taking part in a discussion about aspects of his behavior. Your extreme reaction when he does this will probably catch your child off guard, leaving him in confusion as to why you responded so vigorously.

Here are some suggestions to handle your child when he talks backs to you:

- *Don't automatically assume your child is being cheeky.* No such intention may be underlying his behavior. Spend a moment or two thinking about the situation from your child's perspective, before deciding whether his back talk was impertinent.

- *Listen to what your child has to say.* Of course, if your child is simply being a nuisance, then avoid encouraging him. On the other hand, though, if your child has a grievance, then he should be heard.

- *Respond to what your child says.* A sign that you have really listened is to give a reply that is relevant and connected to your child's comments. Reprimanding your child for speaking to you confirms you have not listened to him.

- *Explain to your child why he shouldn't talk back.* Just as you are prepared to hear his side of events, your child should be prepared to listen to you. Explain that talking back appears rude, and that he should think very carefully before doing so.

The best way to tackle a child who talks back to irritate and show his defiance is to simply ignore him. Easier said than done, of course, but failure to response to his challenge is a strong disincentive. Later on, when both of you have calmed down, explain to your child that you were unhappy with his behavior and that you don't want him to do that again

See also *Attention-Seeking Behavior; Discipline; Ignoring; Tantrums.*

Tantrums Young children are prone to temper tantrums, particularly around the age of two, which is why this stage is often referred to as the "terrible twos." At this age, a child begins to assert herself and tries to exert her authority over her parents. In time, the child will learn that family life involves give and take and, occasionally, she does not get her own way. At two, your child still thinks she can rule the roost. When her wishes are blocked, her feelings of anger and frustration may be so strong that they explode into an uncontrollable tantrum.

You may be tempted to give in to your toddler when she loses her temper, if only to calm her down. You won't be doing your child any favors by behaving in this way. Such a response simply teaches your child that when you say "no" you really mean "Yes, but you must have a tantrum first," so it will encourage her to have even more tantrums.

Stick to your guns. If you have said "no," then make sure you mean "no." Although sometimes household rules should be flexible, in most cases where family rules have been set, your toddler should be expected to follow them, whether she is happy with them or not.

Once in a temper tantrum, your child may need your help to get out of it. This does not include your screaming at her to be quiet. Some children calm down quickly when they are given a "time-out" for a few minutes, because they hate losing their parents' attention. A time-out forces them to gain control. Some calm down quickly when they find that mom and dad ignore their outbursts. Some need their parents beside them, to provide calming reassurance. There isn't a right way of dealing with tantrums—a lot depends on the individual child, her parents, and the setting in which the tantrum occurs.

Prevention is better than cure. It is better to try to prevent your child from having a tantrum than it is to calm her after the event. Because tantrums are often predictable, you may be able to take offensive action. If you know that your child is in a situation that usually agitates her (for instance, trying to do puzzles that are too difficult), either give her something else to play with or share the activity with her, all the time keeping her calm. Tantrums tend to be more frequent when a child is tired—so try to avoid confrontations just before bedtime. Of course, sometimes attempts at prevention simply do not work, and your child goes on to have a full-blown tantrum. Try to remain calm at this point. Chances are, your child has little control over her outburst, and so there is no point in your losing control, too.

Most children have fewer tantrums as they grow older. By the age of five, a child is more able to talk about her anger and frustration, rather than rely on actions to release these pent-up emotions. Some, however, continue to have tantrums even when they reach school age—though the size and strength of an older child means that her tantrums are far more harrowing and destructive than those of a younger child. On the positive side, a school-age child has greater insight into her own reactions during a temper tantrum. The child will be more aware of what happens as her temper builds up, and she will probably regret her outbursts afterwards. You may be able to use this awareness to help your child gain control of her anger (for example, by encouraging her to walk away when she feels her temper building).

Relaxation techniques have become increasingly popular for helping older children control their frustration and rage. Such techniques involve learning how to induce a feeling of calmness through muscle exercises and breathing exercises. Although these methods have been widely used for many years by adults as a way of managing stress and anxiety without the use of drugs—in circumstances ranging from prenatal classes to treatment for phobias—only in recent years their potential for helping children has been recognized.

A child around the age of five or older is more likely to respond to strategies that put her in charge of controlling her temper, than to methods that her parents may use to control her. That's why teaching your child preventative methods of temper control—such as avoiding potential frustrations or using relaxation techniques—is the best course of action.

See also Aggression; Discipline.

Teeth Every tooth consists of an outer coat of hard, dead enamel and an inner core of soft, live dentine. We start to feel a toothache when decay is so severe that it bores its way through the enamel into the inner living core. Dental care, therefore, is very important for your children.

While occasionally a baby is born with a tooth, most babies don't have their first tooth until around six months, although some children don't get their first tooth until they are at least a year old. This first set of teeth (known as baby teeth) is found in girls earlier than in boys, but boys tend to lose their baby teeth earlier. All twenty baby teeth are already formed at birth. You may be able to feel them as bumps in your baby's gums before they actually break through.

The teething stage (when your baby's teeth begin to erupt through his gums) can cause your baby extreme discomfort. You may notice he salivates a lot, or chews hard on his rattles. In many instances, a teething baby has red cheeks, diarrhea, and even a rash on his bottom. Be careful not to attribute every ailment at this stage to teething, since another cause may be responsible for your baby's distress. You may be able to ease your baby's discomfort by gently massaging the gum area with your clean finger. Some parents recommend giving the baby something hard and cold to chew on, such as a cooled teething ring.

Baby teeth are particularly vulnerable to decay, which is why you should avoid giving your infant sweet drinks and foods. His first teeth should be treated with care, as they lay the foundation for subsequent healthy jaw and gum growth. They also guide the second teeth into place.

From the age of five, your child's baby teeth will begin to loosen and fall out, usually in the front lower jaw first. You may be able to see the second tooth as soon as the baby tooth comes out. And by the time your child is seven, a good many of his first teeth will have fallen out—ask a group of children this age to smile, and you'll have great difficulty counting all the gaps between their teeth! The legend of the generous tooth fairy comes to the fore at this point. Although your child may have a hunch that, in reality, you are the tooth fairy, he'll be quite willing to push these doubts to the back of his mind as he savors the prospect of finding a coin in place of the tooth he left under his pillow the night before.

Since dental care is so important, introduce your child to toothbrushing as soon as his baby teeth appear. At first, simply let him chew on a small, soft toothbrush, and let him watch as you brush your teeth in the morning. This sets a good example. Don't let your child use toothpaste until he learns to spit, not swallow. Then make sure the toothpaste contains fluoride, and ask your dentist's advice on the proper technique for brushing teeth (regular dental appointments should be made when your child is three or four years old). Good brushing does not involve scrubbing the teeth as hard as possible—rather, you should be gentle, but thorough. When your child reaches the toddler stage, make toothbrushing a regular routine after mealtimes and before bedtime. Never let your child have sweet products, juices, or milk in his mouth once he has brushed his teeth at night.

Despite your best intentions about not letting your child develop a sweet tooth, chances are he will want to eat more candy than you would like. Try to reach a balance on this. If you forbid him to have any candy, he will probably get some from his friends. The best strategy is to give your child candy or dessert after a meal and just before he brushes his teeth. His teeth are most at risk from decay when he eats a small number of candies throughout the day than when he eats a large number all at once.

Encourage your child to have good dental care habits, right from the start.

See also *Eating; Healthy Eating; Snacks.*

Television Statistics indicate that, on average, a preschooler watches twenty-five hours of television a week. Most kindergarten teachers say they know which children have spent the most time in front of the television set, both by their amount of aggressive behavior and their lack of willingness to participate in new activities. Never allow your young child's television viewing to interfere with other essential activities of childhood: playing outdoors, cuddling, playing games with you, running and jumping, singing and dancing, playing with other children, creating with Play-Doh, drawing, making puzzles, and reading stories together.

Never use your television as a baby sitter, or as daily background sound. Use it instead for fun, entertainment, and information. When a show bores your child, turn the television off. Many quality children's programs are available, such as *Sesame Street, Barney and Friends, Reading Rainbow, Mr. Rogers' Neighborhood,* and *Wish Bone.* Lots of wonderful nature shows intrigue young children. Whenever possible, watch these programs with your child. For example, if *Sesame Street* discusses such concepts as "up" or "down" you can make a game together, doing the actions. Try to avoid a steady diet of superhero cartoon characters and prime-time violence. Remember, too, that even quality shows such as *Sesame Street* have a zip-zap pace that some experts feel discourage the development of attention span, and, in fact, can contribute to Attention Deficit Disorder (ADD).

Parents can help children develop "television literacy," the ability to critically evelute what is shown on television. Talk to your child about the violence and the values presented to increase her appreciation and understanding of what she sees. Small children have difficulty differentiating what is real from what is imaginary. Spend time explaining to your child that television is not real, but make-believe. Ensure you explain to her that she should not imitate every action she sees, because some of those actions can hurt others.

***See also** Aggression; Videos.*

Toilet Training Despite what your mother-in-law or great-aunt tells you, children vary in the ages at which they gain bowel and bladder control. However:

- Girls usually achieve success with toilet training more quickly and easily than boys.
- Bowel control usually comes before bladder control.
- Day control usually comes before night control.

- The majority of children achieve the ability to go to the toilet between the ages of two and three.
- Younger children usually want to "catch up" with an older sibling.
- By the age of three, most children have full bowel and bladder control during the day, and 75 percent are trained at night, too. By age five, 90 percent are fully toilet trained, day and night.
- Few five-year-olds wear diapers to kindergarten.

In order for you to help your child achieve the goal of toilet training, you will have to ensure that he is ready, willing, and able. Otherwise, frustration occurs for everyone. Relax, and remember that this is an important part of your child's growth. It is also one of your child's first steps toward independence, and a major part of his social development. Don't rush; toilet training will evolve naturally. Remember, also, that every child is different. Some will want to use a potty; others will want to use the toilet. Others will use a potty as a toy, as a hat, as a place for teddy to pretend to poo, but not him. That's for babies. Your child wants to be a big boy and use the toilet.

A baby of one year cannot possibly be toilet trained because the nerves and muscles involved are too immature for him to control his bladder and bowel. Never rush your child, or expect him to measure up to anyone else's standards. By eighteen months a toddler may know when he wets or soils his diaper, but may still not have the necessary physical control to train. As well, any attempts may be thwarted by the "No, no, no" attitude typical of this age. At twenty-one months, toilet training may or may not have started, but remember, there is no need to rush. And if toilet training is begun too early, it can lead to frustration for all concerned, leading to low self-confidence in your child.

Your child is probably ready to begin toilet training when he shows one or more of the following signs:

- *Your child watches you, or others in the family, use the toilet.* This alone doesn't mean your child has the necessary muscle control for toilet training, but his interest is a positive sign.

- *Your child lets you know his diaper is wet or soiled.* Once your child can draw your attention to the fact that he has used his diaper—either by gesture or words—he is probably ready to start toilet training.
- *Your child knows when he is wetting or soiling his diaper.* When your child deliberately indicates to you that he's filling his diaper, then he has a level of awareness that means toilet training can begin.
- *Your child indicates that he's about to fill his diaper.* There is no doubt your child is ready to learn bowel and bladder control when he is mature enough to let you know he needs the toilet—at this stage, muscle control is well developed.
- *Your child's diaper is dry even though he's worn it for several hours.* If your child's diaper is still dry late in the morning, even though you put it on first thing, then he has some muscle control. The same applies if you find your child's diaper is consistently dry after being worn during a short nap.

It is essential to provide your child with the simple, consistent language with which to convey the message of what is happening or is about to happen: for example: pee, pee-pee, tinkle, poo, poop, BM. Select one for each function, and be consistent in its usage.

Capitalize on your child's natural curiosity by taking him into the bathroom with you and allowing your child to observe how an adult correctly uses the toilet. At these times it is important to use the simple, clear vocabulary you have established, for instance, "Mommy is going pee now." As well, when boys go with dad, they can observe the raised position of the toilet seat, how to take aim, and how to put the seat down afterwards. Usually, younger siblings are trained earlier, simply because they want to do what big sister or brother does. Make it a point to wash hands, too.

At some point your child will begin to show increasing discomfort with a wet or soiled diaper. You require your child's cooperation, so remind yourself that you have to be encouraging (use much praise and many hugs) and never punish accidents. Say, "Even grownups can have accidents, sometimes." When your child shows discomfort by gesture or words, it is a clear indication that he will be receptive to the idea that the potty or toilet can eliminate the need for diapers.

The following tips will make toilet training more successful:

- *Ensure that you have the necessary equipment before you start.* A potty is essential. You may need to buy a step stool to reach the toilet or sink. You may also need to buy a child-sized insert for the regular toilet seat for the child who prefers this to the potty. Be prepared.

- *Start with day training first.* Night training begins once your child has achieved control for most of the day. Accidents will happen, although they'll become fewer and fewer as time progresses. Remember, you need your child's willingness in the process.

- *Initially, wipe your child yourself.* For girls, wipe from front to back, and teach her that she always wipes herself this way (this discourages yeast infections). Encourage your child to try wiping him- or herself, although some children don't want to do this, quite yet.

- *The summer is an excellent time to begin toilet training.* Your child will be outside much of the time, and you can use this as a good opportunity to remove the diaper and bring out the potty.

- *If you are beginning training in inclement weather, let your child run around the house without diapers.* Preferably, keep the diaperless child in family living areas with easily-washed tile or linoleum floors. Remember, this is not the time to buy a new carpet.

- *Once your child appears to have some bowel and bladder control, give him training pants.* All of your child's clothing must be easy for the child to remove or undo "right now." Your child may be excited by underwear that makes him feel like a big boy. Do everything possible to motivate your child's success.

- *Above all, give your child lots of praise.* Be positive, patient, and persistent. You will have setbacks, possibly caused by starting training too early, or by family stressors such as the birth of a sibling. You can always put your child back into diapers for a break from training. You can always start again.

See also Bed-Wetting; Playing with Bowel Movements.

Twins
Twins are born approximately one in ninety pregnancies—and this number is increasing steadily year by year. Multiple births are also on the increase.

This growth in the rate of multiple births is due to the wider availability of infertility treatment. However, parents rarely undergo this treatment with the hope of having twins or multiple births; their aim is usually to have one healthy baby—more than one at the same time is a bonus. Research confirms the following:

- Twins tend to run in families, so a woman who is herself a twin or has a twin relative is more likely to give birth to twins than a woman who has no twins in her family.
- Women who conceive after the age of forty are four times more likely to produce twins than are women who conceive at the age of twenty.
- It is quite usual for the birth of twins to follow the birth of a single child.
- Doctors are often able to identify twins as early as the sixteenth week of pregnancy.
- Most twins are born prematurely (the average gestation period is thirty-seven weeks) and are underweight.
- There is a higher incidence of crib deaths in twins.
- Twins tend to be slower to acquire speech and are more likely than other children to have speech problems that require professional help.

Twins are either identical or nonidentical. When identical twins are conceived, a single egg that is already fertilized separates into two identical parts. Each part develops into a baby. Since each child comes from the one egg, these twins (monozygotic) are always of the same sex and possess the same inherited characteristics.

When nonidentical twins are conceived, two entirely separate eggs are fertilized by separate sperm at the same time. Since each child comes from different eggs, these twins (dizygotic) are no more alike than any other brother and sister.

Studies show that even identical twins are not exactly the same in every way. While it is true that they have a greater similarity of heartbeat and pulse rate than nonidentical twins, clear differences often emerge in other areas. Parents frequently find that one identical twin is right-handed, while the other is left-handed. The left-handed child is likely to be the smaller twin. Twins often have different handwriting styles, and there are likely to be personality differences. It is normal for twins to pass developmental milestones at slightly different times. The birth order of the twins (which one actually emerged first) has no effect on the children's psychological development. People are often fascinated by the question of which child is a few moments older than the other, especially with identical twins, because it provides a way to distinguish between the two look-alikes. The inherent danger in such labeling, particularly if it originates from the parents, is that it can cause unnecessary rivalry between the children. The so-called older twin may feel pressure to be dominant, even though she would prefer not to be. Or she may feel inadequate if the so-called younger twin develops at a faster rate.

According to a widely held view, twins have a special psychic relationship that allows them to be constantly aware of the other's thoughts. Although no scientific evidence supports this idea, in many instances twins have fabricated a secret language between themselves. They tend to give up this form of communication before they reach school age. But the existence of a special language between children is not unique to multiple births; parents of nontwins often find their young children are able to communicate using terms adults can't understand.

Twins present certain practical difficulties in the early years, difficulties to do with their basic management—for example, whom to give attention to first, whom to feed first, whom to pick up first when both children are crying. Indeed, the main complaint of parents, during the first twelve months after their twins' birth, is the physical strain of managing two feeding and sleeping schedules simultaneously.

Fortunately, this very exhausting phase of the babies' lives does pass quickly, although it might not seem that way at the time! Parents often look back on those early months as a period when they themselves became very close. They have no choice but to share child care, and this sharing process often enhances their relationship.

Once a basic routine has been established, parents then have to manage life outside the home. Have you ever tried shopping with two young children of the same age? Double strollers are available, but they are difficult to get on and off public transportation—and even harder when carrying the week's shopping. The toddler stage carries hazards of a different sort, because the children's increased mobility means that their parents may have two toddlers darting off in opposite directions at the same time. This is probably why twins are usually kept in their strollers for longer periods than single children.

As twins grow older, their parents have to choose whether to place both in the same class in nursery school, or whether to separate them. Separation can make starting nursery school difficult, since each child will have to manage without the support of her twin. This difficulty may be offset by the advantage that each can establish her own identity. At some point, twins do have to develop separate lives, and the longer parents delay, the harder the separation becomes for the children. Parents often report that each child positively thrives when given the chance to be in a class of her own, away from her twin, because each is treated individually.

See also *Birth Order; Independence; Language Development; Zygote.*

U

Ultrasound Scientists have learned a great deal about fetal growth, largely through the development of the technique known as ultrasonography. An ultrasound examination of a pregnant woman involves a probe, pressed against her abdomen, which sends acoustic impulses into her body. These impulses are then deflected at different angles by fetal bones and tissues of varying density. All of this information is fed back to a television screen, on which strong signals from areas of high density are seen as white, while weak signals from areas of low density are seen as black. These techniques have shown that the fetus

- spends a lot of time moving around the womb, and probably has a good sense of balance;
- gives a startle reaction to a loud noise occurring outside the womb;
- has slow eye movements as early as the sixteenth week after conception;
- begins to have rapid eye movement (REM) sleep around the twenty-third week, and this continues until around the thirty-sixth week, when long periods of quiet sleep take over;
- appears to have identifiable facial expressions, such as disgust, unhappiness, joy, and fear.

Psychologists have also used ultrasonography to reduce maternal anxiety during pregnancy. One study monitored the psychological effects of letting mothers see a video of their ultrasound assessment to reassure them of the fetus's well-being. The researchers found that infants of these mothers (compared with infants of mothers who didn't receive this information) were less active in the womb, had higher birthweights, and were less irritable in the early weeks of life.

See also Prenatal Development.

Unhappiness No child is happy all of the time. Like adults, children have ups and downs. There is a difference between a child who is momentarily sad in reaction to a particular occurrence, for instance, because someone has broken her favorite toy, and a child who is regularly unhappy, for instance, because she is unable to make friends, no matter how hard she tries. This latter child is so affected by her sadness that her self-image and her relationships with others suffer. This severe degree of dissatisfaction is quite different from the brief tearful moments that are a normal part of every child's life.

Young children demonstrate their unhappiness in many different ways. One child may show it by being passive and withdrawn, while another may express her distress in the opposite way, by turning her inner turmoil into outer turmoil. At first glance, a child's underlying worries may not be obvious, but the picture becomes clearer when the troubled behavior persists.

The most important aspect of your child's early life that is necessary for later happiness—though by itself will not guarantee it—is the affectionate relationship your child has with you. The quality of this bond determines many of your child's emotional characteristics, including her feeling of inner happiness. A child who has not forged secure emotional relationships with at least one adult before the age of four may be in a constant state of unhappiness and despair, and will find future personal relationships difficult.

Childhood does have its moments of stress, and the way you help your child through these periods will affect her level of contentment. For instance, a first-born may have problems adjusting to a newborn brother or sister, but sensitive and thoughtful handling by her parents can help her through this experience. Similarly, a child whose parents separate wants to remain loyal to both, even though the adults themselves do not get along together. Handled badly, parental antagonism causes the child deep-rooted sadness; but if it is handled well, the child can learn to accept her new family circumstances. Another stress point that some children have to face is the death of a close relative; if the child's grief is ignored or if it is relegated to second place, her unhappiness will deepen.

Temporary unhappiness is an inevitable part of growing up. But if your child is allowed to express her distress as it arises, and is not ignored or made to feel guilty about it, then it will ease in time. Do everything possible to make sure this happens.

See also *Bonding; Emotional Deprivation; First-Born Jealousy; Grief; Separation and Divorce.*

V

Victim One of our greatest fears, as parents, is that our child will be bullied. Take all reports of bullying seriously. True bullying can destroy your child's self-confidence, cause fear, and even create panic about going to school. Yet some children seem to be the victims of bullies, time after time, no matter what the situation. These children appear to attract bullying wherever they go. It's not simply a matter of being small, or of being bookish, or even of being slightly built and underweight. Many children have these characteristics and yet are never constantly picked on. A child who is consistently bullied may behave in a way that actually encourages others to be hostile to him.

Ensure you check out if it is really bullying, or if your child is unable to handle the social interaction at school.

Ask yourself the following questions:

- Is my child seeking attention in other ways?
- Do I constantly have to reprimand my child at home?
- Is my child willing to take the blame for something that he hasn't done?
- Does my child seem to deliberately provoke me into punishing him?
- Does my child get bullied by more than one child?

If you answer yes to most of these questions, it is possible that your child makes himself a victim of bullying to meet his psychological needs. Talk to your child about it, and try to find out why he feels this way. A child who is often a victim may also be the recipient of authoritarian discipline and know no other way to behave. Look to your own style of discipline.

If you answer no to most of these questions, then it is highly unlikely that your child is in any way responsible for being bullied. Probably you should talk to your child's teachers and principal, and role-play with your child about how he can better handle the situation.

See also *Attention-Seeking Behavior; Bullying; Discipline; Scapegoat.*

Videos Parents, educators, and social workers are concerned about the influence of movies on young children. The advent of the home video means that young children can now access films as never before.

Few parents, of course, intend their five-year-old to watch a film rated R, restricted. Three main factors make this sort of viewing a possibility:

- *The "morning after the night before" scenario.* Parents watch a video the night before, and the next morning their children—who are up and out of bed while the parents are still asleep—have ample opportunity to watch it themselves.

- *Although movie theatres adhere to age guidelines when admitting audiences, many video stores are less rigorous.* This makes it easier for children to obtain films that they couldn't see in the theater.

- *A child may watch an inappropriate video at a friend's house.* It's not easy to control your child's viewing when she stays with a friend.

Without a doubt, a horror film can have a disturbing influence on the impressionable young mind of a four-year-old. This is precisely why you must provide some degree of supervision over your child's home-video diet, especially when she is young.

See also *Aggression; Nightmares; Television.*

Violence Hardly a day goes by without news broadcasts carrying a story about a child who has been physically abused. This doesn't mean that violence toward children is a phenomenon of the 1990s, or even the 1980s. One of the earliest-recorded court cases of a child being repeatedly beaten and cut with a sharp implement happened in New York in 1874.

The whole issue of violence toward children is controversial because of people's varying attitudes. Some argue that any physical assault on a child should be regarded as an unacceptable act of violence and should be treated as such, while others maintain that parents have a right—and a duty—to spank their child when he misbehaves. Right now, society is moving toward a zero tolerance of hitting a child under any circumstance.

The problem is that no clear line divides a justifiable spank (is there ever such a thing?) and a violent assault. In many cases, parents hit a child, only to be subsequently shocked by the level of injury they had inflicted upon him.

It's a myth that all parents who are regularly violent toward their children are seriously psychologically disturbed; less than 10 percent come into this category. No single explanation accounts for the reasons why some parents hit their children. However, analysis of over 20,000 cases of child physical abuse in the United States revealed a strong association between violence against children and environmental deprivation (unemployment, poor living conditions, inadequate housing, young parents, and large families). All the same, this cannot account for all instances of violence toward children, since many families living in these circumstances do not assault their children, while more-affluent parents do.

Violence and abuse toward children does not have to involve direct physical assault. Neglect is an equally damaging form of violence, which results in physical and emotional scars. Depriving a child of adequate diet, adequate hygiene, and adequate warmth are subtle forms of violence that hurt all the same and will have a long-term effect on the child's growth and development. Likewise, deprivation of love and attention makes a child feel unhappy and insecure, and this impact can last throughout the child's life. Every child has a right to receive physical and psychological nourishment from his parents.

See also Discipline; Sexual Abuse; Spanking.

Vision Sight is only one of five senses—yet it is possibly the most important, since a great deal of learning takes place through vision. A baby uses her eyes to explore the environment; an infant uses vision to judge the expression on her mother's face; a toddler uses sight as she wanders about the room, avoiding the hazards as she goes; a preschool child uses vision to fit blocks into her shape-sorter; a school-age child uses sight to learn to read. Vision, therefore, is central to a child's development, and a child with impaired vision may be slower to learn basic skills than a sighted child.

William James, one of the first psychologists, believed that a baby is born with very little visual ability. He described a new baby's visual experiences as a "buzzing, blooming confusion." But we now know that James was wrong; research has shown that a baby arrives in the world already preprogrammed to attend to specific features in the environment. At birth, a child

- *is sensitive to light.* If a very bright light shines into a baby's eyes, she will shut them tightly and keep them that way until the light source is removed.

- *can track large moving objects.* A baby is able to notice movements of large shapes, and may watch her mother as she crosses from one side of the room to the other.

- *detects contours.* If a baby is shown a solid, black shape against a contrasting white background, she will spend most of her time looking at the points where black and white meet.

- *prefers patterns to colors.* A new baby will look longer at a patterned picture than she will at a solid-color picture.

- *focuses on objects between eight and ten inches (eighteen to twenty-three centimeters) away from her face.* This means she can look closely at her mother's face during feeding.

A major change in the way an infant uses vision occurs when the baby is about two months old. Until then, she uses her "secondary visual system": she is concerned only with the whereabouts of an object. She will watch an object as it moves around, will focus on something that comes near to her, and will look at edges of things. After this, a baby's "primary visual system" takes over: she now becomes more interested in what an object actually is. She starts to attend more to details, such as whether an object is straight or curved, light or dark, and so on; and instead of peering at only one specific feature of a picture (as does the very young baby), an infant of two months and older begins to scan the whole picture.

These early visual skills enable a new baby to begin to make sense of the world around her, to distill meaning from all that is happening in her immediate environment. Lack of such visual skills hampers this process.

In the remaining preschool years, your child's vision skills become more finely tuned. Even if you do not suspect a problem, have your child's eyed tested by an optician before she starts school. This routine screening will pick up minor visual problems, allowing corrective action to be taken if required.

Glasses will be prescribed for your child if it is thought she would benefit from them, but you might have difficulty encouraging her to wear them. Your child could find glasses uncomfortable and irritating; she might be afraid others will make fun of her. Build up your child's tolerance of glasses gradually, perhaps by having her wear them for only a minute or two on the first day, then for a minute longer the next day, and so on. Try to avoid this becoming an area of confrontation between the two of you; you can't win because your child can remove the glasses as soon as your back is turned. Better to reinforce the times she does use her glasses, than to punish her for the times she doesn't.

See also *Bonding; Eyes; Visual Difficulties.*

Visual Difficulties Although total blindness in childhood is rare, many children are partially sighted—they have sufficiently bad eyesight to require some form of visual aid over and above the normal range of glasses obtainable by prescription from an optician.

Partial sight in childhood has many causes, including the following:

- *Cataract.* This is an opaqueness in all or part of the lens (the bit of the eye that lets the light shine through, allowing it to activate nerve ends in the retina). Corrective surgical work is possible, but this is rare for a baby unless there is a genuine risk of blindness in both eyes.

- *Glaucoma.* This condition occurs when the eye's natural fluid can't drain away. The build-up causes an unnatural pressure, resulting in blurred vision. Treatment can remedy the potential loss of sight.

- *Squint.* With this condition, a child's eyes appear to look in opposite directions. In a baby under six months, a squint is normal. However, if a severe squint continues and remains untreated until the child is two or three years of age, blindness in one eye may occur. Treatment for squints varies from temporarily covering up the good eye to surgery.

- *Toxocariasis.* A rare disease passed to a child through contact with dog or cat excrement, usually when the child plays in a public park or a garden used by animals.

Many children have much less serious visual defects, but these instances give little cause for concern because wearing prescription glasses remedies the difficulty.

Common remediable defects include short-sightedness (a child sees objects that are near, but has trouble seeing an object far away) and far-sightedness (a child sees objects far away clearly, but has trouble seeing a nearby object). Routine medical screening is a worthwhile and efficient means to detect these minor visual defects.

Sight is possibly the most important of the five senses, since a great deal of learning takes place through vision. A child with

impaired vision may be slower to learn basic skills than a sighted child. Your baby has to learn to use whatever vision he has,
no matter how slight it may be. Unlike a baby with normal
vision, who can sit unaided and use his eyes to observe his environment, a partially sighted baby needs the environment to
come to him. Objects have to be brought close to him, and
people have to be nearer than normal when talking to him.

A baby with partial sight needs a lot more touching and
other physical communication with his parents. He will rely on
sounds and smells to gain understanding of what is going on
around him. Talk to your baby while playing with him. Just like
a sighted baby, he must be placed in different positions to
encourage his physical development. A partially sighted baby
should have a normal range of opportunities to be in his stroller
or play area. He should also experience rolling about on the floor.

Don't become overprotective of your partially sighted toddler. He must be allowed to move around his environment. As
long as normal baby-proofing safety precautions are taken (for
example, a baby gate across the top of the stairs, covers for the
electric outlets), then the few bumps and bruises that your child
acquires will be more than offset by the benefit he gains from
exploring.

Toys are as important to a partially sighted child's development as they are to a sighted child's, although buying a toy for
a child with limited vision requires more thought. Some toys
are designed specifically for a partially sighted child, but such
toys are not readily sold in most toy shops. When choosing
toys, consider the following features:

- *Stimulation.* Your child will prefer toys that are interesting
  to touch, that rattle or make any sort of noise when played
  with, and that even have an interesting smell.

- *Colorfulness.* A partially sighted child may have some vision,
  however slight. Toys in vivid yellow, blue, red, or green are
  easier to see than dull colors.

- *Play potential.* Some toys, such as puzzles, are only usable in
  specific ways, whereas other toys, such as building blocks,

Play-Doh, and paper and paints, can be used in a variety of ways. This latter group has the greater play potential and is most suited to the needs of a child with partial sight.

- *Purposefulness*. Toys aimed at developing specific skills—toys such as finger puppets, pedal-cars, and shape-sorters—are as appropriate for a partially sighted child as they are for any other child.

- *Safety*. A partially sighted child is more vulnerable to every-day hazards, and the choice of toys has to reflect this. Avoid play objects that have sharp edges, that are easily breakable, or that are small enough to be swallowed.

- *Washability*. All children go through a phase of exploring objects by putting them in their mouth. A child with a visu-al difficulty is likely to continue with this habit for longer than a sighted child, and so toys should be easily cleanable.

See also *Bonding; Eyes; Hazards; Overprotectiveness; Vision.*

Weaning Weaning your baby from bottlefeeding or breast-feeding to solids is an exciting time because it symbolizes a tran-sition in childhood. But avoid rushing into this new phase. Milk from the breast or bottle provides all that your baby needs for the first four or five months of life. Some parents are tempted to introduce solids before the age of three or four months in the mistaken belief that their baby doesn't get enough nourishment from milk alone. However, the introduction of solids too early can be harmful, as your baby's kidneys and liver may not be mature enough to cope. The sign that your infant should be introduced to solids is her continued hunger despite feeding, or her need to have more-frequent feedings.

Helping your baby learn how to eat solids from a spoon is great fun, and will result in a huge mess! You don't have to sterilize the silverware and bowl, but do keep them clean. Start off by giving your child a very small taste of a baby food (such as baby rice) mixed with her usual milk, from a plastic teaspoon. If she resists this by pushing the spoon away with her tongue, try putting a little of the food onto the tip of your (clean) finger, then put the finger into her mouth.

Your baby has to get used to the new tastes and the new method of feeding. At first, her face might contort into a grimace of dissatisfaction; this will soon pass, however, as she quickly adapts. These small amounts of food should be given in conjunction with your baby's bottle- or breastfeeding. Over a period of weeks, gradually increase the amount of solids. And vary the texture of the solids. Your baby will prefer mashed food to finely chopped foods at first because she doesn't yet know how to chew, but she'll learn this skill eventually.

When giving solids, be careful to avoid giving too much salt (your baby's kidneys are not strong enough yet to process a high level of salt), too much sugar (this will cause unnecessary damage to her baby teeth), and nuts (which can easily choke a child under the age of five).

See also Eating; Fussy Eaters; Healthy Eating; Overweight; Snacks.

Whining No matter what age your child, his constant whining and moaning will drive you to distraction. Some children are, by nature, prone to complain, and rarely have a smile on their face even they enjoy themselves. But in most instances, a child whines constantly for a reason, which might be

- boredom,
- sadness,
- loneliness,
- ill health,
- physical discomfort or pain,
- need for attention, or
- anxiety.

First, have your child medically examined to rule out any health problems. This is absolutely essential since young children are often unable to specify the source of their discomfort (for example, an ear infection might result in irritability, and the child might not be able to tell you he has a pain in his ear). You may be surprised to discover that your child is whining constantly because he is ill.

Having ruled out the possibility of illness, then consider the circumstances in which your child's whining occurs. Is it when you are busy with household chores or shopping? Is it when he can't decide with what toy or game to play? Is it when he is with his friends? Is it when he is hungry? Could it be he is unhappy in your relationship with him? Think about these and any other potential sources of emotional discomfort. This analysis will help you see a pattern in your child's whining. You may be able to identify the cause of his moaning, and then to follow a course of action that reduces your child's need to relate to you in this way.

In the end, you might discover that whining of this sort is simply part of your child's personality. If so, it is likely to become less evident as he grows older because he'll soon learn that other children prefer to be with peers who are pleasant, not complaining. In the meantime, let your child know how pleased you are when he doesn't whine or moan, and try to ignore him when he does.

See also *Attention-Seeking Behavior; Crying Baby; Discipline; Ignoring; Spanking; Tantrums.*

Working Mothers The number of mothers who return to full-time employment continues to increase. In many instances, a mother goes back to work because she needs the money; in some instances, she does so because she doesn't want to risk losing a promising career; in some instances, she is the sole support of the family. Whatever the reason, no evidence shows that a mother's returning to work—even during the child's preschool years—inevitably has an adverse effect on a child's psychological development.

This lifestyle is not without its problems. From a woman's perspective, being a working mother may mean managing double the normal amount of tasks, with increased stress and demands. Very few working mothers would say that their partner actually agrees to split the domestic chores evenly down the middle. Generally the prime responsibility for running the house continues to rest with the woman. The woman's job is frequently given a lower priority. Some couples exercise a much more even balance, but this is difficult to achieve, and requires consistent determination from both partners. The net effect of the usual imbalance in task allocation is that a working mother's role has expanded, rather than changed. Now she does more. In addition, she may have postponed pregnancy until her thirties or forties, or she may be dealing with aging parents or in-laws, as well. In such situations, the physical and emotional strain of being a working mother is high, and a woman can be at risk for depression, illness, or addiction to tobacco, alcohol, or drugs.

Critics of working mothers express concern that a child will lose out psychologically by not having her mother with her during the preschool years. While it is true that the preschool years see the formation of the child's fundamental characteristics, the fact is, nothing suggests that the quantity of time a woman spends with her baby is critical. Research findings indicate that what matters is the quality of the mother's time with her baby. An uninterrupted hour with a loving, relaxed mother is worth more to a baby's psychological development than is a day spent with a rejecting, tense mother who simply parks her infant in front of the television.

If going out to work or back to school improves a woman's self-confidence, and consequently helps her relate more positively to her child, then the child will benefit psychologically.

New mothers face two challenges:

- *Some women who want to give up their job to be a full-time mother are aware of social pressures against such a move.* They feel embarrassed to admit to others that they do not want to go back to work after the birth of their baby.

- *Some women who opt to combine parenthood with full-time employment are not completely comfortable with their choice.* They will have chosen this course of action only after weighing the pros and cons, but that doesn't mean they are entirely happy about leaving their baby in the care of someone else during the work week. Women in these circumstances often experience guilt feelings, which may persist.

See also Fathers; Mothers; Quality Time; Postnatal Depression; Single-Parent Family.

X-Ray The X-ray is the most common medical procedure carried out in childhood, largely because of the high number of children under the age of seven admitted to the hospital as a result of broken bones, and because of routine visits to the dental office.

Unfortunately, many children are upset and uncooperative during this procedure—even though having an X-ray isn't painful. This lack of cooperation makes the radiographer's job extremely difficult.

X-rays are most prevalent in dental offices. A lead apron should be worn—especially for girls—when this routine procedure occurs. Explain to your child that the dentist will take a picture of his teeth, to make sure they are growing in the right way and are healthy. Tell your child that the X-ray will not hurt, but he might be slightly uncomfortable for a few seconds because he must keep inserts in his mouth in awkward places.

When a more serious medical situation exists, a child's agitation is probably due to a combination of factors: the clinical surroundings, the protective robes that the medical staff have to wear, and the fact that his parents may not be allowed to accompany him while the X-ray is taken, especially if he is in an emergency room. Whatever the cause of his distress, your child's reaction may mean that proper medical treatment is delayed.

Psychologists have found that the most suitable strategy to help a child through this situation is patience and calmness; not easy when you know your child is injured and needs immediate treatment. However, when accompanying your child to the hospital, reassure him that he will only have a picture taken of his arm (or whatever), that it won't hurt him at all, and that he'll be perfectly safe. Try to be with him in the X-ray room, if possible, because your presence will help to calm him.

The use of physical restraint or punishment in the X-ray room in order to coerce a child into cooperating with the radiographer rarely works. In most instances, this tactic simply upsets the child even more, further delaying important treatment. Never use threats to cajole your child into cooperating with medical staff.

See also Hospital; Illness.

Y

Young Parents The average age of first-time parents continues to rise steadily, as more and more couples prefer to acquire financial security and broader life experience before starting their family. Even so, statistics suggest that up to 10 percent of new parents are under twenty years old, and up to 27 percent of all new mothers are single. Most of these are teenagers.

Young parents are no different psychologically from older parents. They tend to share the same values, and have the same hopes for themselves and their children. They are particularly likely to be isolated from important family and social networks, for the following reasons:

- *They may be single and without financial or emotional support.*
- *Their families may disapprove of the partnership and, therefore, reject them.*
- *Their friends probably have no children, and so have a more flexible lifestyle.*
- *Their neighbors may not approve of them and may regard them as irresponsible.*

Unemployment is an additional stress young parents often have to face. Untrained under-twenties rarely find jobs easily, and many young parents have trouble making ends meet because of dual unemployment. Sociologists call this the "spiral of disadvantage"—the young parents' inability to find work, plus their inability to relocate easily in order to do so, often results in a low income, which in turn results in poor housing. The cycle of poverty is hard to break.

These psychological and environmental influences can combine to place young parents in a vulnerable situation, although many do manage parenthood effectively. Child-care professionals should be prepared to give young parents and their child extra attention and advice whenever necessary.

See also *Fathers; Mothers; Older Parents; Parents; Single-Parent Family; Working Mothers.*

Z

Zero-Sum Games Most games that your child plays, beyond the age of three or four, are competitive (such as soccer) and generally have winners and losers. Psychologists term these zero-sum games because they offer a mixture of positive outcomes (when your child wins) and negative outcomes (when he loses).

Activities of this sort have an important place in childhood, and can encourage a child to develop very positive characteristics, such as determination to succeed, an ability to withstand pressure, and tolerance of failure. Zero-sum games can also encourage your child to develop negative qualities, such as aggression, selfishness, and the desire to win without thought for others.

Positive-sum games provide an alternative. Here children work together cooperatively, rather than against each other competitively. The outcomes for each child are always positive.

The following positive-sum game involves minimal preparation. Get an empty juice bottle and four chunky pencils or clothespins whose diameter is slightly less than the neck of the bottle (one pencil for each child who plays the game). Tie one end of a piece of string around one of the pencils and lower it into the bottle, leaving the other end of the string trailing down the side. Repeat this with the other three pencils.

When your child plays with two or three friends, tell them that you want them to play a new game. Using the equipment you've prepared, ask each of them to hold one piece of string. Explain that when you say "Go" they have to pull the strings to get the pencils out of the bottle as quickly as possible, and that the game is won by the whole group when the last pencil is removed. The relative widths of the pencils and bottle-neck mean that only one pencil can be pulled out at a time—so the children have to cooperate in order to complete the game quickly. You may find that they start to bicker with each other at first, because they are competing rather than working together. After a few attempts the children will begin to work more effectively as a team. You can time their performances, and keep a score chart for them. Positive-sum games of this sort encourage desirable characteristics, such as sharing, cooperation, and sensitivity to the strengths and weaknesses of others.

See also Friendships; Kindness; Sociable Play; Social Development.

Zygote Conception occurs when a sperm from a male pierces the wall of the egg (ovum) from a female. This is only possible during a specific physiological phase: once every twenty-eight days an ovum in one of the two ovaries ripens and begins its journey (which usually takes between three and seven days) down the fallopian tube, toward the uterus, pushed along by small hairlike cells that line the tube. If the ovum isn't fertilized by a sperm during this time, it disintegrates in the uterus after a few days and its remains are dispersed.

However, if a male sperm is present in the fallopian tube when the ovum is there, the two may join together, and conception may then take place. At this point, the fertilized ovum—known as a zygote—is only about $\frac{1}{175}$ of an inch in diameter, but it begins to grow immediately. In the next ten to fourteen days the zygote continues travelling through the fallopian tube until it reaches the uterus, where it becomes implanted; by then, it is approximately the size of a pinhead.

With identical twins, a single zygote splits into two identical parts, each of which will develop into a baby. Since each child comes from one egg, these twins are always of the same sex and have the same inherited genetic characteristics. With nonidentical twins, two separate eggs are fertilized by separate sperm at the same time. Since each child develops from different eggs, they are no more alike than any other siblings.
See also Prenatal Development; Twins.

Index

(Main entries are in **bold** type.)

Order Form

Qty.	Title	Author	Order No.	Unit Cost (U.S. $)	Total
	Baby & Child Emergency First Aid	Einzig, M.	1380	$15.00	
	Baby & Child Medical Care	Hart, T.	1159	$9.00	
	Baby Journal	Bennett, M.	3172	$10.00	
	Baby Name Personality Survey	Lansky/Sinrod	1270	$8.00	
	Best Baby Shower Book	Cooke, C.	1239	$7.00	
	Child Care A to Z	Woolfson, R.	1010	$11.00	
	Discipline without Shouting or Spanking	Wyckoff/Unell	1079	$6.00	
	Eating Expectantly	Swinney, B.	1135	$12.00	
	Familiarity Breeds Children	Lansky, B.	4015	$7.00	
	Feed Me! I'm Yours	Lansky, V.	1109	$9.00	
	Gentle Discipline	Lighter, D.	1085	$6.00	
	Getting Organized for Your New Baby	Bard, M.	1229	$9.00	
	Grandma Knows Best	McBride, M.	4009	$7.00	
	Hi, Mom! Hi, Dad!	Johnston, L.	1139	$6.00	
	Joy of Parenthood	Blaustone, J.	3500	$6.00	
	Maternal Journal	Bennett, M.	3171	$10.00	
	Practical Parenting Tips	Lansky, V.	1180	$8.00	
	Pregnancy, Childbirth, and the Newborn	Simkin/Whalley/Keppler	1169	$12.00	
	Very Best Baby Name Book	Lansky, B.	1030	$8.00	
				Subtotal	
			Shipping and Handling (see below)		
			MN residents add 6.5% sales tax		
				Total	

YES! Please send me the books indicated above. Add $2.00 shipping and handling for the first book and 50¢ for each additional book. Add $2.50 to total for books shipped to Canada. Overseas postage will be billed. Allow up to four weeks for delivery. Send check or money order payable to Meadowbrook Press. No cash or C.O.D.'s, please. Prices subject to change without notice. **Quantity discount available upon request.**

Send book(s) to:

Name _____

Address _____

City _____ State _____ Zip _____

Telephone (_____)_____

Purchase order number (if necessary) _____

Payment via:

☐ Check or money order payable to Meadowbrook Press (No cash or C.O.D.'s, please.)

Amount enclosed $ _____

☐ Visa (for orders over $10.00 only)   ☐ MasterCard (for orders over $10.00 only)

Account #_____

Signature _____ Exp. Date_____

A **FREE** Meadowbrook catalog is available upon request.
You can also phone us for orders of $10.00 or more at 1-800-338-2232.

Mail to: Meadowbrook Press
5451 Smetana Drive, Minnetonka, MN 55343

Phone (612) 930-1100   Toll-Free 1-800-338-2232   Fax (612) 930-19